PRAISE FOR *A Marriage That Changed the World*

Addiction has been mentioned in the Dear Abby column practically since my late mother began writing it. Al-Anon and A.A. have been a blessing for many individuals and families. Al-Anon and A.A. have changed countless lives and will continue to do so in decades to come. Those interested in learning more about this life-saving program should read this book.

—Dear Abby, a.k.a. Jeanne Phillips

A Marriage That Changed the World is a deeply insightful exploration of the extraordinary partnership that transformed global addiction recovery. Through meticulous research and compelling storytelling, this book unveils the personal struggles, spiritual evolution, and pioneering contributions of Bill and Lois Wilson, offering a profound understanding of the origins of the Twelve Step movement and its enduring impact on millions of lives worldwide.

—Mike Fitzpatrick
Founder, Recovery Speakers

Tom Adams and Joy Jones have written a beautiful, comprehensive portrait of Bill and Lois Wilson's marriage, highlighting how they—separately and together—contributed to the recovery movement. For the millions of people who've landed in Twelve Step rooms to recover from addiction, this book is a valuable addition to the historical record about recovery's founding couple. Most notably, Adams and Jones have brought Lois Wilson out of the shadow of her larger-than-life husband and let her words and incredible life works stand next to his. This is a must-read tribute!

—Christie Tate
Author, *The New York Times Bestseller Group: How One Therapist*
and *How a Circle of Strangers Saved My Life and B.F.F.: A Memoir of Friendship Lost and Found*

I consider Bill and Lois Wilson to be the First Couple of Recovery. This book reminds us that addiction is a family illness, and that love is the greatest healing force in recovery.

—Mark Sanders, LCSW, CADC
Founder of Online Museum of African American
Addictions, Treatment and Recovery

If the marriage of Bill and Lois Wilson weathered the storms of addiction, their partnership activated revolutionary programs of recovery. Adams and Jones have gifted us with a book that offers perspectives on this relationship that go far beyond the woman-behind-the man narrative, suggesting a harmony that led to a deeper understanding of alcoholism as both an individual and family disease. Lovers of history will appreciate the Wilsons' thoughtfulness in creating local cultures of recovery while designing organizational structures to sustain recovery efforts across the planet and uphold universal recovery principles and values.

—Tom Hill, MSW
Retired Senior Policy Advisor,
Office of National Drug Control Policy (ONDCP)

A compelling page-turner that transports the reader into the shoes of ordinary people who did something extraordinary: They saved themselves from the ravages of addiction and then saved the world. It is a must-read.

—Debra Jay
Author of *Love First* and *It Takes a Family*

Tom Adams and Joy Jones have written a remarkable history of Bill and Lois Wilson and their contribution to the development of Alcoholics Anonymous. Indeed, the millions of us who are now sober owe our very lives to the commitment they made so many decades ago. Their personal struggles ended up serving all of us who have received support in A.A. and Al-Anon.

This book does even more, though. It weaves in the history of the entire early recovery movement. The authors beautifully blend the myriad components of what it was like, what happened, and what it's like now. Their dedication to research and storytelling provide all of us who travel this path with the answers we have hungered for.

Thank you Tom Adams and Joy Jones for showing up in my lifetime.

—Karen Casey, PhD
Author of *Each Day a New Beginning*

A Marriage That Changed the World is a brilliant contribution to the recovery movement, helping the reader understand the process of addiction, hitting bottom, recovery, and the interplay of relationships. It inspires hope, faith, and belief in the power of each human spirit to change the world!

—Dr. Anita Gadhia-Smith
Psychotherapist and Best-Selling Author
of From Addiction to Recovery

A refreshing perspective on the marriages and coupleship of A.A.'s cofounders and their wives. Tom and Joy have taken a deeper dive into the real-life events of these relationships and a behind-the-scenes view of how they contributed to the big picture. Through much research and effort by the authors, we are drawn into a closer understanding of their lives, sacrifices, and a detailed narrative of the sequence of events that led to the founding of A.A. and Al-Anon. This book is a wonderful addition to our understanding of the roots of this great spiritual movement.

—Gail La Croix
Archivist, Dr. Bob's Home, Akron, Ohio

Tom Adams and Joy Jones have written a book that tells the recovery story. This book is fantastic! I have read some history books, but this one has soul about it. I loved it. Stories and storytelling are a part of our native culture. Thankful it's what we do in Alcoholics Anonymous as well. You have told a story that has moved me. Thank you.

—Francis (Big Man) Old Rock Jr.,
Mandan, Hidatsa, and Arikara Nation, North Dakota

Abstinence alone is not recovery, and long-term recovery from addiction happens in community, most often reflected in essential relationships—most importantly, including marriage.

A Marriage That Changed the World begins to fill a different, yet obviously important, gap in addiction recovery research—a focus on the relationship and marriage of Lois Burnham and Bill Wilson—and its impact in the creation of Alcoholics Anonymous and Al-Anon Family Groups.

—William (Bill) Lammers
Member of the Board of Governors of the Hazelden Betty Ford
Graduate School and past member of the Hazelden
Betty Ford Foundation Board of Directors

There is no larger mental health issue than addictions. I have personally and professionally seen the destruction caused by alcoholism in my family and in my six decades of nursing practice and global policy work. Tom Adams and Joy Jones have offered us a fresh and broader look at how addictions destroy individuals and families and why and how recovery is possible. This book offers hope and guidance based on the amazing marriage of Lois and Bill Wilson and the recovery movement they launched. We all learn from their journey.

—Sally Raphel, MS, APRN-PMH, FAAN
International Society for Psychiatric Mental Health Nurses

The immense power of unconditional love, unwavering faith, high determination, absolute tenacity, selflessness, and compassion are meticulously illustrated in this book. These salvaged Bill and Lois Wilson's marriage from the cruel claws of alcoholism. The union has saved lives and continues to be a beacon of hope for alcoholics and their families across the entire globe! The book gives hope to the hopeless and instills a sense of compassion for the alcoholic in a world that is filled with judgmental people. It's surely a must-read for everyone!!!

—Lemohang Ntsinyi-Mtshali
Eswatini, Southern Africa, person in long-term recovery
from impact of addictions on families and advocate
for recovery services for all

As an individual blessed with over three decades in long-term recovery, a hopeless romantic, and a female empowerment advocate, I found this work compelling and relevant to anyone who has/is/will be touched by addiction, especially the insidious disease of alcoholism. Given the chance, love can heal!

—Janice Ferebee, MSW
Founder of Ferebee Enterprises International, LLC, a global female
empowerment social enterprise. Recognized by BET Teen
Summit, *The Oprah Winfrey Show*, and *Essence Magazine*

Despair, fraught relationships, surrender, and love—the journey to changing the world through A.A. and Al-Anon reads like a highly complex human drama. The lessons of Bill and Lois Wilson's personal evolution and recovery revolution still apply to today's pressing societal problems. This book reveals the uneven path that they travelled in search of deep, meaningful ways of hope.

—Patrick Canavan, PsyD
Clinical Psychologist and Executive Consultant at CNVN
Consult. Former CEO of St. Elizabeths Hospital, Washington, DC

Tom Adams and Joy Jones have produced a long-needed examination of the marriage of Bill and Lois Wilson, with its period of agony for both as they struggled with Bill's alcoholism and their mutual success at founding the two largest mutual aid organizations in the world. I and others applauded their main thesis that these two people were in love from the beginning to the end and that there would have been no A.A. without them both.

—Linda Farris Kurtz, MSW, DPA
Author of *Recovery Groups: A Guide to Creating,
Leading, and Working with Groups for Addictions
and Mental Health Conditions*

I am grateful to Tom Adams and Joy Jones for offering us this book, which documents in poignant detail the struggles of a courageous couple to mobilize a community of mutual support which continues to grow in influence and importance. This book will be of enormous value to academic researchers and clinicians in addition to the members of the recovering community and anyone who may be considering the process of examining the impact of addiction in their own lives or the lives of their loved ones.

—Jeffrey D. Roth, MD
Distinguished Fellow of the American Society of Addiction
Medicine and past member of the Outreach
to Professionals Committee of Al-Anon

Tom Adams and Joy Jones bring to consciousness the depth and importance of widening the lens beyond the simplistic narrative of Bill Wilson and Dr. Smith co-founding Alcoholics Anonymous. This book brings fresh insight and perspective to the importance of the role that the marriage between Bill and Lois Wilson played not just to A.A., but the broader recovery movement taking shape beyond even their wildest dreams.

—Greg Williams
Filmmaker, *The Anonymous People*, *Generation Found*,
and *Tipping the Pain Scale*

I am so excited about this book! As a married man whose recovery date and wedding date are both 2012, I understand that the devastation of alcoholism not only destroys the individual, but their family as well—and both need to go into recovery. In the Twelve Step world, we revere Bill Wilson. However, Lois is sometimes an afterthought, which is unfortunate, because without her steadfast support of not only Bill but the families of the alcoholics they helped, A.A. would not have survived and flourished. This book will not only interest those in recovery (and their families) but history buffs and folks like me who love reading biographies. I appreciate Tom and Joy's hard work, and I am excited for the lives this work will touch!

—James LeBlanc
Author of *The Miracle*

I did not learn until after my father's sudden and unexpected death when I was an adolescent that he was an alcoholic in recovery for several years before I was born. I started to understand him and our family dynamics much better once I started to learn more about this disease and its dynamics. Personally, then as an attorney, priest, and pastor, I came to appreciate the complexity, the insidiousness, and the treatability of this condition. Recovery starts with emerging from isolation, forming relationships, and initiating healthier and healthier relationships. Lois Wilson recognized this; Bill and Lois Wilson lived it. It is no exaggeration to say they have saved many lives and restored relationships and joy to so many. Tom Adams and Joy Jones are to be congratulated and commended for making the story of Bill and Lois Wilson, and the lifesaving and life-enriching work they spent their lives doing, better known.

—Rev. Phillip J. Brown, PSS, President
Rector St. Mary's Seminary and University, Baltimore Maryland

A Marriage That Changed the World

A Marriage That Changed the World

Lois and Bill Wilson and the Addiction Recovery Movement

Tom Adams, msw
& Joy Jones

GREENBELT
PUBLISHERS

GREENBELT, MD

Copyright © 2025 by Greenbelt Publishers. All rights reserved.

Published in the United States by Greenbelt Publishers LLC
GreenbeltPublishers@gmail.com

Additional credits and disclaimers appear on page 370.

Cover photo by Art D. (colorized detail), 1953: Courtesy Stepping Stones Foundation, Katonah, NY, WR-101--35_Y-3_001.

Library of Congress Cataloging—in Publication Data pending.

ISBN (Paperback) 979-8-9921509-1-9
ISBN (Digital) 979-8-9921509-0-2

Cover, interior design, logo design, and photo editing by Sharon K. Miller, www.buckskinbooks.com.

To my (Tom's) wife Geraldine, in gratitude for her love, understanding, and support, without which this book would not exist.

To Doris Beverlin, a friend and recovery guide   to us both.

To Lois and Bill Wilson and the millions of individuals and families who have found hope and the millions more who will.

CONTENTS

FOREWORD

CLAIRE RICEWASSER

Today, more people understand that alcoholism is systemic within families and has an intergenerational impact on the drinkers and their loved ones. Treatment and recovery for all family members and alcoholics are critical to break the cycle of addiction. Hopelessness, fear, and anger can be overcome and replaced with trust, faith, and happiness. Even joy is possible as the past is put into proper perspective.

I am a family member with lived experience and in recovery from a loved one's misuse of alcohol. I believe it is imperative to continue to tell the stories about the importance of family recovery through participation in Twelve Step programs. The marriages of Lois and Bill W. and Annie S. and Dr. Bob continue to provide "roots and wings" to present and future generations of people in recovery and to the public.

As a person in long-term recovery, I have always related to the lives of Lois W. and Annie S. I identified with Lois as the daughter of a physician and to Annie S. and her children living in a medical family. Alcoholism devastates all kinds of families, regardless of education and background. It is cunning, baffling, powerful, and patient! Sobriety is a miracle, and yet it does not resolve all problems in relationships.

A Marriage That Changed the World is the first major study since 2005 that calls attention to Lois W., her marriage, and the evolution of family members' recovery from a loved one's alcoholism. Lois W. and Annie S. were socially, financially, and emotionally dependent upon their husbands. They remained in their marriages at a time when American society looked down upon divorced women. It is easy to apply today's twenty-first-century beliefs to their marriages by asking, "Why did you stay?" or dismissing (or minimizing) the importance of these two women because of their choices. Fortunately for family members of individuals struggling with addiction to alcohol, Lois and Annie's decisions and determination laid the foundation for family recovery and the creation of Al-Anon Family Groups.

Digital technology has made it possible for Tom Adams and Joy Jones to bring together other sources overlooked or not previously utilized in retelling the lives of Lois and Bill W. and other early recovery family members. As a person who has studied the history of family recovery for over four decades, I am delighted with how *A Marriage That Changed the World* brings together the stories of the originating cofounders of Al-Anon and Alcoholics Anonymous.

My hope is that readers of *A Marriage That Changed the World* will come to see addiction as a family disease and find the needed pathways to healing for the family.

—Claire Ricewasser
Person in longtime family recovery with
a passion for Twelve Step history

Foreword

William B. Stauffer

This is the story of a marriage that survived the devastating struggle of addiction, a condition that impacts hundreds of millions of families globally. The marriage evolved into a partnership that has changed the world. Those first conversations of hope at the kitchen table of Lois and Bill Wilson rippled across time and transformed the way we heal from addiction on every continent and in every culture. Entire movements of recovery emanated out of them. Processes of mutual aid, formal treatment strategies, and recovery support across diverse communities have sprung from the union formed of humble origins in this couple's home.

It would have been impossible, in those moments decades ago, to know how this marriage would so powerfully influence our world. Millions of people around the globe are alive and thriving today because of what grew from the Wilsons. Their work has evolved to support global recovery efforts at the individual and community levels.

My own recovery, which took hold at age twenty-one in the mid-1980s, emanated from the recovery capital—a reservoir of resources and support—sown by these pioneers. In my community, those seeds can be traced back to Marty Mann, the first woman in A.A. to stay in continuous recovery, whom the Wilsons invited into their home to help in those early days. She was our nation's first recovery advocate, who spoke out publicly and formed education centers in the early 1950s, including Alcohol Councils to raise public awareness about alcohol addiction and recovery. We had one of the first councils in my community. Without the Wilsons, the help I found decades later would have been unlikely at best. The same is true for millions of people worldwide.

Such recovery capital is clearly still needed today. Death certificates from 2019 and 2020 show that fatalities involving alcohol rose precipitously from approximately 79,000 to more than 99,000 deaths, a 25.5 percent increase.[1] These numbers are staggering, like losing the population of the state of Montana or Rhode Island. As Princeton economists Anne Case and Angus Deaton note, "Americans are drinking themselves to death, or poisoning themselves with drugs, or shooting or hanging themselves" at unprecedented rates, starting around the year 2000.[2]

These deaths fall into an emerging concept known as deaths of despair. We are experiencing profoundly difficult economic conditions, war, supply chain disruptions, social isolation, and a level of vitriol toward each other unrivaled at any point in American history since the Civil War. At the same time, our very system of care focuses on services and support in ways that limit healing to an individual level. In contrast, emerging science is supporting the fact that we need to conceptualize healing from a substance use condition across the family system. We can and should envision the world of the future in which healing is embraced in the context of family and is done so without stigma or shame. Our families can and do heal, and millions more can and should have the resources to do so.

Anything beyond a cursory review of recovery history invariably generates a deep appreciation of the Wilsons' profound contributions and an even deeper sense of humility in respect to our own efforts to support healing in the next generation. Bill Wilson died when I was six, and Lois passed just short of my second Anniversary in recovery. Like millions of people in recovery around the world, I never got to thank them for what they did for all of us, other than to pay their efforts forward in whatever way I can. A commitment to service to others runs deep within us, a practice that legions of us are engaged in worldwide. The Wilsons' healing ripples through us and out into the future. I thank them and all who have served to carry the message of recovery forward across our world. It was a marriage that quite literally changed the world, one life at a time, including mine.

Thank you, Lois and Bill Wilson. You live on in our service to others.

—William B. Stauffer, Executive Director
Pennsylvania Recovery Organizations Alliance

Preface

The story of Bill and Lois Wilson—their marriage, their battle with addictions, and their roles in helping co-create the Twelve Step movement—is astonishing and uplifting, full of both drama and hope.

Bill Wilson, a chronic, near-dead alcoholic, became the cofounder and visionary architect of Alcoholics Anonymous (A.A.). His partner and wife, Lois Wilson, became the cofounder of Al-Anon Family Groups and remained its consistent rudder until her death.

If Bill and Lois lived today, the odds are great that Lois would have divorced Bill. His behavior was so out of control, most wives would have given up. Lois Wilson didn't.

Instead, she committed herself to a marriage that changed the world. Their persistent union connected them with Annie and Bob Smith and other couples in New York, Akron, Cleveland, and other communities to develop an unprecedented recovery movement.

A.A. history, like most history, is told mostly from the male point of view. Bill Wilson and Dr. Bob Smith are championed as its cofounders and heroes. Yet, they both acknowledged that without their wives—Lois Wilson and Annie Smith—they would have died. Instead, with the help of their spouses, they founded a movement that has changed countless lives. Beyond that, these men acknowledged how the strength, warmth, spiritual beliefs, and intelligence of their spouses shaped the movement.

This book also explores what some see as the enigma of Lois Wilson. Lois was an achiever, but in a far different style from that of modern, twenty-first-century women. She was dedicated to Bill's journey yet also trail blazed her own spiritual quest. She followed his lead but also exerted a personal magnetic power. These seemingly contradictory positions might present a compelling paradox for women today.

This book offers a deeper understanding of Lois Wilson and her role in her marriage and in the launching of A.A., Al-Anon, and the Twelve Step movement. We embrace the task of helping twenty-first-century readers understand a woman leader born in the late nineteenth century who was shaped by a different sensibility and spiritual orientation.

Why did we write about Bill and Lois? Without their marriage, there would be no A.A. or Twelve Step movement. Without the Wilsons' attention, along with other Twelve Step pioneers, to healing for the family, family members of those living with addiction would not know there is help, even if someone they love is harming themselves and others through their addictions. Without Lois Wilson and her extraordinary commitment and leadership—in a time when women were not allowed to lead—neither A.A. nor Al-Anon, nor the many other Twelve Step programs would offer the world hope and recovery in the unique way that evolved because of her leadership.

The Wilsons' legacy is not theirs alone. They continuously gave credit to both divine help and others' assistance. Their marriage resulted in an exceptional, world-changing legacy that includes a way to recover from many kinds of addictions and provides choices for families that are confronted with a family member or friend with an addiction problem. That legacy includes approaches to emotional wellbeing, spiritual growth, and organizational life that offer a way forward for individuals, families, and communities all over the world.

Whether you are interested in history in general, in Twelve Step history in particular, or want to better understand the magic and mystery of the Twelve Step and broader recovery movements, you will want to know more about Bill and Lois Wilson and how their marriage is still changing the world.

If you have misused alcohol or drugs, have displayed other addictive behaviors, or are related or married to someone who has, you know the depth and breadth of the pain and chaos out-of-control addictions can cause. You will likely identify with Bill Wilson's hopeless despair as he repeatedly made pledges to himself and to Lois never to drink again, then faced the heartbreak and terror of not being able to keep those promises.

If you are the child, sibling, spouse, or close friend of someone who has misused alcohol, drugs, or other substances, you know a different pain and frustration. You have watched someone you love act in unimaginable ways. You have been hurt, scared, and perhaps despaired at this seemingly inexplicable behavior. If you have experienced the octopus-like pains of addiction and perhaps benefited directly or indirectly from the Twelve Step movement, then a deeper look at the Wilson marriage could provide some insight and hope.

If you have been fortunate enough not to have lived with addiction, your curiosity about this story might serve you well. There are many myths and mistruths about addiction, recovery, and their impact on everyone involved. There are also still societal judgments and stigmas that have blocked some from seeing why the Twelve Steps established by the Wilsons are now used effectively in so many ways to advance mental health. Understanding the roots of the Twelve Steps through the lives of two of the program founders can deepen your understanding of and appreciation for the power of addiction in families and the power of Twelve Step recovery.

Whether you know about the Twelve Steps or not, this book can enable greater appreciation for why the Twelve Steps, pioneered by the Wilsons and others, are now helping people who misuse drugs during the current opioid crisis, people with eating disorders (obesity, anorexia, bulimia), and people who compulsively gamble or spend. You will see the complexity of addiction and recovery and how both can be passed along from generation to generation. The Wilsons' story and their legacy will broaden your understanding of how these principles shape recovery practices today.

Two courageous and creative people—Bill and Lois Wilson—forever reversed for so many the death sentences and the emotional pain related to misuse of alcohol, drugs, food, and other substances. Some people still believe excess drinking or drug use is a problem of self-control or morality. But because of the pioneering work of the Wilsons and other early members of Alcoholics Anonymous and Al-Anon, that view is changing. There is hope for alcoholics, their families, and many others who misuse a substance or practice addictive behavior.

Finally, whether you know about or participate in a Twelve Step recovery program or are new to the topic, we trust you will find something of value here.

Some practical notes:

A Marriage That Changed the World: Bill and Lois Wilson and the Addiction Recovery Movement is a blend of history, biography, and story. Some call this narrative nonfiction. It is not intended to be pure history or biography, and it is not historical fiction. We expect more to be revealed over time about the Wilson marriage and hope to contribute to an ongoing exploration of the Wilsons, the family diseases of addiction, and the growing recovery movement.

This book is based on rigorous research that includes primary and secondary sources, interviews, and previous books on the Wilsons. We use terms like "drunk," "alcoholic," and "addict" to accurately reflect the language of the period. Today, these terms are replaced with terms that do not contribute to the stigma still associated with addictions of all kinds. Later chapters use people-centered language like "person with alcohol-use disorder" or "person who is experiencing alcohol or other drug use disorder."[1]

A.A. traditions include the use of first names and surname initials to respect A.A.'s spiritual principle of anonymity and "principles before personalities."[2] However, in a few instances, we join with other contemporary authors in using the full names for deceased A.A. and Al-Anon leaders.

We also want to acknowledge that while many people provided guidance and knowledge, we take full responsibility for the contents of this book. We see it as a first step in broadening the lens through which addiction recovery is seen in a way that brings hope to more individuals and families.

Now, come and meet the people who started a twentieth-century revolution which is still saving lives all over the globe. We hope you will be inspired and encouraged by knowing more about the extraordinary Wilsons and the birth of the Twelve Step movement.

We have been—and still are.

—Tom Adams and Joy Jones

INTRODUCTION

In the beginning of the marriage, everything was wonderful.

Lois had grown up in a warm, loving family and felt that, in Bill, she had found the next chapter of love in her life. Bill's childhood had been rough, but, in meeting Lois, he believed things had turned around. For both Lois and Bill, this was a beautiful beginning headed for a happy ending.

But the middle sure was cataclysmic.

Part One

Bill and Lois Wilson: Early Life and Early Marriage

1891–1934

CHAPTER 1

LOIS' ROOTS AND CHILDHOOD

Lois Burnham was born on March 4, 1891, twenty-nine years before women could vote, twenty-nine years before Prohibition started, and four years before the birth of the man who would transform her life and the lives of millions.

Lois Burnham's Early Life

On crowded cacophonous city streets at the turn of the twentieth century, boys called out,

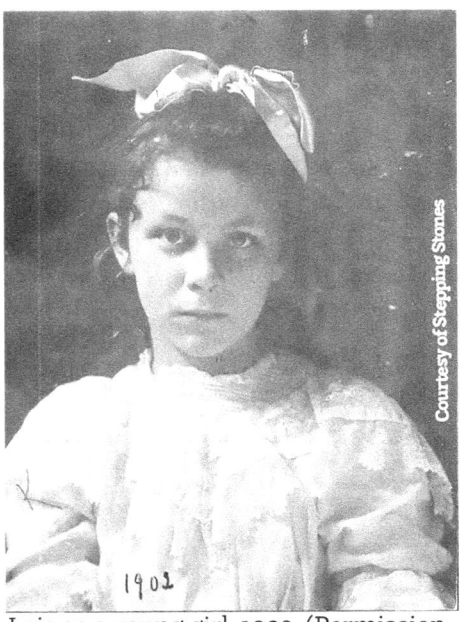

Lois as a young girl, 1902. (Permission required for use.)

5

"Extra! Extra!" while hawking copies of *The New York Tribune*, *The Evening Sun*, *The New York Times*, or another of the dozen or so local newspapers in business at that time. The headlines of the 1890s announced news about the bicycle craze, ads for the Buffalo Bill Wild West Show starring Annie Oakley, or the schedule of the Grays baseball team (later known as the Dodgers) at Ebbets Field.

Lois' childhood was a pleasant, privileged one. The average American went to school until age fourteen because of compulsory school legislation begun in the late 1890s and found in thirty-one states by 1900. Lois and her four younger siblings had access to the best available schools. The German educational practice called kindergarten was a new concept, and Lois belonged to the first set of American children to attend. That was followed by the Friends School, a private Quaker grammar school, then culminated with Packer Collegiate Institute, formerly the Brooklyn Female Academy, which was a college preparatory and finishing school organized in 1845 to improve education for girls.

Lois was a doctor's daughter, and her mother was from a genteel New England family. Dr. Clark Burnham was also the child of a doctor (who was also a lawyer and a minister). Matilda Hoyt met Clark Burnham at her coming-out party.

Matilda was cultured and caring. Lois recalled that "among my most pleasant memories are of Mother's reading aloud to us youngsters before we went to bed and of her reciting poetry or a monologue as we were driving home after a long day in the open. Absolutely without self-consciousness and totally selfless, Mother loved people and people loved her. Everyone told us youngsters that Mother was the loveliest person they knew."[1]

Lois grew up at 182 Clinton Street in Brooklyn Heights, New York. Its tree-shaded brownstones and red-brick facades housed the privileged families of busy professionals. She later described what her home meant in detail in the forty-page booklet *Vignettes of the Past*.[2] Her father had first rented a room in the building as a young gynecologist. Later, when married, he rented the whole home and eventually purchased it.

Her father's work as a doctor and her mother's family wealth provided a life with more privilege than most. Lois' *Vignettes* includes memories of hearing the elephants' footsteps coming down Clinton Street to Prospect Park for the circus each year, the frequent invitations for friends to join them for dinner after church, and her father's valuable wine collection, which grew through contributions from patients.

During the 1890s, the times were changing, and America was changing too. Immigrants were coming to the country in large numbers. Music by African Americans began to seep into the mainstream. Ragtime, radio, and vaudeville entertained the masses, and the upper classes got to hear Pyotr Tchaikowsky play at the Carnegie. Two new stars were added to the flag as Wyoming and Idaho became the forty-third and forty-fourth states in the Union. The twentieth century brought automobiles, home appliances, and increasing automation as American households were introduced to the telephone, toaster, and motion pictures.

The dawn of the twentieth century was an exciting time to come of age! The Victorian period, with its restrictions and constrictions, was unraveling. Female fashions were freer and more flowing. This more relaxed attire made it easier for girls and women to move and express themselves. Lois, in particular, described herself as a "tomboy." In high school, she enjoyed being physical, playing guard in the new sport of basketball. She was proud of her agility and the fact that a school gym test reported she had the strongest back and second strongest legs in the school.

Lois Burnham (second from left) with high school basketball team. (Permission required for use.)

Elise Valentine was Lois' best friend. They met in the Friends School and maintained their strong friendship into adulthood. They both liked sports and played on teams together. They enjoyed each other's company and shared hairstyles, observations about boys, and the joys and wonders of growing up. Later, this sweet and longstanding bond was poisoned by alcohol, although neither of them was a drinker. But for now, they explored the unfolding new century together.

Coming of Age

Lois grew up in a time when women were continuing to organize and fight for equality and the right to vote. In March 1913, when Lois turned twenty-two, 5,000 white women marched on Washington, DC, in a segregated movement for women's rights.

While the seeds for later change in women's rights were being sown, the average woman would not have seen herself in the forefront nor bringing up the rear, but by her man's side as a helper and supporter.

Lois definitely fell in this more classic, conservative category. She reflected in her memoir about how she and her family frowned upon new musical forms like jazz. The Burnhams were adamant in their preference for classical music and the opera.

Lois' grandfather was a minister in the Swedenborgian faith, a branch of Christianity that believes that "the spiritual life involves the active development of a useful and meaningful life in service to the betterment of the world as a whole."[3] Emanuel Swedenborg, an eighteenth-century theologian whose writings shaped Swedenborgian beliefs, also had clear and strong views about the importance of marriage. The Swedenborgian Foundation introduces a video called *Spiritual Marriage* this way:

> After a series of profound spiritual experiences, Emanuel Swedenborg came to believe that marriage is a union that connects everything in the universe—from the lowest material combinations to the highest spiritual levels. He came away with an immense respect for "de amore conjugiali" (Latin for "the love of marriage")—and authored a book called *Conjugial Love*, also translated as *Marriage Love*, so that others could learn how two souls can reflect and express the fundamental connection of the universe, leading them to the greatest joy a human being can experience.[4]

This worldview would have strongly influenced Lois' sensibilities around marriage and her commitment to a partner and to doing good through service.

Lois' parents modeled a loving relationship. They were much more open about their affection for one another than most parents at the time. Lois witnessed firsthand the love of her parents from how they looked at each other, talked to and about each other, and affectionately greeted and touched. Lois commented in her memoir about how her parents demonstrated what love meant between a man and a woman in marriage. Physical affection was expressed easily and often between Matilda and Clark, providing an example for their children of healthy devotion in a married couple.

Lois Meets Bill

In the summer of 1913, when Lois met Bill, she was twenty-two years old. The typical young woman of that era got married around age twenty-one and men around age twenty-four. In her memoir, Lois doesn't mention any sense of the ticking clock, but certainly marriage had to be on her mind.

However, she wasn't desperate. "I was different," she wrote. "There were several young men to whom I was attracted physically, yet I knew I didn't love them. Sometimes it was hard for me to keep to our strict rules. When young men sat with me all evening long in the front parlor, they frequently tried to spoon. But I did hold quite faithfully to our conventions, although it was often difficult to find enough conversation to interest a young man otherwise."[5]

Even Bill Wilson didn't command her attention when he first came on the scene. Lois' brother brought the two together, but she almost immediately dismissed Bill because of his age. What could a mere boy offer her? It's easy to sense the probable disdain and disinterest in her attitude. After all, Bill was four years younger and still a mere teen.

Lois and her family were enjoying the summer of 1913 on Emerald Lake near Manchester, Vermont. Bill's grandparents lived in East Dorset, which was about three miles away. Emerald Lake was the ideal setting for Lois because she loved the outdoors and being active.

The man who could capture Lois' attention needed to be someone who appreciated field, forest, fresh air, and physical activity. Plus, he had to have some personality, along with some purpose. One man, Norman, had a crush on Lois. Norman was quite serious in his intentions, and her parents approved of the match. But Norman lacked dash and drive.

Bill's upbringing, including parental divorce, depression, and the premature death of one he loved, had marked him with rough edges. Yet despite this—maybe because of this—there was something in him that clicked for Lois.

Some of the appeal probably lay in Bill's adventuresome nature, his competitiveness, and his ambition. Bill could do a lot of things. He not only played the violin; he had made a violin with his own hands. During that fateful summer when it all began, Bill challenged Lois to a boat race. Her boat was a well-made skiff with a mast and sail, while Bill was making do with a rigged-up rowboat. The outcome of the race was predictable—to everyone but Bill—given the advantages of Lois' boat.

While Lois was perhaps entertained by Bill and his aggressive charm, she was by no means swept off her feet. It would take some getting to know this local youngster before Lois fell for Bill. In the beginning, for Lois, that elusive quality that coalesces in the connection between two people, that soulful rapport that confirms you have met your mate, was not yet there.

Furthermore, Lois was not pressed to marry. In fact, Lois probably had a more balanced understanding of marriage than most girls (she was the daughter of a gynecologist, after all) and had work that she enjoyed at the Young Women's Christian Association (YWCA) in Brooklyn. She began as a receptionist, then was promoted to assistant to the head of the employment bureau. She was replacing Ethel Smith, a woman who was about to get married and was terrified at the prospect.

Lois and Ethel became fast friends. As good girlfriends are prone to do, they held heart-to-heart talks. We can draw a picture of one possible exchange, based on Lois' comments in her future memoir about her friend. Ethel was worried about getting married and confided in Lois. Other women had told her men can be beasts in the bedroom! Lois asked Ethel if she thought her fiancé loved her. "Yes, for sure," she replied. "Then you have no worries," Lois might have assured her. "Your wedding and wedding night will be lovely."

Things did work out for Ethel, who reported back to Lois after she and her beau married. Just as Lois predicted, he was sensitive and kind.

Eventually, Lois left her job at the YWCA to work for her Aunt Marian, who operated a small progressive school in her home in New Jersey. Lois taught lessons designed to match each child's needs and interests. When she left that job to get married, Lois seemed to find her calling and her destiny with Bill Wilson. But if she thought she was in for a life of tender lovemaking, tending house, and rearing children, she discovered that her life would be something different.

Very different.

CHAPTER 2

BILL'S ROOTS AND EARLY YEARS

While Lois Burnham had a happy childhood, Bill Wilson's childhood was marked by anguish and anxiety. His first romantic experience ended in tragedy and left him struggling with depression. Meeting Lois Burnham would become the antidote for this loss.

Bill Loses Bertha

Bill's heart turned as cold and hard as granite the instant he heard the words of Burr & Burton school's headmaster: "I am

Bill Wilson, age 4. (Permission required for use.)

13

saddened to inform you that your classmate Bertha Banford won't be returning. She died unexpectedly from surgery while home in New York for holiday last week. Let us bow our heads and remember her and her family in prayer."

Bill didn't budge. He couldn't move. He felt the tears deep inside and refused to let them out. He couldn't believe God would do this to him again. His fist clenched in anger at everything and everybody: God, the headmaster with his cold words of comfort, his parents, Bertha's parents. "I am alone again," he thought.

Assembly ended, and Bill headed to his room, speechless. He didn't have many friends, and no one knew how much he loved Bertha. She was his everything: his best friend, his hope for the future, the one person he could trust. Connecting with her was the only time he'd had any idea about what love might be, and now she was gone—Bang!—in an instant. His love was gone, his life over.

In his autobiography, written later in life to describe his first forty years, Bill described himself as amazed Bertha took an interest in him "despite my homely face and awkward figure."[1] Bertha's father was the minister at nearby Manchester Zion Episcopal Church. Bill described how he felt at home and welcomed during visits to the Banford home.

Bertha died on November 19, 1912, shortly before Bill's seventeenth birthday. Her parents had taken her to Flower Hospital in New York to have a small tumor removed. Though it was considered a minor operation, she died from postsurgical hemorrhaging.

Bill tried to return to class and spent his nights alone, staring at the stars, trying to make sense of this loss. All conclude that he fell into a depression. He could not focus on studies, sports, or anything. Though he was president of his class, he was forced to drop out of school and did not graduate with his classmates.

Bill Wilson later described the loss of his first love and his ensuing depression this way: "The healthy kid would have felt badly, but he would never have sunk so deep or stayed submerged for so long.... I could not be anybody at all. I could not win, because the adversary was death. So my life, I thought, had ended then and there."[2]

Later in life, Bill applied hindsight to why he was so ecstatic about being in love with Bertha and so depressed when she was suddenly gone. Bill puts this tragic loss in the context of what he calls

> the triad of primary instincts which result in primary drives. The drive for distinction and power; the drive for security—physical, financial and emotional; and the desire to love and be loved, romantically or otherwise.... Now that I am in love, I am fully compensated on all these primary instinctual drives. I have all the prestige there is to have in school. I excel, indeed I'm the number one where I choose to be. Consequently I am emotionally secure.... And now I love and am loved, fully and completely for the first time in my life. Therefore, I am deliriously happy and am a success according to my own specifications.[3]

Bill Wilson's Early Life

Given that his grandfather Wilson and his father were both heavy drinkers, Bill might aptly be described in today's language as the adult child of an alcoholic. Fear of abandonment and isolation are common traits of such children.[4]

Bill Wilson's life began in East Dorset, Vermont, in 1895. His father, Gilliam, called Gilly Wilson, was a hard-drinking, storytelling quarry manager. His mother,

Emily, was the daughter of a proper New England family, the Griffiths. Emily had hopes for a brighter future for herself and her family. She quickly saw that wouldn't happen while she was married to Gilliam Wilson.

Bill described his early memories and family roots in detail in his autobiography.[5] Bill's grandparents owned the Wilson House, a hotel and tavern frequented by New England travelers. Some, including Bill himself, found it ironic that Bill Wilson, the cofounder of A.A., was born in the back room of a tavern! East Dorset was a town of less than 1,500, and Bill and his younger sister Dorothy later attended the one-room school within walking distance of the tavern, where they lived.

East Dorset was considered the working-class neighbor to the more affluent town of Dorset. After describing his early interest in science and dangerous experiments with chemicals, Bill described his views of his heritage. He fondly described his father and his paternal grandparents as "very amiable...popular...tolerant folk. Good-natured, good managers, good organizers.... Incidentally alcoholism ran pretty rife on the Wilson side. My grandfather Wilson was a very serious case of alcoholism, and it no doubt hastened his death, although some years prior to this he had, to everyone's great surprise hit the sawdust trail, to speak figuratively, at a revival meeting at the Congregational Church and was never known to drink afterwards."[6]

Bill described his mother and her father and heritage quite differently. The Griffiths were intelligent people who ended up in professional positions—lawyers, teachers, and judges. Bill regarded his parents as people considered decent and proper but not particularly easy to get along with.

In a letter to Bill when he was an adult, Emily Wilson described the drama of his birth. "When they brought you to me you were cold and discolored and nearly dead. And so also was I but I held you to me, close in my arms and so we were both warmed and comforted and so we both lived."[7] Concerns about health, and, some would say, hypochondria, followed Bill and his mother throughout life.

Bill didn't say much about his parents' relationship and struggles. Bill described his father as a "work hard and drink hard" kind of guy. After a day at the marble quarry, Gilly and his friends enjoyed a few drinks at the tavern.

Emily was a no-nonsense woman and not shy about speaking her mind. She got angrier and angrier about her husband's drinking, coming home late, and alleged running around with other women. And she wasn't particularly happy living with her in-laws at the Wilson House.

In 1903, Gilly got a promotion to manage a quarry in Rutland, Vermont, twenty-seven miles from East Dorset. He thought he might patch over the rough spots in his marriage by buying a home in Rutland. Bill, Dorothy, and their parents moved to a bigger city and a home of their own when Bill was seven and Dorothy was four. Being in a bigger city, Bill's education moved from a one-room schoolhouse to the Longfellow School.

This experiment didn't last long. A couple years later, Bill and his mother and sister were back at the Wilson House, and his father was taking a job on his own in Canada.

As the only boy, Bill kept his feelings about this to himself. The one person he could confide in was a friend ten years his senior, Mark Whalon. Whalon started out working in a general store where he had access to a horse-drawn wagon for deliveries. He later became a local mailman and got a college degree. He had a voracious interest in learning. Bill liked to go on wagon rides with Mark and listen to his stories. Like his dad, Bill loved a good story and eventually became good at telling them himself. Mark became a lifelong friend and "wise older person" that Bill turned to, even when Bill was guiding the growth of A.A. In later years, Bill became a confidante to Mark as well in his difficult times.

Mark liked to take Bill out after work for a ride on crisp New England fall evenings. Bill described Mark as an idea guy and dreamer like himself. We might imagine Mark, with one hand on the horse's reins and the other pointing to the sky, saying something like this: "Look at all those stars, Bill. Which ones do you think have life? We think this earth is the center of everything. But how can it be, with all those stars and unknown universes out there? I don't know if there is a god or not. But this night sky is pretty amazing, isn't it?"

Bill was fascinated with Mark's knowledge of the world and equally curious. He might have responded with his own fantasy: "Do you think there are people like us or creatures different from us on those faraway planets?" Then they might talk about the stars or politics for hours. Mark was old enough to drink and offered Bill his first drink. Bill was tempted, but at that time in his life, he said no.

The Pain of Divorce

But it wasn't a wagon-ride conversation with Mark that changed Bill's young life the most. It was his parents' divorce. While there are different versions[8] of exactly when and how Bill and Dorothy learned their parents were divorcing, the pain for Bill and his sister was clear. Divorce was very rare and viewed as a weakness and a disgrace.

Bill had already experienced the anguish of separation from his mother when she and his sister spent almost a year in Florida in 1902–1903 while his mother was recovering from one of her frequent illnesses. Bill was seven and

18

missed his mother terribly. Now, he was facing an incomprehensible final separation from his father.

One biographer speculates that Gilly Wilson said good-bye to little Bill in 1905 with a short wagon ride and a simple question: "You'll take care of her, won't you, Billy? You'll be good to your mother and little Dotty, too."[9] Gilly took a big sip from his jug, smiled at his son, and concluded their ride and their relationship in quiet.

Once Emily had figured out how to gain independence (by studying to be an osteopath), she took Bill and Dorothy on a picnic and told them she was moving to Boston. They would go to live with her parents, the Griffiths, not far from the Wilson home in East Dorset. Thus, two short conversations changed Bill's life forever. With no more explanation or discussion, Bill's father and mother had both abandoned him and his sister.

Bill's hunger to be loved and appreciated was no doubt fueled by these devastating and sudden losses. Today, such a loss would be called childhood trauma. Another biographer described what Bill himself, as an adult, called his "mommy issues" this way: "Bill Wilson was always his mother's boy. He was always asking for her permission or trying to find a way to get her attention. He abandoned projects she didn't approve of and responded to her cheerleading with redoubled efforts. He remembered her round face contorted in anger as she beat him with a hairbrush, and her determined voice raining down on the contrite husband who was always just a little bit late, always just a little bit too happy."[10] It seems that, from infancy, Bill had done everything he could to get his mom's attention. It didn't work—and then she left.

In his autobiography, Bill described this challenging time of adapting to living with his grandparents, missing his parents, and doing the things young boys did in the early 1900s in Vermont. Bill described how the decline of the marble quarry resulted in him growing up in a community of farmers. His grandfather encouraged him to do the things everyone else did. Bill learned to fish, trap, and hunt, then to swim. In each, he sought to excel, suggesting he needed to be like Ty Cobb (the best baseball player of the time) or whoever was the best in whatever he was doing. While striving through these normal boyhood activities, Bill ached as he tried to understand why his parents divorced.[11]

He wrote of overhearing his grandparents discussing the divorce. But it was his neighbor, Rose Landon, from whom Bill heard the most about the divorce. Bill described her vividly as a regular user of morphine but only "a moderate drug user," which Bill thought fueled her imagination and informed her propensity to gossip. Consequently, a lot of what Bill learned about his parents and their life together came from Rose. According to Bill, "She rather took the side of my father against my mother.... And it was her talk to me, well intended of course, which no doubt accelerated my feeling of being different from other kids who had their own fathers and mothers."[12]

Bill's childhood shaped him in several ways that persisted for much of his life. His parents' abandonment triggered the first experience of deep emptiness he later came to call depression. At times, Bill turned inward with his shame about his parents' divorce. He felt he could tell no one of his deep loneliness. He found ways to isolate and stay busy. And his grandfather, recognizing this need for distraction, became a great source of new ideas and opportunities for Bill to learn.

Another impact, which developed over a longer time, was a strong-willed determination to succeed, to win, to "show 'em," no matter the cost. Bill acknowledged a fierce sense of competition in everything he did. His grandfather looked for every opportunity to suggest something new for Bill to try.

For A.A. members, one of the best-known of these projects is Bill's success in carving a boomerang at the age of eleven or twelve. Given Bill's quickness and obsessive follow-through on projects, his grandfather looked for difficult—some might say impossible—challenges. Bill described how his grandfather told him that only people who lived in Australia could make boomerangs. Bill reported how "my hackles rose when he said that nobody but an Australian could do it.... Well I will be the first white man ever to make and throw a boomerang."[13]

Thus began Bill's single-minded, six-month focus on building a boomerang. His grandfather began to worry that he had given Bill too difficult a challenge, and it was making him feel worse. Finally, after cutting a piece of wood out of the headboard of his bed, Bill was successful. Bill and his grandfather had to fall to the ground to avoid being hit by the returning boomerang. Bill arose and began shouting, "I did it!"

This amazing feat both improved Bill's self-confidence and helped his grandfather get over the death of his only son, Clarence, who had died the same year Bill was born. Fayette Griffith was still grieving when Bill and Dorothy came to live with him, but the boomerang success became a turning point. He was proud of the fact that his "Willie" was the first man in America to construct a boomerang. That motivated Griffith to spur Bill to try other things, including unearthing old Uncle Clarence's violin from the attic and learning how to make music with it.

While Griffith was seen as gruff, Bill explained how his grandfather taught him to love reading: "All during this period my grandfather was really the soul of kindness. He loved me deeply, and I loved him as I have few other people. One of my earliest recollections, was that of sitting on his knee and later at his knee, while he read me books of travel. And then came the Heidi books [by Johanna Spyri] and the [Horatio] Alger books, and all kinds of books kids used to read in that time."[14]

When a neighbor opened a circulating library, Bill became a compulsive reader, occupying himself with voracious study of anything on the library shelves, especially projects that involved building with wood and experimenting with chemicals. His desire to learn fueled these interests.

The Challenges of School

It wasn't long before Bill faced another change—a move to a boarding school. His grandfather wanted to help Bill, but he didn't know what else to do about Bill's moods and compulsive attention to reading and projects. So, he decided to see if a good school would make a difference.

By the early 1900s, school attendance was becoming more commonplace (around 79 percent of children attended school in 1910). Many attended one-room schools, where younger children sat in the front and older students sat in the back. Lunch pails were actually pails—small metal buckets for carrying food—and corporal punishment was the norm.

Most kids in East Dorset went to the public school. In contrast, Burr & Burton was a nearby private school, founded in 1829.[15] His grandfather applied for Bill to attend Burr & Burton without telling him. Bill was accepted and sent off in the fall of 1909, where he boarded during the week and went home on the weekends. While Bill often characterized himself as coming from a working-class family, his grandfather was the wealthiest person in East Dorset. He owned the local waterworks company, a lumber company, and several rental properties. So, he made sure Bill went to a fancy school.

But Bill wasn't thrilled about it because he was separated yet again from his family and those who were supposed to love and care for him. As Bill struggled to get over his depression and tried to adapt to being with rich kids whose families were very different than his, he continued to develop his unflagging willpower.

Bill's strong will and determination served him well at Burr & Burton. He was passed over for the baseball team his first year. Was he discouraged? Yes. But daunted? Absolutely not. He practiced pitching all summer. The following year, he was the starting pitcher and, by his senior year, captain of the baseball team. Music was the same way. Bill had, with his Grandfather Griffith's encouragement, taught himself to play the violin. Other boys made fun of how he sang, so he got voice lessons from the wife of the principal.

As described above, Bill's first love for Bertha Banford was so powerful, so poignant, and so painful when it ended in her unexpected death. Bertha was more than a first love for Bill. Like Lois would become, Bertha was someone Bill could talk with. They shared ideas. More than an attractive sixteen-year-old, "there was a glow about the girl, a promise.... There was a rare and special quality about Bill's loving, and there was a very special quality about Bertha.... Bill instantly forgot he'd ever been shy, and he never again thought of himself as a man who could plan only for himself. And that spring he made a miraculous discovery; When someone thinks you handsome, you are handsome."[16]

His broken family tried everything to get Bill out of his depression over Bertha's death. His grandfather had been a Union soldier in the Civil War, so he took Bill on a trip to Gettysburg to celebrate the fiftieth anniversary of the Civil War battle. Bill slept in an Army tent and heard President Woodrow Wilson give a speech on the Fourth of July. His grandfather was excited to be there and asked Bill how he felt hearing the president of the United States speak at such an important battleground. Bill was so depressed he didn't respond.

Bill's mother was outraged at his depression and poor school performance and blamed the school. She contacted her father and demanded Bill come to live with her near Boston. She enrolled Bill in the local high school. Following his mother's direction, he applied to attend Massachusetts Institute of Technology to study engineering. Bill didn't argue with his mother. He didn't know how to stand up to her and was too depressed to try. It didn't matter, since he failed the entrance test.

When summer came, his mother's fury and frustration resulted in her sending Bill to see his father in Canada. Gilly had no idea what to say to him. After a few days of mutual torture, Gilly sent Bill back to his mother, who sent him back to Grandfather Griffith, where he stayed and returned to Burr & Burton.

Bill's educational career was a mixed bag. He was initially successful in school, sports, and romance with Bertha Banford. After she died, his school performance was negatively impacted by his depression. He failed courses, but, despite spending part of his senior year in Boston, he received a diploma from Burr & Burton on June 24, 1913. He barely had enough credits to be accepted at Norwich University, a military school located in Northfield, Vermont, about ninety miles from East Dorset.

Bill's first semester at Norwich was, by all accounts, a disaster, as he was "still in grave mental trouble. On the train to school he suffered a massive anxiety attack." Bill reported shortness of breath and heart palpitations and the infirmary could find nothing wrong with him. During his second semester, he injured his elbow and insisted on going to Boston to be treated by his mother.[17]

Bill attended Norwich until 1917, when the school was closed, and students joined the military. As a result, Bill Wilson never completed college. He was commissioned a second lieutenant in the Coastal Artillery on August 14, 1917.

Fortunately for Bill, his romantic life had taken a much more positive turn, starting in 1913.

CHAPTER 3

FALLING IN LOVE

L ove at first sight? No. It took some time for Lois and Bill's relationship to form. Lois' brother, Rogers, had encouraged her to pay attention to Bill in 1913, even though Bill had two strikes against him—his younger age and his lower status as a "native" from Vermont. And Bill's ego must have taken a hit when he lost the sailboat race to Lois. While there were initial obstacles, an attraction nonetheless began to take hold.

Bill and Lois Get To Know Each Other

Bill's approach to Lois was a combination of accident, intention, and perhaps divine intervention. While no instant connection moved either of them, spending time together slowly built a passion that became undeniable. Bill described his slide into loving Lois this way:

> Well, summer came and Lois appeared and she lifted me out of this despond and we fell very deeply

in love—now I loved and was loved and there was hope again. Lois was the daughter of a very dominating father and she was four and a half years older than I. Moreover, she represented areas in which I had always felt a great inferiority. Her people were of a fine family in Brooklyn. They were what we Vermonters called city folk. She had social graces of which I knew nothing. People still ate with knives around me; the back door was still a lavatory. So, her encouragement of me, and her interest of me did a tremendous amount to buck me up.[1]

Once Lois got over her initial resistance to Bill, she fell hard for him. The summer of 1914 found Lois and Bill frequently together with friends and going to dances, hayrides, and movies. Her dad liked Bill's determination and drive but wasn't sure he was the one for Lois.

In May of 1915, Lois was excited to be back in Vermont and near Bill. She opened a small refreshment stand (Lois called it a tea arbor) that offered tourists tea and small sandwiches. Bill became her unpaid partner, suggesting ads in the paper to increase business. The business never grew, despite Lois' unshakable determination. Like Bill, she played to win, but she was happy to have more free time with Bill after her summer employment venture failed.

Bill's mom returned from her schooling in Boston that summer. She rented a cottage not far from the Burnhams on Emerald Lake. This made it easier for Bill to spend time with Lois. The long walks got longer as love deepened between Bill and Lois. They went to dances together and both enjoyed playing musical instruments.

Lois summed up becoming smitten with Bill this way: "Bill was very different than anyone I had met before. He had ideas, he was always intriguing, I mean he'd talk about all kinds of things that surprised me. I don't know what draws two people together. I thought he had great ideals, I just got crazier and crazier about him. And what he found in me I can't answer that at all."[2]

Courtesy Stepping Stones

Lois Burnham as a young woman. (Permission required for use.)

Then came the proposal, which happened suddenly. At the end of the summer of 1915, Norman, the wealthy Canadian about Lois' age, was going home. As Norman was preparing to board the train, he took Lois' hand, looked her in the eye, and asked her to marry him.

Lois was flabbergasted. Norman was nice, but certainly not the guy she wanted to marry. She realized clearly that she wanted to spend any time she had with Bill. Being decisive, Lois said no to Norman's proposal.

Norman, dejected, got on the train home. Later that same evening, Lois told Bill about the surprise proposal. Bill was also shocked and, for a moment, scared. What if he lost Lois, his love? Determined not to let this possibility happen, he immediately took action. While we don't know Bill's exact words, we might picture him saying, "Lois, I have never loved anyone more than you. My heart races, and I am so happy when I'm with you. I can't imagine spending my life with anyone else. I wasn't planning to do this tonight, but it seems the perfect time. Will you marry me?"

While Lois provided many details on the courtship in her memoir, she summed up their decision to get engaged very simply: "The same evening [after rejecting Norman] we told each other of our love."[3]

Courtship after Commitment

Lois reminded readers in her memoir that courtship was very different in the beginning of the twentieth century. She explained how couples weren't allowed to hold hands because it wasn't considered "proper." But she acknowledged that when she and Bill walked, their hands kept touching each other. Given what Lois did say about her love for Bill, including about writing him daily love letters, her imagination must have been going wild. Lois saved many of her thoughts during this period and throughout her life in her diary.[4]

As she imagined their future together, she envisioned a houseful of kids with Bill as a successful businessman. They'd travel and hike and summer on the lake. Lois admired Bill's big plans, and the thought of being part of his dreams appealed to her. She believed they would continue to share their ideas and make real the life they talked about every day. It was not hard for Lois to say yes to loving Bill Wilson.

The lovers decided not to tell anyone about their commitment just yet. Bill's love letters after the engagement became more direct: "O believe me, dear Lois, I love you more than anything in the world. May we kiss together tonight? Fondly, Bill to Dear."[5]

Two days after the proposal, Bill headed back to college at Norwich University. Lois and her family packed up the cottage and headed back to their home in Brooklyn. Lois soon began her new position at the YWCA. The prospect of a major war loomed, so Bill and Lois had no idea when they might get married. Bill had dropped out of school for a semester the year before and was still only a freshman. They continued to keep their engagement a secret.

Letters flew back and forth as the two lovers struggled to accept being separated. Bill repeatedly professed his love for Lois, though he occasionally missed the evening mail train. Lois wrote at least daily, causing Bill's grandmother to comment that at the rate those letters were coming, there'd soon be enough to wallpaper the kitchen! Bill's letters told of his love, of his dreams, and of his ideas about a better world: "I love you from head to foot. Don't you wish you were taller? I don't, for then my love would have to be divided among more feet. To sum it all up, less love per square centimeter."[6]

Lois, in her letters, expressed her love and added short notes to herself about any questions or worries. For example, she noted that Bill had not told his mother about their engagement. In another place, she mused about Washington, DC, as a possible honeymoon location. Lois eventually confided about her engagement to her close friends Elise, Helen, and Edith.

Over their many summer conversations and walks, Bill had told Lois about his pain over his parents' divorce and his father leaving the family. There were no secrets between Bill and Lois. Lois knew the hardships Bill had already faced in life and was certain her love would be enough to overcome them. But she kept Bill's story secret from her parents. If her parents had known Bill's whole sordid story, perhaps there would have been no Bill and Lois Wilson.

However, Lois' feelings were not hidden. She was prone to bursts of anger. Frustrated by not hearing from Bill for a few days, her temper erupted one night when a male friend who was escorting her to the movies insisted she not wait for Bill's telephone call. Lois confessed to being so upset by this insistence that she tossed a book at Emil.

Bill's friend Mark Whalon encouraged Bill in his love for Lois. In a 1915 letter to Lois, Bill shared Mark's advice. "Dear Darling girl, ... [Mark] said 'Bill it is the big thing. Go to it. Make good for the girl. She is a woman thru & thru.' Then he gave me sound advice as follows *'She loves you because you are Bill Wilson nothing more or less. Never try to be anything but your plain ordinary self. You are enough.'"*[7]

Lois and Bill Prepare for Marriage

Despite the uncertainty posed by the possibility of war, Lois eventually told her parents about her engagement. They gave their approval, though her father reminded her of the differences between Bill and Norman.

Later in the fall of 1915, after Bill returned to school and Lois to New York, the engaged couple deepened their sharing in their letters.[8] Bill enthusiastically agreed with Lois' views about religion: "Darling, Your dear letter of last night at hand. Have been reading over your letters for the 99th time and note what you say about religion. 'I prefer my own prayers to that of the minister. I prefer my own thoughts to those of the sermon. I believe that we live after death.' Dear heart you could not have stated my attitude more clearly. We agree on so many things."[9]

Bill went on to say he agreed with Lois about "spooning" (romantic cuddling) and what is appropriate before marriage. He continued by confessing to some inappropriate flirting with Lois' sister Barbara a few months earlier. Some back-and-forth communication about Barbara and Bill's flirting continued, concluding with Bill detailing for Lois other girls with whom he had flirtatious or perhaps "spooning" experiences.[10] Some have interpreted these letters as Bill's sharing about sexual intercourse he had with other girls. It is difficult to know for certain whether he was merely flirting or was sexually intimate with the girls he mentioned to Lois. "In Vermont at the turn of the century, there were many different cultural attitudes toward sex. Bill Wilson came from a quarry family, and his father had defined masculinity through sexual activity.... Bill straightforwardly shared his sexual history (with Lois). These letters to Lois are startlingly eloquent, and they set their pattern for their long marriage. Bill was passionate, and abashed by his behavior; Lois was forgiving and comforting."[11]

At this distance, it's impossible to determine whether Bill was faithful to Lois or not. Whatever the truth, this exchange did not dampen Lois' enthusiastic love for Bill.

As 1916 progressed, their love and excitement about marriage grew. In one of his letters, Bill foreshadowed two shared interests that would keep them together and sustain them throughout their marriage. "Pal what shall I get you for Christmas. I'm at my wits end. *It would be nice to get a set of books perhaps.* If we could only decide on something that we will want to have in our home. Books or perhaps music would be as fine as anything to get now as we can't start yet with furniture."[12]

Once the engagement was public, Bill went to New York to spend time with his future in-laws and look for an engagement ring for his beloved. Bill had no way of preparing himself for his first visit to Lois' Brooklyn home in early 1916. Their whole romance had occurred at the summer cottage on the lake—a warm, informal setting. The Burnhams' home and fashionable neighborhood in Brooklyn were stunning for Bill.

First, the warm, bright finishings in the sprawling 1848 brick house absorbed Bill. He'd never seen a home so gorgeously decorated. And everyone was so lively and talkative—a big home filled with love. He'd yearned for that forever, as Bill's maternal grandparents came from quiet, reclusive Yankee stock, not the garrulous storytellers like his dad and the Wilsons. His only prior taste of being part of a "real" family was his brief friendship with Bertha Banford and her family.

"Try to do and say those things only which will be agreeable to others." So stated Emily Post in her 1922 book on etiquette.[13] Bill certainly wanted to be agreeable, but, despite his private school attendance, Bill hadn't grasped all the conventions of the upper crust. Refined gentlemen of that era did not wear their hats indoors and always stood when a lady entered the room. Bill had a few things to learn.

His first dinner presented some unique challenges, though Lois did her best to help Bill feel at home. Bill gulped when he saw all the forks and spoons by his place. Lois, ever attentive, gently nudged him under the table and nodded toward the outside fork as she picked hers up. That was enough of a start for Bill. He was often intimidated by new situations and felt off balance. Lois, from the beginning, sensed his anxiety and comforted and directed him.

Bill's ideas and imagination often outran his pocketbook, and ring shopping was no exception. Lois wanted to take Bill to some less-expensive jewelry stores in Manhattan to look for her engagement ring. Bill had been working cutting wood and playing concerts and had saved $25. He insisted they go to Tiffany's for the engagement ring. Bill didn't know much about the place other than it was the best of the best, so that's where he went to get Lois' ring. They selected a classic amethyst stone set in a gold band. The cost—$25—made their engagement official. Lois gave Bill a ring in exchange too—her Packer Institute class ring. A February date was set in 1918, and plans were soon underway for a large, very fancy wedding. After all, Lois was the oldest daughter of one of Brooklyn's best doctors.

As 1917 was ending, Bill's love letters continued: "Every night I hold out my arms to you in the dark and whisper for you to come to me. And then gather them in thinking I hold you close and hear you whisper wonderful things— *then fall asleep thinking and dreaming of the time when these wonderful things shall really be.* Oh Lois I love you. I love you. I love you. Bill."[14]

Bill and Lois Marry

Early in the new year, there were rumors that Bill's unit, the 66th Coastal Artillery Corps, Battery C, would soon be shipping out for the war in Europe. Lois and her family made hasty calls to relatives and friends and approved emergency overtime for Lois' seamstress, and the wedding was moved a week earlier to January 24, 1918.

The nuptials took place in Lois' family's place of worship, the Swedenborgian Church, followed by a reception at her family home. The wedding day was cold and cloudy, and there was the cloud of Bill's imminent departure, but Lois and Bill were ecstatic. Nothing could interfere with the glow of their love. There was no holding back. They were meant to be together and thrilled to be married. Bill's transition from his troubled family of birth to his new life with Lois was complete.

Bill's mother and sister were unable to come to the wedding, reportedly due to colds. On their way north to Bill's first army assignment at Fort Rodman in Bedford, Massachusetts, shortly after the wedding, Bill and Lois stopped to visit Bill's mom. Bill had been open with Lois about his childhood and strained relations with his parents. She knew his early life had not been easy and was probably not surprised that his mom and sister did not attend the wedding.

After an engagement with too much time spent apart, the married couple cherished the months between their wedding and Bill's departure for war, which was delayed until August 1918. At Fort

Wedding day picture. (Permission required for use.)

Rodman, the young lovers shared a furnished apartment just off the base. "They began married life in a state of near ecstasy. They became each other's world. They made love. For the first time in a long time, Bill felt he might become the man he dreamed of being."[15]

In April, Bill's unit was transferred to Fort Adams in Newport, Rhode Island. Lois lived off base and saw Bill only on weekends.

Bill was completing officer training and, as an officer, was invited to parties hosted by the members of

high society in Rhode Island who wanted to show support for the war effort. According to some, Bill had his first beer at one of these parties given by a wealthy Rhode Island family. When Bill returned to his apartment, he told Lois about his first beer. He described this life-changing beginning as no big deal. "Everybody had a beer, so I did too," he explained.

A month or two later, Bill was again at a social gathering hosted by the wealthy of Newport, Rhode Island.

A happy Bill Wilson before leaving for war. (Permission required for use.)

Here the drinks were different, including a new drink popular in New York called the Bronx cocktail. This was hard liquor—gin—mixed with vermouth and orange juice. This new drink had a different impact than the beer. After the first, Bill recalled all the warnings he had received about the trouble that drinking caused his father and other relatives. But he also recalled how the beer had not hurt him and kept on drinking.

That weekend, Bill got more honest and told Lois about his first major hangover. Perhaps he described how the bed moved, making him dizzy and so sick to his stomach he couldn't eat the entire next day.

Lois reflected in her memoir about how Bill drank occasionally after they married, mostly at parties. He didn't imbibe excessively, although when invited by a young lady to partake, he usually said yes. Lois wasn't perturbed—well, maybe a little—by his drinking habits. She was sure that her love and her good Christian example would be the fence that would keep him sober and satisfied.

As was to be the case many times in their marriage, Lois smiled and put a positive face on Bill's drinking or acted like it wasn't happening. Drinking was also on Bill's mind, and he raised it in an early letter to Lois which she marked "First Drink": "I'm trying to figure out this drinking business. I am sure we're going to run against it a good deal. Of course there are a great many times when one can refuse gracefully enough, and there seem to be times when you can't. What do you think dear? Should we be teetotalers or shouldn't we? I couldn't see that beer did anything to me and I can't say I was crazy about the taste of it. Tell me dear just what you think of it. I love you, old pal."[16]

We don't know whether or how Lois replied to Bill's question. She seemed to ignore his suggestion. She remained infatuated with her new husband and was confident her love was more than enough for Bill. At the time, she didn't see anything, including Bill's drinking a little alcohol, as blocking her all-consuming and all-powerful love for him.

Little did Bill and Lois know this was the beginning of nearly two decades of drinking and hangovers.

After he got sober, Bill would describe his drinking experience this way: With the first drink, "that strange barrier that had existed between me and all men and women, even the closest, seemed to instantly go down."[17] Bill had found the magic that overcame all his shyness and feelings of separateness. Alcohol was his new best friend.

Courtesy Stepping Stones

Bill and Lois enjoying time before the war separates them in 1917-1918. (Permission required for use.)

Alcohol may have been his new best friend, but Lois was his brand-new wife. "I wanted to be the best possible wife and mother, as much like my own mother as possible. When Bill, knowing I idolized Mother, wanted to please me, he would say, 'You're just like your mommie.'"[18]

Lois prepared herself for Bill's unavoidable departure for war in many ways, one of which was captured in a love poem written in the spring of 1918:

(Permission is required from the Stepping Stones Foundation for any further use, display, or duplication of the following material from its archive.)

Dear Bill: A poem for you;
The robins sing, 'tis spring, dear heart,
And soon you'll have to go
To that over "over there" where guns do flare
And the price of life runs low,

The robins sing 'tis spring dear heart,
God gives us powers that we
In our hearts most deep that song may keep,
Whatever the road may be.[19]

Every great wartime movie has a scene where the women run alongside a departing train, waving handkerchiefs to their men as the locomotive pulls out of the station. But in August 1918, it was no Hollywood gimmick when Lois waved farewell to Bill at the depot. The romantic farewell had begun the night before. Lois and Bill had enjoyed dinner together, along with other couples, before peeling off to be alone. They sauntered by the sea, admiring the August moon. They probably did more than merely walk hand in hand that night.

After only six months of married bliss and living on or near army bases, Bill left for England in August 1918 as a second lieutenant in the US Army. Military life separated Bill and Lois Wilson for the first time. It was just the first of several ominous changes for the idealistic newlyweds.

Lois wrote frequently to Bill, keeping him informed of her life and her deep love and longing for him. Because not all letters were saved, it is likely, but not certain, that Bill wrote less frequently to Lois.

And being at war led Bill to further embrace the relief he found in drinking.

CHAPTER 4

FINDING THEIR WAY AFTER THE WAR

Bill's military orders sent him to France, where everybody drank rum and brandy all day and night, even the children—or so it seemed to Bill. He could not understand why the French weren't always drunk. In his autobiography, he described in detail his increasing reliance on wine and rum.[1] Lois came to understand, as she got fewer letters from Bill than she hoped, that this was because his drinking was growing.

Lois wrote to Bill regularly. They spent their first anniversary apart because of Bill's military service. Lois wrote:

(Permission is required from the Stepping Stones Foundation for any further use, display, or duplication of the following material from its archive.)

My husband I love you, I love you dear with all there is in me, with my whole heart & my whole soul & my whole body. This is our wedding day dear & I have never been so lonesome in all my life. Did you remember it & did you long for me my darling? I had to work like the dickens today to make myself forget how I wanted you.... In one way I hope you forgot it was our wedding day because it would be harder for you. Off there by yourself. I keep wondering where you are, I have had no word from you in so long dear. Just thinking a year ago today, how happy we were! But wait until we get together again we'll be even more happy won't we dear? I can't understand why I don't hear from you unless you have started for home & I can't see the 66th listed as being on any of the transports. It doesn't seem as if you could ever really come home to me. I have wanted you so long. It seems as if I must always continue to want you. Mother has just this minute brought me some candy to celebrate. Mother surely is wonderful. I love you my dear husband. I love you more than I can tell. I long for you, for some word from you. I love you dear I love you Lois.[2]

Lois initially tried to see if the YWCA would send her to Europe so she could be closer to Bill. To her surprise, her application was rejected because of her religion. Her Swedenborgian faith was not considered Christian. Lois was indignant and put her energy instead into learning the emerging profession of occupational therapy. She moved to Washington, DC, and worked at the Walter Reed General Hospital, serving wounded soldiers. Lois wrote about the emotional toll it took on her, seeing all those wounded soldiers and worrying about Bill and his safety.

Bill's wartime service was short. The war ended less than five months after his arrival in Europe. The highlights of his time there were what he called a spiritual awakening while reading a poem about drinking on a tombstone in England[3] and the gift of a pocket watch with a chain and ring given to him and his captain by the men of the battery he led. Bill loved to be appreciated, and this unexpected recognition was a memory he shared often.

Bill was part of the transition force in France and returned home to an eagerly awaiting Lois in March 1919. Lois got a letter telling her Bill would arrive in Norfolk. She raced there to meet him and found out he was arriving back north in Hoboken, New Jersey. Lois described the reunion as sweet, despite some awkwardness after living apart during this traumatic time for the nation and world.

Early Years of Marriage

The early years of their marriage were both normal and unusual for the Wilsons. The normal part was establishing a home of their own. Like many young couples, they gradually moved from Lois' parents' home to a tiny apartment and then a slightly nicer place on Amity Street in Lois' childhood neighborhood of Brooklyn Heights.

Bill had a hard time adjusting to being home and without a job. He wrote in his autobiography about riding the subway and being shocked when the guards didn't salute him. Lois' father tried to use his influence to find Bill employment, but he hadn't finished college, and there were lots of war veterans looking for work. Bill tried bookkeeping for the railroad and got fired. Next, he worked as a laborer and did not like it. As his frustrations grew, his drinking increased.

On January 19, 1920, Prohibition began in the United States, making the sale of alcohol illegal. Bill, like many, quickly found the speakeasies, so Prohibition posed no detriment to his drinking.

Lois and Bill, both still in denial about his growing drinking problem, decided in 1921 on a solution they came back to often—spending some time alone in nature. They decided to hike the 300-mile Long Trail in the

Green Mountains. Bill later described their itinerary in his autobiography as the happy couple traveled to Portland, Maine, to begin hiking all the way to Rutland, Vermont. It was a magical hike, full of tender moments and intimacy. It gave Bill much-needed relief from the challenge of finding meaningful work.

Bill's curiosity and eagerness to learn were as compelling as his need to drink. His scientific interest and intellectual prowess were evident during this period, though he chose not to pursue engineering or science. Lois enjoyed working with Bill on his ham-radio set. Bill became connected to people in thirty-five communities and introduced relatives and friends to the power of the new ham radios, called superheterodynes.

Before eventually finding his way on Wall Street, Bill was offered a job working as a researcher in the acoustics department of Thomas Edison's world-renowned Bell Laboratory. Bill got this opportunity through a newspaper competition he won, but he turned down the offer because he didn't want to work for someone else. Despite such decisions, Bill never lost his interest in science and in building things.

Bill forgot about Edison and took a job as a criminal investigator of defaults for a surety company, US Fidelity and Guaranty Company (USF&G). Lois' sister Barbara's husband-to-be worked there and provided Bill this job opportunity, which involved investigating defaults by Wall Street stock exchange firms.

During their New England hike, Bill had decided to take his Grandfather Griffith's advice and go to law school. He attended classes at night for four years, alongside his work at USF&G, and struggled due to his heavy drinking.

Lois had worked for the Walter Reed General Hospital in Washington, DC, and Brooklyn Naval Hospital during the war. After Bill got home in 1921, she moved on to work for higher wages in the women's psychiatric ward at Bellevue Hospital.

Struggles with Pregnancy

Stressful aspects of the marriage began to surface. In the summer of 1921, Lois suffered the first of three ectopic pregnancies, all of which occurred in the early 1920s. In her memoir, Lois recounted her experience of these pregnancies rather frankly. She also commented on Bill's attentiveness to her during the first two times she lost a pregnancy. She convinced her dad she was OK after the second experience in 1922 because she "wanted so badly to return to Bill."[4]

After the second unsuccessful pregnancy, Lois and Bill knew they couldn't have children. Given their dreams of a big family, this was devastating news. Lois generously described Bill's "grace and kindness" to her despite the deep sadness they both felt. She acknowledged that, while she knew she had done nothing to cause this inability to have children, she still felt guilty. And she observed how Bill's disappointment led to more drinking. She confessed to trying to understand his drinking and often losing her temper.

While Lois was silent in her memoir about the details of her grief, she was a person who stayed close to her friends. Elise Valentine was among the closest, and she likely would have shared the pain of this loss with Elise. Lois no doubt was crushed by the loss. Elise, who had married Frank Shaw and already had children of her own, would understand her loss as only another mother could. But Elise's consoling words didn't take Lois' pain away.

Eventually, Lois was ready to again pour all her love into being with Bill. She loved being with Bill on weekend hikes and out in nature. They eventually bought a

Harley-Davidson motorcycle with a sidecar to expand the places they could explore.

Bill on Wall Street

As Bill got to know Wall Street, he became convinced of the importance of learning about companies firsthand and in person.

Lois recalled in her memoir how Bill's grandfather had reinforced his confidence in the importance of studying something firsthand before investing, just as you would want to examine a cow before purchase.

Reflecting on this time later in life, Bill wrote: "I began to get in circulation amongst the stockbrokers and wondered why so many people lost so much money and wondered why they acted on so little investigation and suddenly it dawned on me that I would make a very good investigator of security values."[5]

Once again, Bill decided to go all-in. His strong will and Lois' faith in him resulted in a decision to sell everything they had and take a year-long motorcycle trip to visit companies. While it seems unlikely that Dr. Burnham, Lois' father, was a big fan of this idea, Lois was clear about her reason for agreeing to what some would call a crazy trip. She would have more time with her Bill, and there would be less temptation for him to drink. She was sure a year with her on the road, camping and having fun, would rid Bill of his need to drink.

Lois chronicled their trip in a book she titled *Diary of Two Motorcycle Hobos*.[6] While April in New England would be too cold for many to consider swimming, Lois noted how refreshing their morning bath was on the first morning and described running to Lake Emerald for a skinny dip the next morning, despite there being snow on the ground. Skinny dipping, picnicking, then hitting the road to do it again. This trip was a success, beyond Lois' or

Courtesy Stepping Stones

Lois and Bill Wilson camping near Schenectady, New York on the motorcycle hobo trip, 1925. (Permission required for use.)

Courtesy Stepping Stones

Lois and Bill on their "motorcycle hobo trip," 1925. (Permission required for use.)

Bill's wildest hopes. They both loved being outdoors. They slept on the ground many nights and bathed together in nearby brooks or streams. Water temperatures that varied by thirty degrees did not bother the young lovers. Bill had his business suit with him, and the next day he would dress up to go visit executives at General Electric or Portland Cement.

But it wasn't in the formal meetings with company managers that

47

Bill learned the most helpful information. Meeting with workers in the evenings at nearby taverns resulted in invitations to come see the plant. This formula of using his social skills to make friends made Bill one of the first successful stock analysts.

After an insider's visit to Giant Portland Cement in Egypt, Pennsylvania, Bill reported to Frank Shaw (Lois' friend Elise's husband), who worked at Rice & Co., on the great untapped potential of this company. While not formally employed by Frank, Bill kept Frank informed about what he learned during his trip. On Bill's recommendation, Frank immediately bought 5,000 shares of Giant Portland Cement stock. Frank bought the stock at $15 a share and sold it at $75 a share. Frank rewarded Bill by buying 100 shares for him. This was the beginning of Bill's short-lived success on Wall Street, including eventually going to work for Frank at Rice & Co.

This trip was successful in that Bill drank less than when in New York and made progress and connections that aided his Wall Street career. But the trip ended abruptly in a motorcycle accident that put Lois on crutches for her sister's wedding in October 1927.

Bill's Drinking Grows

Thereafter, Bill's problem drinking began to surface more strongly. At first, it didn't seem too bad. He showed up for work. He didn't hang out with slackers. He didn't drink every day, it just got out of hand sometimes. But it was the Roaring Twenties, after all—the decade that introduced the car, the airplane, movies, and jazz music. New forms of technology and new styles of entertainment were exploding onto the scene. Everybody was a little bit outrageous.

And Bill was a stock analyst. He made deals, took risks, and, because he was talented, they paid off handsomely.

He described it this way: "The great boom of the late twenties was seething and swelling. Drink was taking an important and exhilarating part of my life."[7] When Bill drank, he couldn't just drink a little. He would drink until he got completely drunk. Once he started, he couldn't stop. Sometimes it made him act in embarrassing ways. Often, it made him spend—or lose—his money.

It wasn't just his own money that Bill was spending. Bill was building a reputation as a brilliant stock analyst. Given his early success and the "sky's the limit" attitude of the 1920s, family and friends turned to Bill for investment advice. Picture Bill in his Wall Street office around 1925, getting a call from his brother-in-law, Rogers Burnham. Grabbing the phone as his long, lanky legs hung over the corner of his mahogany desk, he heard Rogers ask: "Bill, what do you think of my buying more GE stock?" Bill might respond, "Rog, GE is like gold. You can't own too much."

Lois, like many loyal wives of that era, joined Bill for important business dinners to entertain clients and potential clients. Since Frank Shaw was Bill's boss and married to Elise, Lois loved entertaining clients with the Shaws. Like with the motorcycle trip, Lois saw the dinners as both a pleasant time with friends and an opportunity to keep an eye on Bill's drinking.

It is understandable why Lois did not say a lot about her anxious moments during such dinners in her diary. But if Lois were to describe a typical evening, it might have gone like this.

The Green Room was a legitimate restaurant off Madison Avenue, with a speakeasy and nightclub in the back. Lois and Elise would meet their husbands at the restaurant and be introduced to two potential clients and their wives.

The evening would proceed to one of two outcomes. On a good night, Bill would be able to stop after three or four drinks, and the business dinner would be a great success for everyone, including Lois. More often, as Bill's drinking got worse, the evening ended agonizingly. After bragging to the prospective clients early in the evening about how big the steaks were, by the time the steaks arrived, Bill would be slurring his words.

An hour or two later, as Bill became louder and dominated the conversation, Frank Shaw would take over. He would try to put the best spin on the evening and emphasize again Bill's skill in analyzing stocks through on-site visits. Most importantly, he would likely emphasize the potential financial gains other customers were enjoying as a result of Bill's research.

While Lois tried to ignore the evenings when Bill lost control, it is likely Elise said something to Frank. Frank remained loyal to Bill, despite occasional embarrassments. Lois could sometimes still feel romantic with Bill while trusting him became harder and harder as his drinking progressed.

A Third Pregnancy

After two miscarriages and despite Bill's drinking and passing out many nights, Lois got pregnant a third time in 1923. She increasingly felt the pressure to have children, as she visited her friend Elise Shaw and saw her joy with her three children, as well as the satisfaction of other friends. Lois held onto Bill's often-stated desire to have a family. She knew in her heart that Bill still wanted their courtship dream of a big family and recalled when he said he hoped their children would have Lois' eyes and disposition.

Three months into this third pregnancy, in May of 1923, tragedy came once more. Lois was stricken with a terrible pain in her belly and called Bill's office. He wasn't there. She called her father and told him she was in labor. He told her to get to the hospital.

By the time Lois arrived at Skene Sanitarium, a women's hospital in Brooklyn where her father was on the staff, Dr. Burnham had arranged for his partner, head of the obstetrics department, to see his daughter.

Three hours later, his partner emerged and told Lois' father he could not save the baby. He confirmed once again that Lois and Bill could not have children. This third, unexpected ectopic pregnancy drove home what Lois already knew: She and Bill weren't going to have children.

Lois cried for quite a while, something longtime friends report she did rarely. A nurse explained she was not responsible for her inability to have children, yet she still felt guilty about not being able to give Bill the family they both wanted. Somehow, this recognition helped her become a little more understanding of the guilt Bill felt each time he broke a vow to not drink.

Lois was despondent for the next three weeks and didn't have much to say to Bill.

A Temperance Pledge

On Christmas Day, 1923, Bill made his first written "temperance pledge" to Lois in their family Bible. He wrote: "Thank you for your love and help this terrible year. For your Christmas, I make you this present: No liquor will pass my lips for one year." Two months later, he drank again and wrote another vow.[8]

Three years later, Bill made a similar pledge, this time in a New Year's resolution:

> Between you and me I've made a New Years resolution: *No booze in 1927.* I sure mean business and I'm going to give it the effort of my life. It's got to be done and *I know that it will make us both very happy*—I love you and you know it don't you darling—*I'm out to best this thing and I'm sure*

trying hard for you dear one—Things are going very nicely and I will be home Saturday PM tho just what home I don't know yet. I love you. I love you dear one. Bill.[9]

Lois' concern about Bill's increased drinking caused her to suggest over dinner one evening that they needed some time out of the city. Bill was eager to get out of the doghouse and please his young bride, so he quickly agreed.

Before they left, Lois suggested that Bill see her brother-in-law, Dr. Leonard Strong. Leonard was married to Bill's sister, Dorothy. Lois trusted him and asked him to talk with Bill about his drinking before the trip. Bill normally would have resisted, but he knew he had hurt Lois deeply with his drinking, so he went along.

Dr. Strong insisted on a full physical and affirmed what Bill already knew: He was in good shape and needed to cut back both his drinking and smoking. Relieved and still believing he could cut back on drinking, Bill eagerly agreed with his brother-in-law's diagnosis.

Eventful Road Trips

Frank Shaw enthusiastically authorized another road trip for Bill. After all, he was making money from Bill's travels, and he was beginning to agree with Lois that Bill drank less on the road.

The first part of the trip went spectacularly. In her memoir, Lois described how Bill didn't drink and was successful at his stops in upstate New York and Connecticut. Next was a stop in Holyoke, Massachusetts, to visit the America Writing Paper Company. The company was in receivership. Bill had a hunch that with new management, this company could be another cash cow for Wall Street. He bonded so well with one of the company's board members, he offered Bill and Lois a cabin in the woods for a week. This was no normal cabin. Lois recalled it with delight. Besides running water and heat, there was a big patch of blueberries and elderberries. As in past trips to Emerald Lake or camping, the Wilsons rediscovered themselves and each other.

Lois was discreet in her diary about their intimacy

during these trips. Their love of nature got them outdoors. Once outdoors, a quick dip in a cold lake often followed, then a snuggle and warming-up session, making sweet love. This trip was an opportunity to forget their pains and savor their love, and Lois made sure they had plenty of opportunities to do that.

Lois Wilson prepares to take a dip.
(Permission required for use.)

Bill didn't drink all week. The next stop was Montreal, which had also been a respite for the lovers in the past. Bill's luck with his investigations began to change in Montreal. He came up against a company that refused him any information. He assured Lois he would get the information he needed the next day.

The next day was worse, and the day after that. Bill was told they refused to see him. Despondently, he decided to head home. Bill's somber face and silence made clear how much he hated to disappoint Frank Shaw.

When they got near the US border in their Packard, Bill said he wanted to stop and get some cigarettes. Lois was suspicious, since cigarettes were cheaper back in New York. Thirty minutes later, Lois began to worry about Bill's absence. An hour later, suspicion was replaced with concern. At the two-hour mark, anger took over as she asked herself how Bill could go off drinking after such a sweet week together.

Three hours later, Lois went looking for Bill. Sure enough, in the closest tavern to the cigarette store, she heard Bill's loud voice even before she opened the door. He was out of money and wobbly on his feet.

Seeing Bill's condition, Lois could not hold back her anger. She called him a pitiful drunk. Once they got to the car, Lois gave Bill the silent treatment all the way back to Brooklyn. She was angry about driving and about her hope in Bill being dashed one more time.

A few days after their return, Frank summoned Bill to his office. Apparently, his lack of success in Montreal wasn't an issue. He asked Bill to go to Cuba and size up the potential for investing in sugar companies there.

In Cuba, Bill and Lois were treated as visiting dignitaries. They stayed at the best hotel, ate the best food, and were wined and dined by the leaders of Cuba. Unfortunately for Bill, Frank Shaw heard stories of Bill's wild partying from a Wall Street friend. This time, he didn't wait for Bill to get home. He told his secretary to get Bill on the phone.

The conversation was sterner than Bill recalled before, with Frank telling him very clearly that if he valued his job, he needed to cut out the crazy behavior and drinking.

Bill was used to Lois shouting and pleading about his drinking. He knew her dad was not a big fan, and he now referred to him as "boss." But Frank Shaw's confrontation scared the hell out of him. Before heading home, Bill wrote to Frank:

> I have never said anything to you about the liquor
> question, but now that you mention it and also for

the good reason that you are investing your perfectly good money in me, I am at last very happy to say that I have had a final showdown [with myself] on the matter. It has always been a very serious handicap for me, so that you can appreciate how glad I am to be finally rid of it. It got to the point where I had to decide whether to be a monkey or a man. I know it is going to be a tough job, but nevertheless the best thing I ever did for myself and everybody concerned. That is that, so let us now forget about it.[10]

Living Their Best Life

Financially, life for the Wilsons could not have been better. They moved from their small apartment on Amity Street to a larger and more prestigious building on Livingston Street. While still only blocks from Lois' childhood home on Clinton Street, Bill and Lois were established and making it on their own. Big-idea guy and spender that he was, Bill decided to rent the apartment next door and break through the wall. They needed a bigger living room for the deluxe $1,600 baby grand piano he bought for Lois.

Lois was a little nervous about committing to the big rent increase for three years. She asked Bill for assurance and got his confident reply. It was 1926, and of course there were no signs yet of the Great Depression lurking a few years away.

The Roaring Twenties were a time of prosperity and optimism. It was that speculative over-enthusiasm that led to the calamitous stock market crash in 1929. But three years before that disaster, the Wilsons were enjoying their prosperity.

Lois loved music and likely was both delighted to have her own piano and concerned about the cost. To have a room big enough for it and be able to play any time she wanted—that was heaven. This piano followed them for the rest of their lives. Even when they were homeless, they kept it in storage.[11]

Bill and Lois loved to entertain. As the holidays of 1926 approached, Lois suggested to Bill that they invite all her family over for dinner to enjoy their new home. Bill agreed and likely saw this as an opportunity to prove to his father-in-law that he was a successful businessman and good husband.

Lois later recalled what happened at this memorable dinner.[12] The day started pleasantly enough. Dr. Burnham and Matilda were complimenting Lois on the beautiful piano and the finely carved moldings and pressed-tin ceilings that adorned the living room.

Over dinner, the conversation turned to the stock market. Rogers Burnham (Lois' brother) and Leonard Strong (Bill's brother-in-law) were both complimenting Bill on his ability to pick stocks. Rogers could not praise Bill enough for his knack for picking stocks. "I don't know about you, Len, but I rest better at night thanks to your guidance, Bill."

Bill, caught up in the enthusiasm, invited his father-in-law down to Wall Street "to see how your son-in-law works his magic." Bill offered a toast with his wine.

To this, Lois recalls Dr. Burnham replied, "Not on your life. I hear it's like watching a herd of wild buffalo stampede."

"Well, he can go to hell," Bill mumbled as he excused himself and went to the parlor for a drink. Lois did her best to normalize the rest of the evening, but one more time, the ideal family picture she had created fell apart because of Bill's drinking.

Bill couldn't believe it. He so much wanted Dr. Burnham's approval. Here he was, making money for all of them. They were sitting in his beautiful home, enjoying his food and wine. Nineteen twenty-six had been a remarkable year. Calvin Coolidge was in the White House. Clara Bow, the "It Girl," was lighting up the silver screen. With a $70,000 contract, Babe Ruth had become the highest paid baseball player ever, and Bill was doing well too.

As the Roaring Twenties got wilder, life for the Wilsons continued to be a roller coaster. Lois would convince Bill to go camping for a few days, and he would dry out. She would get a little hope. He would come back to Brooklyn and quickly go back to getting drunk every night.

Bill proudly told everyone he did not drink until the bell sounded at 3 p.m. each day on Wall Street. With a fistful of cash, he would make his way home, sometimes a little drunk, sometimes barely able to unlock the door. Lois vacillated between angry taunts and passionate pleading. At times, she moved back to her parents' home and told Bill she would return when he was sober for two weeks. Bill would again plead for another chance, and Lois would eventually relent.

As his reputation advanced on Wall Street, Bill got to know a lot of wealthy and powerful people. Bill enjoyed being in the company of influential people and became quite skilled at making connections. Among them was Joseph Hirshhorn.

Joe Hirshhorn began his career as a runner on Wall Street. He was from Brownsville, a poorer part of Brooklyn. Like Bill, he mastered the art of picking stocks with potential and making a lot of money. Hirshhorn was Frank Shaw's largest client. Hirshhorn had on occasion hired Bill on the side to investigate stocks he was considering. Joe's wealth grew rapidly, and he moved out to a prestigious estate in the posh Great Neck section of Long Island. Hirshhorn got interested in art by framing a picture he found for his mom. As his wealth grew, so did his art collection. (Hirshhorn's wealth would later result in the Smithsonian Institution opening a Hirshhorn Gallery to house and show his extraordinary art collection.)

A Fateful Party

Frank Shaw knew Joe liked Bill. Bill helped Joe make a lot of money. So, one Friday in the spring of 1928, as work ended, Frank invited Bill and Lois to join him and Elise for a party. It was a big fundraiser Joe Hirshhorn was hosting at his Long Island estate to benefit his synagogue.

Elise Shaw liked Bill, but she was a bit worried about Bill's behavior when he drank. Elise wasn't speculating; she had lived with a drunk father and knew that embarrassing the family was predictable when men drank the way her father and Bill did. She was so concerned about her friend Lois that she had lunch with her earlier that same week at the Metropolitan Museum of Art.

Elise casually mentioned Frank's concern about Bill's drinking. Lois dismissed the concern because Bill had once more assured her he was stopping forever. Elise tried to explain her experience with her own father's drinking and how he often promised to stop and never could. His drinking kept getting worse, Elise explained. Lois did not want to believe that was true for Bill.[13]

Lois shifted the topic back to Joe's party and confided to her friend she was having trouble finding the right dress. Knowing Lois' love for art and decorating, Elise understood her desire for the "right" dress.

Elise, as always, assured her friend of her beauty and charm and told her not to worry. After frantic visits to four shops, Lois indeed found the perfect dress at a store new to her, on the seedier part of Fulton Street.

At the party, Elise welcomed Lois with a hug and complimented her on her gorgeous red dress. During the beginning of the party, Lois and Bill thoroughly enjoyed themselves. Lois led Bill through the house and pointed out all the details of the upscale furnishings. When it came to the art, she stood in awe. Bill smiled and nursed his first glass of champagne for a while. They danced to the soft, soothing music and held each other close.

A couple of hours into the party, Bill excused himself to get a smoke and find his friend Clint from the firm. He assured Lois he'd be right back.

Lois didn't know that Clint was a hard drinker like Bill. Bill and Clint began throwing down the champagne. Bill and Clint then apparently connected with a very attractive divorcee from a nearby estate. Allegedly, she approached Bill and Clint and invited them to check out Joe's wine cellar.

While Lois was chatting with strangers in another part of the house, Bill, Clint, and the divorcee were on their way to trouble.

The divorcee opened an elegantly wrapped bottle of wine. "Here's to you, boys." They passed the bottle around, taking big swigs. The more they drank, the funnier everything became. When they got to the third bottle, Clint became impatient with one swig at a time. He grabbed a case of wine and began cracking open the tops. Amazingly, he could do that and leave a lip for drinking. Now, they each had two bottles, and the drinking got intense. They proceeded to drink and destroy two cases of Joe's best wine.

Meanwhile, Lois' barometer for trouble was on high alert. She was avoiding Elise and Frank, but in desperation, she finally asked Elise if she had seen Bill. She said something about seeing Bill and Clint heading toward the wine cellar. She was trying not to alarm Lois.

Lois could hear them whooping it up as she approached. As she saw them, she screamed at Bill. There he was—

carousing with Clint and an attractive woman Lois had never met. Lois dragged Bill upstairs, found a room away from the party, and sat her drunk husband down. He was in no shape to head home, and he was too big for Lois to carry or drag. Bill likely tried to apologize, if he was conscious enough, in that pitiful, helpless, little-boy voice familiar to many who live with an alcoholic. Bill might have said: "Come on, Lo. I was just talking with Clint, and we got a little wild."

For Lois, this incident was much too humiliating to tolerate: "I must admit I became a bit hysterical for a moment. I remember running at Bill and pummeling him on the arms and slapping him in the face.... I had never felt so low, so upset, so angry, so terribly humiliated in all my life. We had to sneak off from that lovely affair like thieves in the night."[14]

Lois went outside to avoid running into Elise and Frank and made Bill stay still to sober up for a few moments. She eventually got Clint's wife to give them a ride home. She said nothing to Bill the entire drive and did nothing to help Bill stagger to the living-room couch.

The next morning, Bill woke up to a huge hangover and a note from Lois: "I am going away for a while. I will let you know where I am. I will not return until you are sober. Lois."[15]

The train ride south to Washington, DC, was painful for Lois. Her mind kept replaying the scene from the night before. She couldn't decide what hurt the most. How would she ever face Elise and Frank again? They had to find out. How would Bill ever do work for Joe Hirshhorn, or Frank, or anyone? And who was that blonde? How many other women did Bill drink with? What happened when she was not there?

Lois repeated to herself over and over a story familiar to anyone who loves an alcoholic. She thought about Bill's many talents, the joy he brought her when sober, her hope. She colored that with remarks from a friend who predicted Bill would keep on drinking and get worse. Lois concluded her reflections this way: "I do know that I am going to have faith in the ultimate success of our struggle."[16]

Chapter 5

The Broken Dream

Before the train reached Washington, Lois knew she couldn't leave Bill. *We will figure out how to beat this drinking. I know we will*, she told herself with less hope than usual.

Lois had worked and lived in Washington, DC, before she was married and loved it there. People in DC were talking about the new craze for kids, the yo-yo, and everywhere people were amazed by Charles Lindbergh's latest flight from St. Louis to DC. She spent nearly a week revisiting the Smithsonian American Art Museum and the Phillips Memorial Gallery and catching up with some friends. Toward the end of the week, as her anger was subsiding, she walked past a playground.[1]

Lois stopped and watched the mothers with their toddlers enjoying Washington's spring sun. As she admired how much fun those mothers and children were having and felt the love between them, her next move became obvious.

"That's it!" she thought to herself. She knew what would give them a focus and end all of Bill's crazy drinking.

Lois called Bill, who was back at work. They had only talked twice since she left him, so he was probably expecting more of her cold shoulder.

She surely reminded Bill in the conversation how hurt she was, but Lois couldn't stay mad at Bill for long. As one biographer summed up the relationship: "The real truth was that Lois would rather be unhappy with Bill than unhappy without him and no matter what happened she knew she would return to him."[2]

So, after telling Bill how mad she was at him, Lois shifted gears and told Bill her solution. She shared her story of seeing the mother and two young children at the playground. She explained how powerfully clear it was to her when she saw the mother and child. She probably told him something like this: "I knew what we have to do, my Bill. We need to adopt a child and start our family."

Lois was sure adopting a child would be enough to stop Bill's drinking.

On the other end of the line, Bill felt redeemed and hopeful once again. He enthusiastically agreed with Lois. He told her adoption was a terrific idea and wondered why they hadn't thought of it sooner.

Seeking to Adopt

Lois was back in New York the next day and went directly to Spence-Chapin foundling hospital in Brooklyn. The excitement from her conversation with Bill grew as the nurse in charge showed Lois around and let her hold two of the babies.

It's not hard to picture Lois pulling a tiny little girl close to her and cooing something like, "Aren't you precious. You are the cutest baby in the world. I can't wait for my Bill and me to have a baby just like you." *This would give me and Bill a focus and stop his crazy drinking forever*, she thought. She confided to a friend that if it had been up to her, she would have brought that baby home that day!

But there was a lot of paperwork, and adoption required cooperation from Bill. He had to bring home a letter from his job with proof of his employment and income. But Bill's drinking made it hard for him to get things done in a timely way. Each day he returned home empty-handed.

The old disappointments and fears returned for Lois. Bill resumed his habit of missing dinner and coming in drunk after the speakeasies closed. Lois went back to staring at the clock and getting angrier by the hour. She might have started dinner so that he could have a hot meal when he came home, thinking, *I can still be a good wife to him*. But the rage and fear over once again not having a baby overwhelmed her. Eventually, Lois would blow up and give Bill an ultimatum about the paperwork. She might have stated the obvious and asked Bill if perhaps drinking and his work friends were more important than adopting a child.

Bill, of course, like most remorseful alcoholics, would protest and deny this reality. Eventually, Bill did produce the proof of employment, and the agency had everything it needed from the Wilsons to proceed. Next came the home visit and reference checks.

After the heartbreak of the miscarriages, finally being able to have a child meant so much to each of them. Lois couldn't wait to have a baby. Bill couldn't wait for Lois to be happy and have what she wanted.

But wait they did. Three weeks went by without any word. Lois' excitement and impatience overcame her. She called the agency. She was told they hadn't finished the references.

Little did Lois know that when she asked her best friend Elise Shaw to be a character reference, she was ending forever her chances of adopting a child.

Another two months, and still no word. Finally, Lois headed back to Spence-Chapin and asked to see the administrator.

Lois was direct and explained her frustration at the long wait. It's hard to know if the administrator was avoiding the Wilsons or too busy to get back to them. Confronted by Lois, the truth came out. Spence-Chapin had denied the Wilsons' request for adoption. Lois undoubtedly was incredulous and may have asked if this was a temporary delay. If she did, the administrator would have been forced to say no. "We will never place a baby with you and Mr. Wilson."

It's hard to know exactly what Lois felt after this devastating news. She certainly felt shock and sadness. Perhaps her tears made it hard to find her way to the subway. At some point, her rage took over, and having no one else to blame, she blamed the agency. *How dare that agency deny Bill and me. Who do they think they are? We will show them.*

Lois had no clue why their adoption request was denied. They hadn't said, "Come back in a year." The agency was clear the Wilsons would never be able to adopt. Her friend Elise was the farthest thing from her mind. Lois didn't know what a mistake it had been to ask Elise to be a reference for the adoption.

A Broken Friendship

Elise knew Lois would be a wonderful mother. But she knew too much about Bill to believe he could ever sober up and be a loving dad. Her husband was Bill's friend and business associate. He knew all about Bill's drinking, including his latest drunken spree involving landing a private plane at a new airport that wasn't open yet. Elise's skepticism about Bill's ability to be a parent went deeper than stories from her husband about Bill. Elise's father was an alcoholic. She knew firsthand the pain alcoholism causes children and family members.

But the adoption agency didn't tell Lois any of that. Neither did Elise. All Lois was left with was no baby and no explanation. She spent weeks in a fog. She would get up, go to work, try to eat, ignore Bill—whether drunk or sober—and go to bed. This went on for weeks. There was no way to get this grief to lift or even to understand it.

The following August, Elise could not hold back her secret any longer. One day, she stopped by to see Lois. After some catch-up on their families, Elise gently tried to warn Lois that her husband was becoming impatient with Bill's drinking and that his job was at risk if he didn't sober up.

Lois had heard this before. She likely nodded and assured Elise she knew Bill drank too much but explained that their trips to the country were enough to keep him sober most of the time. She might even have told Elise of Bill's writing a pledge not to drink in the family Bible.

Baffled and totally discouraged by her friend's denial of her husband's drinking problem, Elise knew she had to confess to Lois. In her frustration with her friend's denial of reality, Elise burst out with her story. She told Lois she was the one who prevented their adoption. She explained how her own experience with an alcoholic dad and seeing Bill's drinking continue to get worse left her no option but to tell the agency she didn't think Bill could be a responsible father. With tears running down her face, Elise apologized and said one more time to Lois, "I am sorry, Lois...but I had to do it. And...you still don't understand."[3]

Elise quickly departed. Lois was stunned and cried all afternoon. She couldn't believe her best friend had done this to her. She couldn't believe Bill's drinking had ruined her dream of a family. Lois sat speechless and stunned for days, avoiding Bill. It took years to let go of her resentment of Elise and to accept the life God had given her—with Bill and without children.

Instead of a family, Lois had multiple miscarriages and a rejected adoption. There were missed opportunities, misgivings, misfortunes, and more misery to come.

It was the same, sad scenario repeated so many times: the eternal drama with the endless unhappy ending. Anyone who lives with a person with a drinking problem knows the daily torture.

Lois' reflections on Bill's drinking progressed in intensity. Midway through these years, she reflected:

> My life is richer than most, but the problem is not about my life, for probably the suffering is doing me good, but about his—the frightful harm of this resolving and breaking down and resolving and breaking down again and again. How can he ever accomplish anything with this frightful habit?
>
> After writing all this, where am I? Have I made anything clearer? I don't know. But I do know that I love my husband and that I am going to have faith in the ultimate success of our struggle; that I am going to appeal to the good in him and keep on everlastingly trying.[4]

Later, as the drinking progressed, she wrote:

> Come home to me, do come home to me—My heart is breaking. How can we go on like this day after day. What's to become of us. I love you so and yet, my love, it does not seem to do you any good. Still I have faith that it must someday. God grant that day be soon for it doesn't seem as if I could keep going on like this night after night. That I had wisdom to know what is best to help you for I am sure that you can be helped if I only knew how.[5]

Yet Bill kept on drinking.

CHAPTER 6

WALL STREET AND THE WILSONS FALL APART

The financial foundation of the Roaring Twenties began to show signs of weakness after a peak in September 1929. On Thursday, October 24, the *Brooklyn Daily Eagle* headline proclaimed: "Wall St. in Panic as Stocks Crash." Bankers quickly bought shares and propped up the market on Friday. Monday and Tuesday, October 28 and 29, brought the decline back with a vengeance. The market declined 25 percent over these two days, triggering the Great Depression which resulted in a 42 percent decrease in wages and 25 percent unemployment in the United States.

The Great Depression Hits

Bill sat at his desk on Black Tuesday and watched the ticker tape. He knew almost immediately that this would wipe out everything he and Lois had saved. Bill, like many other

71

investors at that time, took advantage of a law that allowed investors to put up only 10 percent of a stock purchase (the margin) and borrow the rest.

The collapse of the market left Bill $50,000 in debt (equivalent to over $907,000 in 2024). It also devastated Lois' family—her dad and her brother—and other friends who had followed Bill's investment advice. Her dad never recovered.

Also, it did Lois no good that at the end of 1927, depressed over his drinking, Bill had signed over to Lois his stocks and investments. He had holdings at two brokerages, but it wasn't long before both his money and hers had evaporated.

That fateful Tuesday, as Bill packed his briefcase, he looked out the window to the office building across Park Avenue. To his horror, he saw two men trying to pull another man back from jumping. *Not me. I will beat this*, Bill thought to himself.

He packed his briefcase and left without saying anything to Frank. There was nothing to say. Bill knew there would be no work for a long time, if ever. He began drinking immediately and never made it home that night.

When Bill finally got home Wednesday evening, Randolph, the building doorman, had to help him up to their double apartment. Randolph had looked after Bill and made sure he got home many nights. The year before, in better financial times, Bill was so appreciative, he bought a piano for Randolph's daughter when he heard she was taking piano lessons.

Bill needed Randolph this evening. Lois was greatly dismayed upon seeing Bill. His clothes were in disarray, his appearance awful, and he looked beaten, almost berserk.

Bill, like many, tried desperately to find work. There was none. Lois asked him about the impact of the Depression on Canada and suggested to Bill that he consider going to Canada to work.

While Lois was deeply concerned about the hardships her father and family were enduring from the stock market crash, she realized there was nothing she or Bill could do for them. When Bill agreed to her suggestion, she reluctantly prepared to go to Montreal, hoping that Bill meant it when he said he couldn't even have one drink.

Bill found work with his friend R. O. Johnson at Greenshields, an investment company. The first couple of weeks went well. Bill earned enough that they could move from a hotel to an expensive apartment on the cliffs overlooking Montreal. Next, Bill joined a country club. Quickly, he forgot the pain of Wall Street, and the Wilsons were living high.

Unfortunately, Bill gradually resumed his drinking. Lois tolerated some of Bill's drinking buddies better than others. At one dinner, Lois and Bill were the guests of Harry, a charming English playboy. Charming English playboys can be highly entertaining—and can get highly drunk, which is exactly what both the Englishman and Bill Wilson did. When it was time to go home, both Bill and Harry fell on their faces trying to get into the cab. The hotel doorman stepped over the two fallen drunks, opened the door for Lois to enter, and then assisted the two men in getting up and into the cab.

The economic downturn eventually hit Montreal, and Bill's drinking predictably got worse. His position at Greenshields was eliminated in the fall of 1930. Bill and Lois now faced fully what they had temporarily avoided.

Lois headed back to New York ahead of Bill to be with her ailing mother. A call from her sister Barbara let her know her mother had serious health problems. Bill stayed behind to sublet their luxury apartment and sell the convertible Packard he had bought on impulse before the crash.

Stories vary on how and when Bill got back to New York. One story has Bill ending up in Vermont at the Burnhams' cabin, drunk, with an unknown male friend and no money left. Lois stated that she and Bill stopped in Vermont on their way home. Another version is that Lois had to go to Vermont to pick up Bill because he had no money and was in no shape to make it back to Brooklyn.

Back in New York City

Regardless of the story, the Wilsons arrived back in New York with no money and no home, and Lois' mother was fighting for her life against cancer.

Lois had to ask her father for help. It's hard to know if she asked, embarrassed, to stay with her parents, or her father saw her desperation in her eyes and, with his usual combination of compassion for his daughter and rage at his son-in-law, invited them to move back into her childhood home on Clinton Street.

Either way, it's certain both Lois and Bill had trepidations about living at Clinton Street. Lois was happy to be closer to her failing mother, yet constantly in fear of Bill's drinking upsetting her father and causing her mother unneeded pain.

Bill was a smart man and knew he couldn't stop, despite his assurances to Lois that he could drink safely. As anyone who has dealt with an alcoholic knows, Bill's intelligence was no match for his addiction. The repeated dire situations he found himself in when drunk did not teach him not to get drunk again. His pledges to stay dry did not prevent him from breaking those promises. No matter the high personal price and the bad experiences, he could not stop drinking.

Once they had moved to Clinton Street, Bill stayed mostly dry for a couple weeks with an occasional night out or afternoon walk for cigarettes that bled into the evening. He called Frank, and there was no work. He called other friends on Wall Street. The stock market was decimated. Thousands were unemployed. A problem employee like Bill was not in demand.

Lois could not get her occupational therapist job back, so she applied for a job in the interior decorating department at Macy's. She was told she wasn't qualified. So the daughter of a doctor father and a wealthy mother ended up demonstrating folding card tables and chairs at Macy's. Her salary of $19 per week plus a small commission kept the Wilsons going.[1]

Bill did a lot of fast talking to get credit in the speakeasies and to get a few dollars from Lois. When desperate for a drink, he stole money from her purse.

Meanwhile, Matilda Burnham's cancer progressed quickly. When she wasn't working, Lois sat with her mother. This helped her not think about Bill and his drinking and recall all her mother had taught her.

By Thanksgiving, Matilda was bedridden and on morphine to keep the pain under control. The family gathered and said a prayer with her in her room before Thanksgiving dinner. Barbara and Lois had a whispered conversation about the woman their dad was seeing. Their grief over the impending loss of their mother was magnified by their anger at their dad's repulsive behavior.

The day before Christmas 1930, Matilda Burnham died. While realizing her death was imminent, Lois was still devastated. And once again, Bill was not there for comfort.

The week before Christmas was a tough one for Bill, even before his mother-in-law died. While Lois spent her last few days with her mother, Bill managed to get into a barroom brawl. Bill's big ideas and strong opinions made such events increasingly frequent as his drinking got worse. Most of his disagreements stayed verbal; occasionally, an old-fashioned slugging contest was required.

The brawl on December 22 wasn't the first such scuffle, but this altercation came with a twist. Bill had obtained a bookkeeping job with an old drinking buddy and was bringing the books home with him. Apparently, Bill had been jumped by thugs, who somehow got his phone number and called him daily, making demands and threats. During the fight, he lost the books. Despite much desperate searching, he never found them. Bill Wilson was scared to death of these thugs and lost his job at Stanley Statistics three days before Christmas.[2]

Bill started drinking as soon as he heard Matilda had died. He knew she cared for him and that he had disappointed her. He had no words to explain his behavior to Lois or her family. So he drank.

Christmas dinner was quiet. Bill had wine with the family, then excused himself. He was gone for two days and missed Matilda Burnham's funeral.

In a later interview,[3] Lois showed a deep measure of compassion for her husband. Of course she was embarrassed, angry, and injured by his behavior. But Lois knew that Bill loved her mother, and she knew he had a sincere heart. So, for him to fail to show up, he had to be extremely sick indeed but hopefully not beyond help.

A few days before she died, Lois' mother had expressed her concern to her daughter about Bill and the negative impact of his drinking on her life. It was as if she suspected that her lesson that her daughter was to love, no matter what, had gone too far. She told Lois that Bill's drinking would likely get worse, and she needed to look out for herself. From her deathbed, her mother encouraged Lois: "You must find what can truly fulfill you otherwise...one day you will wake up and be consumed with anger and resentment for being cheated out of that life. Please don't let that happen to you, my child. Don't let that happen to you."[4]

Despite Lois' understanding, the days after her mother's funeral had to be tough. Besides facing her mother's death, she learned from her brother that her father's finances were nearly depleted. He was struggling to pay the mortgage on Clinton Street, and his medical patients could not pay him. He was considering selling their cherished family cottage on Emerald Lake.

Lois Struggles to Cope

Lois felt the pressure to get a job and not be more of a burden on her father. Bill felt remorse and mostly drank, with an occasional call or two to look for work. Work was hard to find, even for the able-bodied. Unemployment was near 16 percent in 1931 and grew to 25 percent by 1933. For someone like Bill, with his reputation for drinking, finding work was nearly impossible.

Her mother's deathbed talk gave Lois the courage to pledge to herself that she would go to school to study interior design. But first, she needed a job to help pay the household bills, even though her father's pride made it hard to accept money from his daughter.

Two other changes occurred not long after her mother died. Her dad's anger at Bill's drinking began to soften. After years of seeing Bill's drinking as a moral failure, it was as if Dr. Burnham could see that a person had to be very sick to keep drinking the way Bill did. So, while he still hated what the drinking was doing to his daughter, he was less hostile and occasionally even kind to Bill.

The second change had been developing for a while. No one in the Burnham family wanted to talk about it. As his wife was dying, Dr. Burnham began spending more time with Joan James, the ex-wife of the former minister of the church the Burnhams attended. As Lois' siblings learned of this, they were shocked. In conversation with Lois, Dr. Burnham explained that Matilda knew of the relationship and approved of it.

Less than two months after his wife died, without much discussion, Dr. Burnham moved out of the only home he'd ever owned. He deeded the home to Bill and Lois. The bank had foreclosed but were not taking it back because of the New Deal mortgage forgiveness program.

The New Deal was a set of programs initiated by President Franklin D. Roosevelt to provide economic relief from the effects of the Great Depression. Dr. Burnham was not alone in his economic distress. "Some 250,000 American families lost their homes in 1932; the following year, foreclosures stepped up to the ferocious pace of a thousand a day."[5]

Lois felt at a loss with both Bill's drinking and losing her dad to a new woman. She couldn't confide in any of her friends. Her brother and sisters knew her problems and seemed to increasingly pity her. Her sister Barbara instructed Lois that it was time to move on and say goodbye to Bill.

Lois couldn't face that possibility. Her mother had taught her to love and forgive always. Jesus said to forgive seventy times seven times, or forever. As much as Bill's drinking outraged Lois, she still loved him.

Lois' life after her mother's death was an endurance contest. She had nothing to live for. She would get up each morning, take the bus to work at the department store, stand on her feet and wait on people all day, then come home to an empty home and wonder when or if Bill would come home and how drunk he would be.

Lois began to experience headaches that lasted for days. One evening, on her way home in the rain, she raced to get to the corner pharmacy before it closed. The pharmacist knew the Burnham family and Bill and Lois. He welcomed her inside and locked the door behind her. He smiled at Lois and inquired what she needed. Fortunately for Lois, Bayer had invented aspirin in 1897, and it was the most popular treatment for headaches by 1910.

The pharmacist grabbed a bottle of Bayer Aspirin and suggested Lois take two before she left to stop the pain. Lois was touched by his kindness and thought nothing of his suggestion that she have a seat at the soda counter while he got her some water to take with her aspirin.

Lois was relieved and followed his directions. After she took her aspirin, Lois was startled to see the pharmacist was fixing an ice cream float. He explained it was another treatment for whatever ailed her. Lois smiled and watched as he placed the bright red cherry on top of the sundae. *I haven't had one of these in years*, she thought to herself.

Lois usually did not have a sweet tooth, but on a dreary, rainy night, with baked beans and one hot dog to look forward to at home, this treat looked delectable, and conversation with the friendly pharmacist was enjoyable.

As she got ready to leave, the pharmacist took her raincoat and held it for her to put on. When it was on, he rubbed her shoulders gently and slowly spun her around to face him. Lois felt excitement and disgust at the same time.

Her anger overtook her fear. She glared at the pharmacist, told him to get his hands off her, fumbled to unlock the pharmacy door, and ran toward the bus stop.

Given all that Lois was dealing with, it would not be surprising that Lois felt some excitement at a man's attention after dealing with a drunk husband for so many nights. Along with that excitement, she likely felt some guilt at her unfaithfulness to Bill in even thinking those thoughts.

Bill, of course, wasn't home, so she was alone with her thoughts about her undesired pursuer and all her conflicting feelings.

Bill's drinking was nearly nonstop now. After Lois admonished him yet one more time to quit, Bill tried again. This time, he stopped drinking at four in the afternoon and planned to stay dry until the morning. That night, he began to sweat and to hallucinate. In such dark moments, Bill was afraid he would shake to death. He would beg Lois to call her brother-in-law, the doctor, or to hug him to stop the shakes. Lois learned that if she found his bottle and gave him a short drink, he would calm down and pass out again.

Bill's inability to get work got worse. Even the occasional job for a day or two became harder to find. Eventually, his reputation as a drinker completely destroyed his reputation as a stock analyst. He would have been even more demoralized if he had realized that he would not have a job for another five years.

Things were desperate. Lois' job at the department store barely paid the electric and food bill. As she thought about all her sacrifices for so little impact, Lois felt anger displacing her hope.

In the midst of all this chaos for Lois, her dad married his new woman friend in May 1933. In her biography,[6] Lois acknowledged the family's disappointment with their father moving so quickly into a romantic relationship and leaving his family home so soon after his wife's death. She attributed their disappointment to a reaction to her parents' wonderful marriage.

At one point, Bill's drinking was so out of control, Lois worried that he might commit suicide. Lois imagined the worst: Bill drinking himself to death, deliberately taking his life, or having a deadly accident. Bill had started having mad imaginings that wild people were coming after him and his only means of escape would be to catapult through the bedroom window. She got so concerned that she pulled their mattress downstairs to the basement. That way he couldn't fall—or jump—out a window to his death.

In the early fall of 1933, Lois reached out in desperation to her brother-in-law, Dr. Leonard Strong. Dr. Strong could see Bill's desperate condition and recommended Lois send Bill to see Dr. Silkworth at Towns Hospital. Dr. Silkworth was in charge of one of the country's best-known programs for alcoholics.

Most people at the time felt drinking was a moral problem. Bill's bosses and friends thought Bill was a weak man who lacked the willpower to stop drinking. Dr. Silkworth was pioneering a belief that drinking was a sickness that needed to be treated like any other sickness.

Lois hesitated, and Dr. Strong suspected she could not afford Towns Hospital, which was expensive, so he offered to pay for this visit. Bill reluctantly went to Towns Hospital. He was detoxed using the standard method of the time: belladonna, a hallucinogen, aided with castor oil, which induced vomiting.[7]

Bill heard the doctor's admonitions about not drinking. But, shortly after being discharged, he couldn't not drink.

Bill's Drinking Worsens

Thus this long and painful period continued for Bill and Lois Wilson. Bill would wander and then stumble from bar to bar, looking for old acquaintances or new suckers to buy him a drink. If he wasn't shaking too much, he'd make a call or two to a pal on Wall Street to see about a little work. He hadn't worked for over a year, so even his optimism about things getting better was beginning to ebb.

Bill was slowly facing the truth that his life was over. He was washed up. Lois was right, he told himself. "The curve of my declining moral and bodily health fell off like a ski-jump" was the way he described his wretchedness. "My weary and despairing wife was informed that it would all end with heart failure during delirium tremens, or I would develop a wet brain, perhaps within a year. She would soon have to give me over to the undertaker or the asylum."[8]

Hopelessness fueled his insatiable need for just one more drink. Weeks and months went by—same story. Some days, Lois tried to be understanding and compassionate. Other days, she yelled and screamed relentlessly, telling him he was worthless. Still other days, she sat with her needlepoint, feeling depressed and thinking about her dreams of being an interior decorator and having children. While having frequent and painful feelings, Lois seemed to also grow in her appreciation of the depth of Bill's illness. She knew Bill loved her and would not repeatedly hurt her intentionally.

By the summer of 1934, Bill was back in Towns Hospital again. Lois didn't know where she'd get the money to pay for Bill's hospital stay, but she knew there was no alternative. Once more, she hoped and begged Bill to make this his last detox.

Dr. Silkworth treated Bill and reminded him again he had an allergy to alcohol. He went so far as to say it was a disease, a restlessness, that led to compulsive cravings and mental obsessions about drinking. Bill was sincerely grateful to the doctor for this explanation and told him how it helped him understand himself and his behavior better. Lois had hope that Dr. Silkworth had given Bill the insight he needed to stay sober.

Dr. Silkworth knew Bill was whistling in the cemetery, hoping to be able to do something he suspected he couldn't.

Bill went home sober and without the shaky hands and jaundiced face. This time, he made it four days. Again, with no reason or excuse, he went out for a walk and ended up in a pub where they were celebrating the end of Prohibition. Bill raised his glass to the jubilant guy next to him and had a drink to celebrate the end to that despicable government abuse called Prohibition. In reality, Prohibition had made little difference to Bill and drinkers like him. He kept on drinking.

CHAPTER 7

BILL HITS BOTTOM AND SURRENDERS

The year 1934 was a milestone for Bill Wilson and his friend Ebby Thacher—and it changed Lois' life.

Ebby Thacher and the Oxford Group

Ebby and Bill were friends from Burr & Burton. Ebby was the youngest of five boys from a prominent Albany, New York, family. His grandfather was quite successful, starting a business to provide car wheels to railroads. With their wealth, his family also enjoyed political success.

Ebby was the most mischievous of the Thacher boys. In fact, had he not done so poorly at the local Albany Academy, he would never have gone to Burr & Burton and met Bill Wilson.

But they did meet, and, though they were together in school only a couple years, they became great friends. Ebby, like Bill, developed a drinking problem. So, when they met after their school years, drinking was usually involved.

Bill recalled one time that had been quite memorable.[1] Back in 1929, Bill visited Ebby in his hometown of Albany, and they got drunk at a speakeasy. One of their drinking buddies was a pilot. So Ebby and Bill decided to fly up to the new airport in Manchester, Vermont, where Bill and Ebby had spent time together as young boys. Unfortunately, the airport had not yet opened. When the townspeople heard a plane was going to land the day before the grand opening, they all came to see it in disbelief. Bill and Ebby were so drunk, they stumbled onto the runway from the plane.

Ebby's mother and father both died in the late 1920s. Ebby inherited $150,000, as did his brothers (over $2 million each in today's currency). Ebby lost most of that money in the 1929 stock market crash and from his drinking sprees. By the summer of 1934, he was living in an empty house, with no furniture, that was owned by his family.

Ebby's drinking got him in trouble with the local police twice in a few months. The first time, he drove his car into a neighbor's kitchen. The other time was even more bizarre. His sleeping was disturbed one night by pigeons. In a fit of anger, he went outside with a shotgun to shoot at the pigeons. Not sober, he slipped and fell in the yard, then proceeded to begin shooting at the pigeons while lying on the ground. The neighbors called the police, and Ebby was arrested.[2]

While humorous, this story is important because it led Ebby to begin to get help for his drinking and eventually try to offer his friend Bill a remedy for drinking. Ebby had two friends, Cebra and Shep, who were part of a newly forming Christian movement called the Oxford Group. It was founded by a Pennsylvanian minister, Frank Buchman, while he was in Europe. The intent was to recreate in the twentieth century the fervor and devotion that existed among the early Christians in the first century after Jesus died. Buchman had struggled in his early career as a minister and was traveling in search of himself and God. His life changed while at a retreat led by Jessie Penn-Lewis, a Welsh evangelical preacher, whose talk on the cross of Christ resulted in a religious experience for Frank Buchman.

Given the influence the Oxford Group would have on the founding of Alcoholics Anonymous and Bill Wilson's getting and staying sober, Jessie Penn-Lewis is considered one of the first of many women who influenced A.A. history.

Those involved in the Oxford Group attended regular prayer meetings and committed to a life of self-examination of their behavior, daily spiritual reading and meditation, and helping others. It was in the spirit of helping others that his two friends encouraged Ebby to come with them to the Oxford Group meeting. Ebby was polite, but resisted until his legal problems made it likely he would end up in jail.

Another wealthy man, Rowland Hazard, also had a problem with drinking. Unlike Ebby and Bill, he desperately wanted to stop drinking. He flew to Switzerland to meet with an internationally recognized psychiatrist, Carl Jung.

Rowland Hazard was able to stay sober for only a short time after his first visit to Dr. Jung. Bewildered, he returned to Switzerland to see Dr. Jung again.

Hazard begged Dr. Jung to tell him the whole truth. Jung replied, "You have the mind of a chronic alcoholic. I have never seen one single case recover, where that state of mind existed to the extent it does in you." When pressed by Hazard for exceptions, the doctor added, "Exceptions to cases such as yours have been occurring since early times. Here and there, once in a while, alcoholics have had what are called vital spiritual experiences. To me these occurrences are phenomena. They appear to be in the nature of huge emotional displacements and rearrangements. Ideas, emotions, and attitudes which were once the guiding forces of the lives of these men are suddenly cast to one side, and a completely new set of conceptions and motives begin to dominate them."[3]

Rowland Hazard went to the Oxford Group and stopped drinking for a while. Ebby's two friends talked with Rowland about Ebby and his predicament at an Oxford Group meeting. They explained the possibility of his going to jail. Rowland Hazard, as part of his desire to abide by the Oxford Group principle of serving others, agreed to take responsibility for Ebby. Being the wealthy and well-respected man he was, the judge agreed.

This experience scared Ebby into not drinking. He became an active and zealous member of the Oxford Group. He moved to New York, where Rowland lived most of the year, and began going to Oxford Group meetings at the Calvary Episcopal Church in Manhattan. Ebby eventually moved to the Calvary Mission nearby and lived with the homeless.

Ebby and Bill Reconnect

Once in New York, Ebby heard his friend Bill Wilson was having an awful time with drinking. As Bill later explained it,[4] Ebby called Bill in late November 1934 and asked if he could visit. Lois was at work, and Bill, surprised to hear from a sober Ebby, invited him over. Bill was shocked as he greeted Ebby:

The door opened and he stood there, fresh-skinned and glowing. There was something about his eyes. He was inexplicably different. What had happened? I pushed a drink across the table. He refused it. Disappointed but curious, I wondered what had gotten into the fellow. He wasn't himself.

"Come, what's all this about?" I queried.

He looked straight at me. "Simply, but smilingly, he said, 'I've got religion.'"

I was aghast. So that was it—last summer an alcoholic crackpot; now, I suspected, a little cracked about religion.[5]

Ebby tried to explain: "It was really more of a spiritual than it was a religious movement. I listened to what they had to say, and I was very much impressed, because it was what I had been taught as a child and what I inwardly believed but had laid aside."[6]

Bill didn't know what to say. He was not a big fan of religion. It seemed to always disappoint him. Why did so many bad things happen?

Ebby talked some more about the Oxford Group and the meetings. He encouraged Bill to go see the New York leader, the Rev. Sam Shoemaker, at the Calvary Mission where Ebby was living.

Bill tried to be nonchalant as he raised one big, bushy eyebrow, looked over at Ebby, and poured a tumbler full of gin for himself. Ebby was careful not to sell too hard. After a few more minutes of desultory conversation, he said good night to Bill.

As Ebby was leaving, he met Lois, who had returned and was in the downstairs parlor. He briefly explained about the Oxford Group and told her Bill's fate was up to God and the best they could do now was pray.

Lois recalled, "I thought to myself as I watched him walk down the steps, what good would more prayers do when they hadn't worked all these years? I didn't know at the time I had a soul-sickness too."[7]

As much as Bill hated anything that had to do with religion, he couldn't deny that Ebby looked better than he had looked in years. Ebby hadn't preached. He had told Bill how two friends had come to see him when he was on trial, offered to help him, and persuaded the judge to suspend his jail time. "They had told of a simple religious idea and a practical program of action. That was two months ago and the result was self-evident. It worked!"[8]

Bill was confused after Ebby left. He wanted to dismiss what Ebby had said, but it was clear that Ebby was sober and Bill wasn't. Later, after he sobered up, Bill recalled, "The good of what he said stuck so well that in no waking moment thereafter could I get that man and his message out of my head."[9]

No, Bill could not dismiss Ebby's sobriety. He was desperate. So, he started asking himself why he didn't trust religious people.

Memories surfaced of his grandfather's disdain for religious people and his objection to anyone telling him what was right or wrong. Bill recalled how his grandfather's stance remained strong, even on his deathbed.

Bill was not an atheist. He recognized the laws in science and believed there must be a power greater than himself. But Bill had a line he could not cross. "With ministers, and the world's religions, I parted right there. When they talked of a God personal to me, who was love, superhuman strength and direction, I became irritated and my mind snapped shut."[10]

In his personal story in *Alcoholics Anonymous*, Bill jumped directly from Ebby's visit to his surrender to his powerlessness over alcohol. Lois told the story another way: First, Bill retreated back to his dirty mattress in the basement and gulped his gin straight out of the bottle.

Bill Attends an Oxford Group Meeting

Bill was knocked off balance by Ebby's visit. He didn't want to believe Ebby's story, but he was dying, and he knew it. The next day, he decided to visit the Calvary Mission and find out firsthand about the Oxford Group. On the way, he came across a drinking buddy, and they had enough beers to be high when they got to the church. The leaders were about to throw Bill and his friend out when Ebby arrived and took charge of Bill. Bill made a drunken admission of his drinking problem as all testified to their weaknesses.

Ebby took Bill home after the meeting and stayed long enough to sober him up. When Lois got home from work, Bill told her he might give the Oxford Group a try. Later that same night, he got drunk and belligerent, accusing Lois and Ebby of plotting to force religion on him. His hallucinations that night were worse than any Lois had seen.

Lois lost her cool and blurted out, "You are nothing but a drunken sot, just like the other bums you keep talking about. But I don't have to live like this anymore. I should have put you in a sanitarium a long time ago, when my father told me to do it and then Dr. Silkworth. That's where you belong—in an insane asylum—because you're crazy. You hear me? You're crazy."

Bill got even angrier and threw her sewing machine against the wall. Terrified, Lois shrank into the corner. Bill ran out the door, shouting: "I'm not crazy! I'm not crazy!"[11]

Bill rode the subway all night. He begged money to buy a pint of gin. Eventually, he went home and looked at the hole in the wall from the sewing machine. He collapsed and began to cry. He knew he was at a decision point. He would die, or he could force himself to try something like the Oxford Group and Ebby's path.

He knew he needed help, and he believed that Dr. Silkworth at Towns Hospital was his only hope. He wrote a nearly indecipherable note for Lois, telling her he had gone to Towns Hospital.[12] He had five cents left for the subway and bought four beers on credit to keep the shakes away. He drank one on the subway. Dr. Silkworth saw Bill and admitted him, without much hope.

Detoxification Once More

Bill went through detoxification after finishing his three beers—the last alcohol he would drink for the rest of his life. As he sweated and his body shook, the staff of the detox ward provided barbiturates to sedate him and paraldehyde to ward off the DTs (delirium tremens). Without these precautions, Bill's withdrawal from drinking alcohol could have resulted in full-body shakes and an elevated blood pressure, which could have led to death. It took two days to get Bill sober enough to move to a regular room.

Meanwhile, Lois came home and found his note, which triggered first relief and then despair. "I thought, what good would it do anyway? He would only get drunk again the moment he left the hospital. And who was going to pay the bill this time?... There wasn't much left in the house to sell or pawn. All I could think about over and over again was what possible permanent good would it do for Bill to go back to Towns again. I had so little faith left in the good Lord just when He was about to show me his miraculous power."[13]

Physically detoxed, Bill Wilson lay alone in his cold hospital bed and thought about his future. He knew he was close to insanity and that death was not far off. Ebby visited, and Bill's spirits improved. Ebby talked with passion and conviction about the moral principles of the Oxford Group. Shortly after Ebby left, Bill's depression deepened. As he would later tell many people with drinking problems, his ego was deflated. In despair, he cried out, "If there be a God, let him show Himself!"[14]

What happened next is hard to explain and harder still to understand. As Dr. Jung had explained to Rowland Hazard, psychic transformation seems to happen suddenly to a very few people. Such change includes a surrender, a letting go of the hope to control, and a belief in some power beyond the individual's will and ego.

Bill's change was sudden. But as he later learned, it can happen to anybody, in many different ways. For most members of Alcoholics Anonymous, Al-Anon (the Twelve Step organization for families and friends of alcoholics), and millions of others, this surrender comes slowly and after a number of setbacks. In A.A., they call this readiness "the gift of desperation" or "hitting bottom." It took Bill many years—seventeen, in fact—and many failures before he hit bottom, while causing extraordinary harm and pain to Lois and countless others.

Yet, on December 11, 1934, Bill was ready. Within days, he experienced an amazing spiritual transformation that changed his life forever and made possible the founding of A.A. and Al-Anon and the launching of one of the world's largest support groups.

Yes, Bill's experience is not common. Here is how Bill described his spiritual awakening.

> Suddenly, my room blazed with an indescribably white light. I was seized with an ecstasy beyond description. Every joy I had known was pale by comparison. The light, the ecstasy—I was conscious

of nothing else for a time. Then, seen in the mind's eye, there was a mountain. I stood upon its summit, where a great wind blew. A wind, not of air, but of spirit. In great, clean strength, it blew right through me. Then came the blazing thought "You are a free man." I know not at all how long I remained in this state, but finally the light and the ecstasy subsided. I again saw the wall of my room. As I became more quiet, a great peace stole over me, and this was accompanied by a sensation difficult to describe. I became acutely conscious of a Presence which seemed like a veritable sea of living spirit. I lay on the shores of a new world. "This," I thought, "must be the great reality. The God of the preachers."

Savoring my new world, I remained in this state for a long time. I seemed to be possessed by the absolute, and the curious conviction deepened that no matter how wrong things seemed to be, there could be no question of the ultimate rightness of God's universe. For the first time, I felt that I really belonged, I knew that I was loved and could love in return. I thanked my God, who had given me a glimpse of his absolute Self. Even though a pilgrim upon an uncertain highway, I need be concerned no more, for I had glimpsed the great beyond.[15]

While it was difficult for Lois to believe this story when he shared it, she knew something was different. "I knew something overwhelming had happened. His eyes were filled with light. His whole being expressed hope and joy."[16]

Bill questioned Dr. Silkworth about whether he was hallucinating. Lois explained that Dr. Silkworth "told Bill he had experienced some great psychic occurrence, some kind of conversion experience he had only read about and that he should hang on to it for it was a great gift, a great blessing. I had no idea which way our lives would go but I now had a strong reason to hope he was finally freed from his addiction. It never occurred to me that I was still trapped in mine."[17]

Bill's sudden ability to resist alcohol was an incredible change for both Bill and Lois and for their marriage, though they were still a long way from living "happily ever after." As Bill so aptly wrote later in *Alcoholics Anonymous*, there is a "long road of reconstruction ahead" for the newly sober individual and their family. Unrealistic expectations abound for the sober individual and their spouse.

PART TWO

STAYING SOBER, LAUNCHING ALCOHOLICS ANONYMOUS

1935

CHAPTER 8

THE WILSONS STRUGGLE WITH EARLY SOBRIETY

Lois' spiritual awakening was not as immediate and direct as Bill's. She was excited to have her husband back and relieved that he stayed sober. Indeed, she was willing to do almost anything to help him stay sober. Adjusting to sobriety took time and proved to be a challenge for both Lois and Bill, as it has been for the many couples who later embraced sobriety and the Twelve Step life.

Learning to Stay Sober for Others

There were probably days when Bill was on fire with doing whatever he thought would help him and others stay sober. Happily, Lois was in full harmony with this focus. When they attended Oxford meetings, Rev. Shoemaker might lead a discussion on the four absolutes: Love, Purity,

Honesty, and Unselfishness. The people gathered would be a mix of other middle-class seekers along with down-and-out drunks that Bill would have recruited.

But although Bill had found sobriety, more often than not, he was unable to persuade his new recruits of the benefits of the abstinent life. Too often, they came for the free cookies and coffee but didn't stay long enough for conversion. Talking about "the Truth," as the Oxford Group members described their path, had helped Bill. So why wasn't he able to help others?

After a few more difficult weeks of failure in reaching other drunks, Bill had a follow-up visit with Dr. Silkworth in April 1935. He talked about his frustration at not being able to get anyone sober. Bill had become as obsessed with getting others sober as he had been with getting a drink for himself a few months earlier.

The wise doctor knew Bill and his type. He had heard lots of people who had gotten sober for a day or two make big promises and share big ideas. So he told Bill bluntly that he imagined the men he was trying to help didn't like being preached at. "For God's sake stop preaching. You're scaring the drunks half crazy. They want to get sober, but you're telling them they can only do it as you did, by some special hot flash.... You've got the cart before the horse. Hit them with the physical first and hit them hard. Tell about the obsession and the physical sensitivity they are developing that will condemn them to go mad or die. Pour it on. Say it's lethal as cancer."[1]

In this way, Dr. Silkworth helped Bill realize he was talking too much about the Oxford Group principles and his own spiritual experience. In emphasizing the physical and mental damage from his drinking, Dr. Silkworth told Bill, "Coming from another alcoholic, one alcoholic talking to another, maybe that will crack those tough egos deep down. Only then can you begin to try out your other medicine, the ethical principles you have picked up from the Oxford group."[2]

In sum, Dr. Silkworth (a hero and legend to many future A.A. members) told Bill to come down off his high horse and try talking to drunks like equals.

Bill bristled at the idea he was preaching. That was the last thing he wanted to do. He had hated people telling him what he could or could not do.

That night, while they ate their dinner of canned tuna mixed with Hellman's Mayonnaise and string beans, Bill told Lois about his talk with Dr. Silkworth. Lois once again reassured Bill, telling him not to be discouraged by the doctor's suggestion. She reminded him why he was enthusiastic.

As a supportive partner and spouse, Lois' encouragement often helped Bill to look with fresh eyes at a situation. Bill might have recalled his first conversation with Ebby and how hard it was to hear Ebby talk about "getting religion." By the end of dinner with Lois, Bill was out of his funk and eager to try a less aggressive approach and talk more from his heart about his own experience.

Bill Develops His Storytelling

Bill tried to follow Dr. Silkworth's suggestion of starting with the medical facts. He knew from his own experience that he had some strange "mental twist" that caused him to think one drink would be ok. He now understood that once he took that first drink, he couldn't stop drinking. As Dr. Silkworth later explained, "We believe...that the action of alcohol on these chronic alcoholics is a manifestation of an allergy; that the phenomenon of craving is limited to this class and never occurs in the average temperate drinker."[3]

With Dr. Silkworth's encouragement, Bill began to develop what he would later refer to as his "bedtime story"—what those in A.A. now call a person's "drunka-logue." For Bill, this was the story of the horror of his life before sobriety, how he got sober, and what sobriety was like now. In these early days, he emphasized the progression of his drinking and how he couldn't stop, including humorous and sad stories to illustrate this point.

It's likely Bill's stories were sometimes painful for Lois to hear over and over again. Still, Bill would tell stories like the incident when he and Ebby chartered a plane while drunk and flew to the Manchester airport the day before it opened.

Another story we can imagine bothering Lois was Bill being too drunk to attend Lois' mother's funeral. To Bill, this was one of the most powerful examples of how drinking caused him to do something he desperately didn't want to do—miss saying farewell to his beloved mother-in-law. Bill thought of her as a mother and loved her dearly. He hoped that sharing this story with the men he met might cause some of them to give the Oxford Group approach a try.

Bill came to accept that he had a physical allergy to alcohol and a mental obsession with it. He tried to follow Dr. Silkworth's advice and let the men he talked with know that he almost died and how horrible his life had become. Instead of telling them they had a problem, he might acknowledge that he didn't know if they were a normal drinker or an alcoholic. If they were an alcoholic, he would explain, they would likely end up insane or dead.

Lois would encourage Bill not to overthink his approach and get too fancy. She would also remind him that the most important thing was for Bill to do what he needed to do to stay sober himself.

One biographer described Bill during this period this way: "With the compulsive dedication of the twelve-year-old boy challenged to make a boomerang, he set off to sober up all the drunks everywhere. There was no besotted derelict who staggered into the mission he didn't buttonhole, no fine executive wanting a drying out at Towns [Hospital] he didn't try to reach.... He was all over New York, at all hours, indefatigable, and incorrigible, totally convinced that if *he* could do it, find a way out, they could do it. And he was spectacularly unsuccessful with everyone."[4]

Yet there was no way to deny that a miracle had occurred. Lois was ecstatic—first Ebby and now her Bill. Why not others? She happily supported Bill in his zeal to help other alcoholics make their miracle happen.

Bill's encouragement from Dr. Silkworth not to preach was tempered by his emerging friendship with the Rev. Sam Shoemaker, minister at Calvary Episcopal Church in Manhattan and leader of the emerging Oxford Group in New York. Rev. Shoemaker urged Bill to spread the word. The more Bill gained understanding about the emotional and spiritual aspects of alcoholism, the more Rev. Shoemaker encouraged him to spread the good word.

Lois Struggles with a New Reality

Lois also acknowledged that while she went to many Oxford Group meetings with Bill and Ebby, she didn't feel any need to embrace the spiritual practices of the Oxford Group movement. "My only problem, Bill's drinking, was being solved so I felt no need for their teachings. I was only too glad to do all I could to help them, but for nearly a year it never occurred to me to apply the program to myself. I had had sound spiritual training, having been brought up in a home where love of God and of my fellowman was the guiding motive. And during my life with Bill, I had tried to live by that principle. I did not think I needed the Oxford Group."[5]

Lois' resistance to growing spiritually and applying the Oxford Group ideas would eventually change. Later, she admitted: "My sheer arrogance told me I was fine and didn't need to change in any way. Was I due for a serious comeuppance."[6]

In another moment of self-reflection, Lois wrote: "We often fool ourselves into thinking we have no self-pity or resentment but a few acid drops are seeping down to water and fertilize. These primitive weeds quickly grow to maturity, and when they do, there is not much control over them. The control is done only in one way: by love. Love of husband, or wife, family, of fellow man, and love of God."[7]

Bill's enthusiasm for saving men with drinking problems continued to influence his marriage, and not always for the good. Despite his daily efforts to save others from their addiction, he had not helped anyone get sober. Fortunately, Bill and Lois had supportive informal gatherings at a nearby cafeteria with Ebby, Rowland, and a few others.

Bill began to invite the men he met with drinking problems to come live with him and Lois in their Clinton Street home. It's hard to think Lois would be excited about this idea. She had just gotten her husband back, and he wanted to invite men who drank into their home as guests. As usual, Lois did not spend much time in her memoir talking about her misgivings. Rather, she again appeared willing to do whatever Bill thought was needed to keep him sober.

Many of the men Bill was now befriending were not the kind of guests Lois grew up expecting to host. Her parents had often hosted other members of their upper-middle-class set. Her mother had taught her how to be a gracious hostess, how to set the table, and proper topics for polite dinner conversation. Her Christian upbringing taught her to be a Good Samaritan. But the Good Samaritan had put his downtrodden charge in a hotel. He didn't bring random strangers home with him, and the conversations she overheard from the men camped in their home could range from scripture quotes to bawdy jokes.

Lois never knew whether they would have two guests or ten on any given day. She got up early each morning and made some bread and oatmeal for breakfast for herself and the men, then headed for work. Home at 5:30, she made dinner for everyone. Bill and Lois continued to attend Oxford Group meetings one or two nights each week and hosted the Tuesday meeting in their home. But where was their life as a couple?

Lois knew Bill considered his witnessing to the down-and-out to be important, but it wasn't bringing in any money. Lois must have had incredible physical and emotional resilience.

While Bill kept talking with drunks without much success, he was also looking for work on Wall Street. He could see how hard it was for Lois, working and running a boarding house for men with drinking problems.

Later, Lois acknowledged that this new life became difficult for her. Yes, Bill was sober, but they had no life together. Her days were filled with the drudgery of low-paid work, her nights with tending troubled, transient men. Bill got deep satisfaction from being with them, but it left little time for Lois. When would her needs get met? "Gradually, she became deeply frustrated and less affable about hosting a household of itinerants. Bill sensed her feelings."[8]

Indeed, it is hard to believe that Bill was oblivious to the new pain his actions were causing Lois. A few years later, he would write very clearly and eloquently that selfishness and self-centeredness is central to the alcoholic personality. "Selfishness—self-centeredness! That, we think, is the root of our troubles. Driven by a hundred forms of fear, self-delusion, self-seeking, and self-pity, we step on the toes of our fellows and they retaliate."[9]

It may well have been Bill's self-centeredness that blinded him to Lois' mounting frustration. She was clear that life with Bill sober was not the honeymoon she had desired. In fact, it was in some ways a different form of loneliness and frustration.

Bill Goes Back to Work

In May 1935, Bill's search for work began to show some promise. He was approached by a stockbroker friend, Howard Tompkins, and invited to go to Akron, Ohio, to lead a proxy fight for control of the National Rubber Machinery Company (NRMC) for one of his clients. The pay was modest, but there was a sizeable bonus available to him if he was successful.

Bill had mixed feelings about accepting this offer. He was embarrassed that he had no money and was relying on Lois to support him, along with whatever drunks were staying with them. When he got the call from Howard Tompkins, Bill knew he needed to go to Akron to lead the proxy fight. But his friend Ebby was worried about Bill staying sober away from home, and Lois also had some initial concerns. Eventually, Bill said yes out of a desire to bring home some money again and reduce the pressure on Lois and their marriage.

The day before his departure, the reality of his constant failure to get anyone sober and his fear of being away from Lois sent Bill into an emotional nosedive. He and Lois had a difficult exchange that haunted them both for days. Bill described himself as a failure. Lois countered that he was sober. Bill wondered out loud if his life was really a sober life. He got on a train and obsessively went over the discussion. Lois sat at home, fretting over her Bill and this separation. "I thought I'd be glad once he stopped drinking.... I thought we'd be happy and close and loving like we once were earlier in our marriage. Now I just sat and wondered and waited for letters to arrive from Akron. I waited and I waited."[10]

CHAPTER 9

BROADENING THE LENS:
THE IMPORTANCE OF DR. BOB AND
ANNIE SMITH TO THE WILSONS' STORY

Bill and Lois needed a community of support so they could grow and recover once Bill stopped drinking. Annie and Dr. Bob Smith offered that initial community, as did early New York members of the Oxford Group. The beginnings of A.A. and the launch of the modern alcoholism recovery movement[1] is the story of two marriages that joined two communities—New York and Akron.

Bill Arrives in Akron

If Bill could convince a majority of the stockholders to vote with Tompkins' New York-based partnership, he thought he might well make good money again and possibly become the head of a major Akron business. That would show Lois and the world that he not only was sober, but he also was back to being a successful businessman.

Unfortunately for Bill's finances and ego, the proxy fight did not go well. This challenge, however, was offset by the germination of Alcoholics Anonymous. Bill was about to meet Dr. Robert Smith, a leading Akron proctologist.[2] He specialized in diagnosing and treating colon and rectal issues, often related to cancer. Dr. Bob (as he is affectionately called by A.A. members and friends) lived in Highland Square, a pleasant in-town Akron neighborhood, with his wife Annie (also known as Anne) and two children, Robert Jr. (called Smitty) and Sue. Dr. Bob was on the edge of losing his practice, as his drinking was a problem both at home and at work.

Addiction is a disease of isolation. In fact, many in Twelve Step programs state that the opposite of addiction is connection. Recovery is built on forming healthy relationships. Neither man knew it at the time, but meeting each other would lead the way out of their alcoholic misery. The fellowship between Bill and Dr. Bob, which later expanded to include Annie and Lois, established the connections that became the heart and soul of Alcoholics Anonymous.

Dr. Bob Smith

Like Bill, Dr. Bob grew up in Vermont. His family was financially secure, much like Lois Wilson's. His dad was a prominent leader who found success in politics and serving as a judge, school board superintendent, state attorney, and state legislator. In addition, he was on the board of a bank and a savings institution.

His mother was described by Dr. Bob's adopted daughter Sue as a "cold woman." Annie thought her mother-in-law was so exceedingly strict that it might have prompted his drinking, as he strove to break loose from her harsh and oppressive grip.[3]

He began his independent streak by going to bed early and then sneaking out to meet friends when he was in grade school. Like Bill and Lois Wilson, Bob found refuge in the woods and outdoors from an early age. Before heading off to college, he met his future wife, Annie Ripley, at a high school dance. Dr. Bob very slowly courted Annie for seventeen years before marrying her!

No one knows exactly why it took so long for Dr. Bob and Annie to get married. Dr. Bob had to cut back on his drinking to successfully complete his advanced medical training to become a surgeon. We can speculate that Annie had concerns about Dr. Bob's drinking, which were addressed by his staying sober for those few years.

Drinking was frowned upon in his conservative hometown of St. Johnsbury. People who shipped in alcohol from Boston or New York weren't to be trusted. Dr. Bob began to develop his love for alcohol at Dartmouth College. Having excelled in billiards, poker, and other card games, Dr. Bob followed the lead of his fellow students and sought to excel in drinking—and he was very successful in becoming a serious drinker.

Dr. Bob's early love for the taste of cider evolved into a passionate love for beer, then progressed in his graduate days to what today would be considered alcoholic drinking. After graduating from Dartmouth College, he was delayed for three years in pursuing his interest in medicine because his mother was opposed. After three years of working in businesses where his dad had connections, Dr. Bob finally convinced his parents to support his desire to go to medical school. By this time, his drinking had resulted in what he called the morning jitters.

His drinking got worse in medical school, resulting in an expulsion and a return home to dry out. Despite numerous interruptions to dry out and get control of his drinking, Dr. Bob got his medical degree from Rush University in Chicago in 1910 when he was thirty-one years old.[4] Dr. Bob was then able to stay sober for a two-year internship because of the intensity of the work. Once his training was completed, he opened a medical office in 1912, in the Second National Bank Building in Akron, where he practiced until 1948.

Dr. Bob Struggles with Drinking

Stomach troubles evidently led Dr. Bob back to drinking. As Dr. Bob recalled, "If I did not drink, my stomach tortured me, and if I did, my nerves did the same thing."[5]

Dr. Bob's drinking got so bad that over a three-year period, he checked himself into a local drying-out place a dozen times. Finally, out of desperation, his father, Judge Smith, sent a doctor he trusted to Akron with instructions to bring Bob home. Dr. Bob returned to his childhood home and was bedridden for two months. Another two months passed before he felt able to return to Akron and begin work again. The experience devastated him, but it stopped his drinking—for a while.

Still sober as he headed into 1915, Dr. Bob went to Chicago and married his longtime sweetheart on January 25. Annie Smith was "small and reserved but had a cheerfulness, sweetness, and calm that were to remain with her throughout the years. She had been reared within a family of railroad people. It was a very sheltered atmosphere, although there wasn't much money at the time. Annie, who abhorred ostentation and pretense, always pointed out that she attended Wellesley on a scholarship, because her family couldn't have afforded to send her there otherwise."[6]

Annie and Dr. Bob Smith. (Courtesy of Dr. Bob's Home.)

Miraculously, Dr. Bob stayed sober for the first three years of their marriage. The couple savored each other, making many friends, and Dr. Bob's practice grew. In 1918, their son Robert Jr. (Smitty) was born. As Smitty got older, Dr. Bob and Annie decided they didn't want him to grow up an only child. However, having married relatively late for the times, Annie was informed at age forty-five that she could no longer have children.

In 1923, when Smitty was five, the Smiths adopted Sue, who also was five and had been left by her grandmother at Children's Home as an infant. Ironically, given their parents' goal of providing Smitty with a sibling, Smitty and Sue described their relationship as challenging during their youth. It wasn't until later, as adults, that they realized their parents' hope that they would support and rely on each other.

The arrival of Smitty in 1918 coincided with the beginning of Prohibition. This new law gave Dr. Bob increased confidence in his ability to stay sober. He decided that an occasional drink now and then would be OK because alcohol was not widely available. However, he failed to recognize that the government would give doctors permission to prescribe grain alcohol without much oversight or restriction.

Dr. Bob wasn't the only medical professional who flaunted Prohibition laws. "Physicians wrote an estimated eleven million prescriptions a year throughout the 1920s, and Prohibition Commissioner John F. Kramer even cited one doctor who wrote 475 prescriptions for whiskey in one day.... Historians speculate that Charles R. Walgreen, of Walgreen's fame, expanded from twenty stores to a staggering 525 during the 1920s thanks to medicinal alcohol sales."[7]

Like most respectable drinkers of the time, Dr. Bob quickly developed a relationship with his own bootlegger. His drinking progressed quickly, as before, from a drink now and then to daily drinking. In his words, he soon "developed two distinct phobias—One was the fear of not sleeping; the other was the fear of running out of liquor. Not being a man of means, I knew that if I did not stay sober enough to earn money, I would run out of liquor."[8]

Drinking Hell

What followed for Dr. Bob, Annie, and their children was seventeen years of drinking hell. Because of his need to be steady to perform surgery, Dr. Bob developed an addiction to morning sedatives to calm him enough to go to work. This put him on the merry-go-round well known today, though barely acknowledged in his time, of combining drugs and alcohol to stay high and functioning. However, as his drinking became widely known in the community, his practice declined.

While Dr. Bob commented on his own pains, he didn't say much about the torture for Annie and his children. Smitty and Sue later told their story in a book, *Children of the Healer*. Smitty and Sue were both respectful of their parents and their legacy of service but still make clear the tensions and hardships the family experienced during their childhood, which coincided with Dr. Bob's drinking years.

Sue admitted to being scared of her father's tall size (he was six-foot-four) and heavy, strong voice. She described him both as a gentle man who never got rough and as a disciplinarian willing to use the paddle when needed. (At this time and well into the twentieth century, corporal punishment was widely accepted as part of disciplining children.)

She described the paddle as having two ends. Her mom used the end that was larger and didn't hurt as much. Her dad used the smaller end and whittled down the larger part. Ironically, Sue reported that she and Smitty were afraid of the paddle, while their dad was afraid of their dog, who growled when he thought Bob was hurting the children. So Dr. Bob had to close the door so the dog wouldn't hear the paddling.

Sue also made clear her rebellious nature as a teen, particularly in slipping away and spending time with her boyfriend. Like many adolescents, Sue told her parents she was going to her girlfriend's, but instead spent the day with Ray. Her parents didn't like Ray, whose family was blue collar; Ray's dad was a janitor, and no one in his family was educated. Bob and Annie assumed that Ray and his father were lazy men who only lived for having sex and making babies. They hoped for more for their daughter.

Paradoxically, even though Sue's own father's drinking was out of control, the family lived in denial and didn't confront him. They did what he told them to do.

Despite Dr. Bob's physical and economic decline from drinking too much, Annie held onto the status of being a doctor's wife. Despite the economic hardships, the Smiths had a laundress, who came once a week and did all the laundry, washing, and ironing.

Smitty summed up his childhood relationship with his parents this way: "My parents and I didn't have a terribly close relationship. They had a certain way to do things. So when the Depression really got going good, when the poverty really set in on us, they began to get some pretty wild reactions from Susie and me."[9]

The onset of the Depression, when Smitty and Sue were twelve, coincided with their father's downward spiral and inability to earn money as a surgeon. While Smitty never heard his parents have angry words, he reported discussions where "the begging and the promises" took place. Later, he asked his mom why she didn't leave. Her reply was simple and not unusual for the times: "I didn't have any place to go; my parents were dead."[10]

The poverty troubled Smitty the most. Like his dad, he liked nice cars and was eager to have one of his own. In his words, "I had a sense of fighting a second-rate feeling."[11]

Smitty's rebellion was perhaps more overt than Sue's. He was restless and started drinking when he was sixteen. He was arrested for urinating in the mayor's spittoon for fun. When he was eighteen, he got a young girl pregnant and "had to marry her.... We got a divorce after two years, and she's dead now. I paid child support for eighteen years.

When I wasn't able to, my father did. I don't know where my daughter is."[12] Smitty eventually married Betty, who became part of A.A. and eventually led Smitty to Al-Anon.

While the term "adult children of alcoholics" did not emerge in Twelve Step circles until decades later, first within Al-Anon and then as an independent Twelve Step Fellowship (Adult Children of Alcoholics and Dysfunctional Families—ACA) in the late 1970s, Sue and Smitty were among the first children of someone who acknowledged he was alcoholic.

Annie and the Oxford Group

In 1933, as Dr. Bob's drinking got worse, Annie began attending Oxford Group meetings in Akron. Annie had grown up in a Protestant church, and prayer was part of her daily life. She had learned that the son of a prominent family in Akron had gotten help with an awful drinking problem through the Oxford Group. Annie went to Oxford Group meetings hoping her husband might get the same help and sober up.

Another Oxford Group member was Henrietta Seiberling. On the face of it, Henrietta appeared to have a perfect life. A graduate of Vassar College, she lived on the beautiful and spacious grounds of the Seiberlings' estate after marrying Fred Seiberling, the son of a successful corporate executive in one of the largest tire and rubber manufacturing companies in Akron. F.A. and Gertrude Seiberling were involved in most of the important charities in Akron. Henrietta, by marrying Fred, became connected to the people of means and influence in Akron.

Henrietta, her husband, and their three children lived in what was called the "gate lodge" or gatehouse on the Seiberling estate. It was a lovely Tudor Revival style property modeled after elegant English homes.

In 1935, Fred separated from his wife and moved back to the main Seiberling house. Like Annie, Henrietta grew up as a woman of faith. She turned to the Oxford Group both because it was something those in the upper classes of Akron were doing and because she didn't know what to do about her disintegrating marriage.

With Annie's encouragement, Dr. Bob attended Oxford Group meetings for two and a half years before getting sober. Dr. Bob acknowledged he was attracted by the poise and happy dispositions of those who attended. "They seemed to be happy. I was self-conscious and ill at ease most of the time, my health was at the breaking point, and I was thoroughly miserable."[13]

The credibility and standing of the Oxford Group in Akron grew when tire magnate Harvey Firestone took an interest. His friend Jim Newton was instrumental in helping Harvey Firestone get his son to stop drinking with the help of the Oxford Group. Out of gratitude for this amazing change in his son, Harvey Firestone invited Frank Buchman, the Oxford Group founder, to lead an introductory meeting on the Oxford Group for the social elite of Akron in January 1934.[14]

Henrietta came to know about Dr. Bob's drinking problem through Delphine Weber, an Oxford Group member, who asked Henrietta after an Oxford Group meeting, "What are we going to do about Bob Smith?" Henrietta asked what was wrong with him, and Delphine responded, "He's a terrible drinker."[15] Henrietta reported she felt guided to have a meeting specifically for Bob Smith. Until then, the Oxford Group met on Thursday nights in West Hill. With Delphine's encouragement, Henrietta organized a different meeting on Wednesday night to invite Bob Smith and specifically address his drinking.

This meeting was held at the home of T. Henry and Clarace Williams. They were active in the Akron Oxford Group and friends of Henrietta. T. Henry had a ruddy face, which made some think he was alcoholic, but he was not. In fact, T. Henry was quite successful, having invented a new process for tire-making, an important gain for Akron and its many tire-manufacturing companies. T. Henry and Clarace were highly regarded, a couple who were generous, good, and emblematic of the best of genuine Christians.

Annie Smith, Henrietta Seiberling, and Clarace Williams were all women who studied and practiced their faith. "Anne Ripley Smith...was a Wellesley graduate, a former teacher, and an ardent student of the Bible and Christian literature of the 1930's.... Clarace had gone to Baptist missionary school in Chicago, specialized in religious education at Ottawa University in Kansas, and then worked in Akron, Ohio with the young people in a church there."[16] Together, they would have a significant impact on the development of A.A. and its spiritual tenets.

After her marriage to Fred Seiberling, Henrietta attended Westminster Presbyterian Church in Akron, where Dr. Bob and Annie Smith were also members. Their pastor, the Rev. J. C. Wright, was an advocate and participant in the Oxford Group and was in touch with the Rev. Sam Shoemaker in New York, who was providing guidance to Bill Wilson.

"Henrietta was a Presbyterian from childhood but not particularly an avid churchgoer. She was, however, an ardent student of the Bible.... She studied the teachings and story of Jesus, as did Dr. Bob and Anne Smith.... She clung to the inspiring version of First Century Christianity (a name the Oxford Group and early Akron AAs used to describe themselves) as it paralleled Christ's own methods."[17] Henrietta's attitude about forgiveness (seventy times seven), listening through quiet times for God's guidance, and "Thy will be done" came from her Bible study and Oxford Group reading and participation.[18]

Given Clarace and T. Henry's reputation for doing good, it makes sense that Henrietta asked them to host this meeting. In fact, they continued to host Oxford Group meetings until 1954. Meetings were marked by a friendly and receptive spirit, along with delicious refreshments after the meeting.

Henrietta encouraged Annie and others to come ready to mean business. Henrietta took the added step of organizing a planning or set-up meeting on Monday night to prepare for Wednesday. Students of recovery treatment history observe that Henrietta's preparation and reliance on guidance was akin to what would become family interventions to confront family members with alcohol problems.[19]

Dr. Bob Admits His Problem with Alcohol

Henrietta was led in her guidance to believe it was important for others to be direct and honest about their own challenges to encourage Dr. Bob to admit his problem. It worked!

Henrietta's perspective on this important first step to recovery for Dr. Bob was this: "We all shared very deeply our shortcomings and what we had victory over. Then there was a silence, and I waited and thought, 'Will Bob say anything?' Sure enough, in that deep, serious tone of his, he said, 'Well, you good people have all shared things that I am sure were very costly to you, and I am going to tell you something which may cost me my profession. I am a secret drinker, and I can't stop.' We said, 'Do you want us to pray for you?'"[20]

This moment, with Oxford Group members on their knees praying for Dr. Bob, was not the end of his drinking, but a major milestone in moving toward it. The practice of asking new members to admit their problem with alcohol and to get on their knees to pray for release became a part of Dr. Bob's way of working with newcomers when he got sober. Moreover, this first public admission of his problem with drinking is a powerful example of the critical role honesty plays as alcoholics and others who misuse substances face the truth of their inability—their powerlessness—to stop.

This admission was the beginning of the end of Dr. Bob's drinking problem. It did not come overnight. In fact, he stayed dry one day, but by Friday he was back to drinking. Annie shared with Henrietta the following Monday that Bob spent part of the weekend holed up in a motel drinking. He came home Sunday afternoon.

Henrietta assured her friend that, though to their human eyes Bob's drinking looked hopeless, there was always hope in God and God's love and mercy.

Mother's Day was fast approaching. Annie shared with Henrietta in a morning call how she dreaded Mother's Day because Bob always let her down. Like many wives of alcoholics, she wished Mother's Day was never invented.

Annie was in the same boat as Lois. As it was for many wives of alcoholics, the no-shows, low blows, and fiascoes of life with a drinker were constant and dispiriting. Mother's Day was one more heartrending turn on the "sorry-go-round" that so many wives of alcoholics experienced.

But when Annie and Lois and Bill and Bob connected, what had been heartrending would become soul-strengthening.

CHAPTER 10

HOW BILL W. AND DR. BOB MET

Pair the right two things together, and the combination is remarkable. Sunlight plus precipitation creates a beautiful rainbow. In a similar fashion, when a man and a woman wed, the marriage is a synergy greater than that of two people acting alone. Now, imagine what happens when two marriages join forces.

Bill's Lost Proxy Fight

While the Smiths were being readied for a life-changing meeting between Dr. Bob and Bill Wilson, Lois was in New York, dealing with her own emotional roller coaster with Bill. She heard from Bill by phone and letters, but definitely less frequently than she wanted.

One letter from Bill talked of this proxy fight as his best work ever, declaring it had great promise for their future financial security. As Lois noted, "He was dreaming great dreams again and without realizing it, I became swept up in those dreams too. I would go to bed thinking all about his exciting work in Akron and wake up smiling and happy.... And yet I wondered why I still had those old butterflies back in my stomach."[1]

Proxy fights are just that—fights. In this case, NRMC was the result of the merger of four family-owned businesses in 1928. It serviced the significant tire industry in Akron.[2] The Depression had weakened the company financially, which resulted in a group of Beer and Company investors from New York hiring Bill to try to accumulate shares of NRMC stock so their group could take control of management. In Bill's mind, this meant that, if he was successful, he would become the CEO or President of the new company.

Bill thought he had a majority of stock shares lined up; hence his enthusiasm. Unknown to Bill and his colleagues, there was another group of New York investors who were working to take control as well. This opposing group, led by Nils Florman, was contacting shareholders and spreading rumors about Bill's drinking history and his lack of readiness to lead a company. As a result, 40 percent of the stockholders joined forces with the management team, which also controlled shares. Together, this competing group successfully won control of NRMC. While the sale wasn't confirmed until later that summer, Bill knew the fight was over, and he had lost.

From the high of great opportunity, Bill was now left alone as his colleagues from Beer and Company headed back to New York and left Bill to try to legally salvage this failed takeover. It was Friday night, and a scene well-known and oft-told by A.A. members unfolded something like this.

Bill was staying at the Mayflower Hotel and had just $10 left. As he crossed the lobby, he noticed the bar, filled with businessmen joking and carrying on like the best friends in the world. Loneliness overcame Bill. He missed Lois and her assurances. He missed Ebby and his Oxford Group meetings. He could feel the old anxiety growing in the pit of his stomach. One drink would ease the anxiety, and he would make a new friend at the bar. He missed the camaraderie of sitting at a bar.

"Bill faced a solitary weekend in a strange city where he had just sustained a colossal disappointment. He had time on his hands and bitterness in his heart; fate had suddenly turned against him. His self-pity and resentment began to rise. He was lonely.... Now began the personal crisis that was to set in motion a series of life-changing events for Bill."[3]

Most people, feeling these intense feelings, would seek an escape. Bill had done that countless times in his drinking days, and it almost killed him. In telling his own story of recovery, he acknowledged the rationalizing thought of going in the bar for a ginger ale. And through some power beyond his own, he mustered the strength to realize that thought was a lie. He might start with ginger ale, but he would turn to alcohol and be back on the path toward death. He chose in that moment to say no to the seductive lie of the first drink.

Bill reported that despite his deep feeling of failure, "I thought, 'You need another alcoholic to talk to. You need another alcoholic just as much as he needs you!'"[4] Bill recalled how he stayed sober in New York, working frantically to help others who had a drinking problem. Somehow, he knew that was the better path for him than having one drink or sitting at a bar nursing a ginger ale.

Fate Intervenes

Fortunately, Bill saw a directory of local churches near the second-floor elevator of the hotel. It included a list of ministers and their phone numbers. No one knows exactly why Bill selected the Rev. Walter Tunks, an Episcopal minister active with the Oxford Group. This call led to Bill calling a number of people associated with the Oxford Group and eventually reaching Henrietta Seiberling.

Henrietta had recently been led in her quiet time to tell Dr. Bob he could not touch one drink of alcohol. She called Bob, invited him to visit, and shared her guidance. Bob, in some dismay over this message, stated, "Henrietta, I don't understand it. No one understands it."[5] How true and prophetic these words were.

Henrietta was on high alert for ways to help Dr. Bob stop drinking. When she got the call from Bill Wilson, she described it as "manna from heaven." In her mind, this call was a direct response to the guidance for her to pray for Dr. Bob to stop drinking and an outcome from the Oxford Group special meeting where Bob first admitted his drinking problem. Bill was quite direct, as Henrietta recalled: "I'm from the Oxford Group and I'm a Rum Hound."[6]

Henrietta told Bill about Dr. Bob. She called Annie and tried to set up a meeting between Dr. Bob and Bill for Saturday night. Annie reported Dr. Bob had drunk too much and was in no shape for a meeting that evening. She promised to bring him to Henrietta's home to meet Bill the next day.

Bill's desperate call for help to Henrietta led to Bill and Dr. Bob meeting on Mother's Day. Amazingly, this meeting became the foundation on which Alcoholics Anonymous was established.

Meanwhile, Lois slept alone in New York and was worrying more and more about her Bill in the face of the proxy deal going sour. And Annie Smith went to bed grieving over how Mother's Day was so painful and wondering why God had not removed Bob's urge to drink despite their endless prayers and attempts. Even with the chronic lack of evidence to support faith in their husbands, Lois and Annie continued to hope.

A Fateful Mother's Day

We can imagine that Annie Smith woke up on Mother's Day morning of 1935 worried. Would Bob be sober enough to go to Henrietta's and meet this man from New York? Perhaps she sat in her corner chair, smoking the remnant of yesterday's cigarette. Her eyes, too blurred by tears, couldn't focus on her Bible. With a deep sigh, she prayed that morning, as she did every morning, smoked her last cigarettes until only ashes were left, and wondered what the day would bring.

She struggled to hold onto her faith and to pray in that dark corner. She had waited seventeen years before agreeing to marry him. There were plenty of reasons to wait—the biggest one, not said out loud too often, was perhaps her fear of Bob's drinking getting out of control.

Their first years of marriage were so full of hope and the excitement of raising a family. But he had not stopped drinking, or at least gained control, as his faithful wife had hoped. He had paused while he got married and launched a profession.

When sober, Dr. Bob enjoyed lunch and a game of bridge at Akron's City Club. During his drinking years, his favorite hideouts were the City Club and The Portage Hotel. But sometimes days would pass without anyone knowing where he was.

Dr. Bob spent seventeen years decimating his medical practice, his standing in the community, his family relationships, and himself through his drinking. It was seventeen years of a living death.

That Mother's Day was emblematic of the other days on Dr. Bob's miserable journey. By the time Dr. Bob met

Bill, his medical practice had deteriorated almost to nothing. Daily, Dr. Bob was dodging people, flat on his back in bed, getting his wife to lie for him.

Meanwhile, back in New York, Mother's Day was painful in a different way for Lois. Her last letter from Bill was unusually brief and not encouraging about his proxy fight. She had left a phone message, and he had not called her back. She went to a church service in Brooklyn Heights, as she often did. The minister preached about the joys of motherhood, plunging her into a sea of despair, not a state of grace.

Lois was restless and irritable. Why didn't Bill call her? Was he drunk? She considered going to visit one of her sisters. Instead, she stayed home by herself all day, sewing and worrying about Bill when she wasn't stewing over him ignoring her.[7]

Back in Akron, persistent Henrietta called Annie again on Sunday morning. "Will Bob be able to make it today?"

Annie could tell he would not fight the visit and replied that she would get Dr. Bob there.

Dr. Bob recalled how the day began this way: "I don't remember ever feeling much worse, but I was very fond of Henri [Henrietta], and Annie had said we would go over.... So, we started over. On the way, I extracted a solemn promise from Anne that fifteen minutes of this stuff would be tops. I didn't want to talk to this mug or anybody else, and we'd really make it snappy, I said. Now these are the actual facts: We got there at five o'clock and it was 11:15 when we left."[8]

A Life-Changing Meeting

Bill referred to his meeting with Dr. Bob this way: "In our first conversation I bore down heavily on the medical hopelessness of Dr. Bob's case, freely using Dr. Silkworth's words describing the alcoholic's dilemma, the 'obsession plus allergy' theme."[9]

Dr. Bob had been giving the Oxford Group program much time and study, though he was still drunk every night.[10] He was ready for Bill's ego deflation approach. "*He talked my language.* He knew all the answers, and certainly not because he had picked them up in his reading."[11]

Bob realized toward the end of the meeting that Bill had gotten sober through the Oxford Group, the same way he was trying. But there was a difference. "The spiritual approach was as useless as any other if you soaked it up like a sponge and kept it to yourself. The purpose of life isn't to 'get' but to 'give.'"[12]

"He gave me information about the subject of alcoholism which was undoubtedly helpful. *Of far more importance was the fact that he was the first living human with whom I had ever talked, who knew what he was talking about in regard to alcoholism from actual experience.*"[13]

Bill also claimed that "Bob talked to me about himself as he had never talked before." Their talk was "a completely mutual thing." Bill found in this mutuality "the final missing link" and declared, "This was it. And this mutual give and take is at the very heart of all of A.A.'s Twelfth Step work today."[14]

Dr. Bob was working the spiritual program. What he lacked and Bill provided was an opportunity to identify with and relate to another man who had drunk in an out-of-control way and felt the same hopelessness and dread when facing each day. Together, Bill and Dr. Bob realized they gave each other something they could not get from spouses, church, friends, or medical professionals. This principle, of one person with a drinking problem telling her or his story to another, is indeed the bedrock of A.A. and has propelled its growth.

Many speculate about all the coincidences at work when these two men came together. They were both from Vermont. They were both among a handful of people in the US who were familiar with the Oxford Group. Bill's desperation call reached a minister familiar with the Oxford Group. The daughter-in-law of a tire-industry tycoon introduced Bill and Bob. Bill was involved with a proxy fight involving a similar company.

As another biographer described this first meeting of Bill and Dr. Bob, "That [Bill] did not drink under these trying circumstances is itself remarkable. What seems truly miraculous—and so A.A. literature has portrayed it—is the chain of events that led Bill W. to Dr. Bob, as if their blessed conjunction were foreordained by a Higher Power."[15]

What's written about this world-changing meeting does what Dr. Bob would have wanted: It shares the important principles that led to the launch of Alcoholics Anonymous.

The imagination begs for more details. It does not seem right for two men to meet for nearly six hours, and we know only these highlights. Yet it would be consistent with other decisions for Bill and Dr. Bob to agree to keep the focus on the Fellowship and the Twelve Steps and off themselves. The more garrulous Bill sensed the importance of respect for the quiet privacy of his new Midwestern friend.

We don't know exactly how Annie and Henrietta occupied their time. Given that it was prayer that brought them together and a belief in the power of quiet and guidance, it is likely they spent some time in quiet and prayer for Dr. Bob and Bill. There also were children to be attended to.

It is likely that both men were honest from the beginning about how they would be dead had they not married Lois and Annie. There would be no reason not to share how the effects of drinking too much had pained their wives and destroyed their financial security.

The bottom line is that two men who didn't know each other came together and shared their pain from years of mental and physical torture as a result of not being able to stop drinking alcohol.

Both men had tried spirituality and the Oxford Group and couldn't stay sober on that alone. The critical missing link, summed up in three words—"This was it"—was one alcoholic helping another and connecting as humans. Dr. Bob's daughter Sue later put this meeting in historical perspective: "Bill was the writer, so he's been remembered. But I think the only thing Bill brought to Akron that Dad hadn't already thought of was the service part of the program. That was the part that Dad was missing."[16]

However impactful this day was, the birthday of A.A. is not May 12, 1935, when Bill and Bob first met. Dr. Bob had some more drinking to finish up before A.A. could be launched.

Back in New York, Lois thought Bill was still fighting the proxy fight and was worried that he might return to drinking. Little did Lois know that this chance meeting would begin the deepest of friendship and trust between four people that would last until death separated them—two guys with out-of-control drinking problems and their wives. The seeds of Alcoholics Anonymous and Al-Anon Family Groups were now planted.

PART THREE

CO-CREATING ALCOHOLICS ANONYMOUS

1935–1950

CHAPTER 11

GETTING STARTED IN AKRON AND NEW YORK

After Bill Wilson and Dr. Bob Smith met at Henrietta Seiberling's, life at the Smith house was different—but still strained. Bill moved into a room in a country club that was convenient to the Smiths' home. Bill and Bob visited regularly. Dr. Bob was on edge, and his daughter Sue wondered about this New Yorker who seemed to always need a cup of coffee when he visited. She watched quietly as Bill's relationship with her mom and dad took shape.

Dr. Bob's Journey and Early Attempts to Share Sobriety in Akron

Annie watched guardedly, waiting for the restlessness that would come over Bob to return. After a couple of weeks of Bill visiting daily, Annie invited Bill to join the Smiths in their home at 855 Ardmore Avenue. Located in a residential neighborhood northwest of downtown Akron, the Smiths' house was a two-and-a-half-story craftsman-style home built in 1915 with twelve stone and wooden steps leading to a welcoming front porch.[1] Annie knew having Bill stay with them would make it easier for Bill to keep an eye on Bob and for her to keep an eye on both men.

Home of Dr. Bob and Annie Smith, 855 Ardmore Avenue, Akron, Ohio. (Courtesy of Dr. Bob's Home.)

Sue reported that her dad was quite enthusiastic about his first meeting with Bill. "He didn't go into a whole lot [of detail], but I do remember Dad saying that you seemed to hit it off with him more because you had the same thing. He realized that it wasn't just him. He told me that members of the Oxford Group just didn't have the same type of problem."[2]

Sue described their new routine this way: "Bill would come down in the morning and make the coffee; it was good coffee. He was an early riser, and he smoked a lot. I also remember him putting up his feet and we'd see a big hole in his shoe.... In a way, Bill sort of ignored us kids. He didn't have any kids of his own, and he talked more with Mom and Dad."[3]

Annie started each day with coffee and what she called *devotion*. We can imagine her saying, "Come on, Bob, let's pray and have our quiet time."

Annie began the devotion with a scripture reading. "Bill," she likely explained, "this is when we sit in quiet and listen for God's guidance." She often ended with her favorite verse from St. James: "Faith without works is dead."

Bill came to these morning quiet times with the zeal learned from his faith experience at Towns Hospital and memories of his grandfather's "good natured contempt of some church folk and their doings."[4] But Bill's spiritual awakening allowed him to move past his contempt for religion and learn from Annie.

Bill spent three months with the Smiths. This morning prayer, quiet time for guidance, and spiritual reading likely shaped the spiritual development of both men under the mentorship of Annie Smith. These early days spent together would influence profoundly the development of the Twelve Steps and the evolution of A.A. as a spiritual program.

As hopeful as Annie Smith was that Dr. Bob was done drinking, that was not the case.

Dr. Bob convinced Annie and Bill he was ready to go to the annual medical convention in Atlantic City. As daughter Sue told it, Bill was an easier sell on the trip than her mom. Bill had insisted on keeping two bottles of liquor in the dining room to prove they didn't need it. "To [Bill], attending a convention was evidently like keeping liquor on the sideboard; he felt alcoholics had to live in the real world, with all its temptations and pitfalls."[5]

That experiment of facing reality was either a miserable failure or a great success. For Annie, it was a horrendous mistake. She didn't hear from Bob for five days and had to have been deeply concerned.

Dr. Bob arrived drunk in Atlantic City on Sunday night and stayed drunk, with one brief break, until the train dropped him off on Friday in Cuyahoga Falls, a suburb of Akron. He was met by his office nurse and her husband, who found Dr. Bob suffering "some confusion and disarray" after a blackout for more than a day.[6] They took Bob to their home. Bill arrived and stayed with Bob, supervising while he tapered off.

Sue described the devastating impact of her dad's relapse this way: "When he did come home smashed, [Mom] was really crushed. She sat at the kitchen table, lighting one cigarette off another, while Bill kept trying to reassure her. She just thought that Dad had lost it all even though Bill had slipped, too, after Ebby first talked to him."[7]

Dr. Bob was scheduled to perform surgery the day after he returned home. Given his condition, this surgery was risky for everyone involved.

Bill explained preparing for the surgery this way: "It was a worrisome thing, because if he was too drunk, he couldn't do it. And if he was too sober, he would be too jittery. So we had to load him up with this combination of tomato juice and sauerkraut and Karo corn syrup. The idea was to supply him with vitamins from the tomatoes and sauerkraut and energy from the corn syrup. We also gave him some beers to calm his nerves."[8]

Dr. Bob and the patient got through the surgery. Those beers were Dr. Bob's last drinks. He remained sober until his death—and Alcoholics Anonymous was born on June 10, 1935[9] (although the name of the organization would not arise for another four years).

The day of surgery and A.A.'s founding was not without drama for Annie Smith and Bill. They didn't hear from Dr. Bob for hours after the surgery. When he arrived home that evening, he reported he had started the process of making restitution for harms done, an Oxford Group principle.

But it was still not a happily-ever-after story. The Wilsons and the Smiths were both financially ruined. Both men had jitters on a daily basis, so work was difficult, if not impossible. Dr. Bob had cravings for alcohol for over two years.

What happened next has allowed A.A. to help so many people with drinking problems for so long a time.

Bill and Bob started discussing how they could help other men with drinking problems. Bill told Bob how Ebby had convinced him that the way to stay sober was to help other alcoholics. Dr. Bob was practical by nature. While prayer, spiritual reading, and willpower had not worked, conversation with Bill had gotten him sober. So, he embraced and encouraged the idea of helping others, a central tenet of A.A. today.

Their first attempt was Eddie R., who lived down the street from Dr. Bob. Bill and Bob were desperate to get Eddie sober. They locked him on the second floor of the Smith home to keep him from drinking. One infamous afternoon, Eddie interrupted a tuna-fish-salad lunch by chasing Annie to the second floor with a big butcher knife. Another evening, they drove to Cleveland in the middle of the night to rescue Eddie, preventing him from jumping off a bridge in a failed suicide attempt. Unfortunately, none of this helped Eddie get sober.

They tried having Eddie's wife and children stay at the Smiths' for a short time. Bill was shocked to see Eddie's wife come downstairs in the morning with a black eye. Dr. Bob's daughter Sue declared that Eddie "wasn't a real good example, because he was their first attempt and it was a complete flop."[10]

Miraculously, decades later, he showed up at Dr. Bob's funeral having been sober a year.[11]

Early on, Bill wondered where to find more prospects. Dr. Bob told Bill: "They always have a batch down at Akron City Hospital."[12] While the admissions nurse was skeptical because she knew of Dr. Bob's drinking, he convinced her he was sober, and she agreed to let them talk to men drying out. Nurse Hall introduced Dr. Bob and Bill to Bill D., who became A.A. member number three. (Anonymity became a central tenet later, but we begin here to adhere to the rule that members of A.A. are identified only by first name and last initial out of respect for anonymity.)

Dr. Bob and Bill gave Bill D. a couple of days to detox in the hospital. They visited his wife, Henrietta D., which became a standard practice before talking with a new prospect. This way, they knew more about the prospect. Often, in the early days, the prospect had no idea that these two big Yankees, as they described themselves, were coming to visit.[13]

Henrietta D. described her husband this way: "When he's sober, he's the grandest man in the world. But when he's drinking, he's the worst."[14]

On his second visit, Dr. Bob mentioned that his wife wanted her to come visit. Henrietta was reluctant to go, but a friend convinced her she had nothing to lose.

"Anne was so sweet. Everybody loved her. There was never anything to make you feel she was better than anyone else," Henrietta recalled. Following that first meeting,

Annie called Henrietta every day to see how she was doing. Henrietta had figured that, because of Dr. Bob's work, the Smiths were rich. "I remember going there on a Sunday, and there was Bill Wilson eating peas out of a can—not even warmed up."[15]

Dr. Bob explained to Henrietta and Bill D. that the husbands and wives met together. "They didn't want separate meetings, [understanding] that husbands and wives had been separated long enough."[16] From the beginning, Bill and Bob recognized the importance of the family in the recovery process.

As the group of prospects grew, Annie and Henrietta talked with the wives and encouraged them while Bill W., Dr. Bob, and Bill D. talked with the men who drank too much. They also attended Oxford Group meetings on Wednesday nights.

Henrietta D. was a matron at the Akron City workhouse, a prison for women. She began telling the women there about how her husband got sober. Later, visiting jails and institutions for people with mental illness became part of what A.A. called its institutional service.

Another couple began coming to the Akron meeting every week from Cleveland after a sister in New York learned about it from Dr. Leonard Strong, Bill Wilson's brother-in-law. Dorothy S. had given up on her husband Clarence. She was done with tolerating his drinking and gave him an ultimatum. She told him if he didn't go to see this doctor in Akron who was helping alcoholics, she was leaving him.[17] He explained it this way in his story, "Home Brewmeister" in *Alcoholics Anonymous*: "Just at this time [rock bottom] my wife heard of a doctor in another city who had been successful with drunks. She offered me the alternative of going to see him or her leaving me for good and all."[18]

Desperate, Clarence S. reluctantly agreed to meet Dr. Bob. After Dr. Bob and Annie introduced the couple to the basics of staying sober, they made the trip weekly to Akron for over a year.

Lois Meets the Smiths and the Founding Partnership Is Formed

While Bill was spending time with Dr. Bob, excited at the prospects of their new friendship, Lois was back in Brooklyn, worried and in the dark. Bill did not tell her about Dr. Bob at first. In May 1935, Bill wrote to Lois on letterhead from Dr. Bob's office: "I'm writing this from the office of one of my new friends, Dr. Smith. He had my trouble and is getting to be an ardent Grouper. I have been to his house for meals, and the rest of his family is as nice as he. I have witnessed at a number of [Oxford Group] meetings."[19]

For most of the summer, when Bill wrote to Lois, he mentioned the proxy fight and was optimistic about the prospect for a successful outcome. Bill's letter to Lois later in May is illustrative of this optimism:

> Things have been happening at a perfectly furious rate both in business and with respect to the [Oxford] Group - And the two activities have been curiously and wonderfully interrelated. The Group situation has been that I have met some of the S and will presently need the Firestones and all of the other leading people in town - There has been for years a terrific feud among the rubber people here which can be solved by Group action - and I think you and I should have a lot to do with it. I am sure you would like it tremendously out here. Have met some wonderful people and it would be such a grand change for you - And the prospect of coming

here is excellent. With respect to business the situation has been hectic.[20]

Knowing Bill well, Lois could sense, by what he *wasn't* saying, when the proxy fight and Bill's dreams of success began to fall apart. At first, Bill talked about the complexity of the many people involved and the unresolved issues from four prior mergers. Then, he mentioned how his opponents were spreading rumors about his drinking problem and unreliability.

Her separation from Bill made it hard for Lois not to worry about Bill and his sobriety. She wanted him home. Their conversations, both phone and letter, got more tense as days became weeks, and Bill was talking less about the proxy fight and more about his new friends.

Most times, she held back from expressing her jealousy directly. Instead, she increased her pressure on Bill to come home. "All she knew from her husband's letters was that he was in trouble, and she was not there to help him. On the one hand, she was angry he hadn't called, and yet on the other, fearful of his present condition. She wanted to take the next bus to Akron, yet she wanted to believe that her God was taking care of him. She found herself tired and short-tempered from worry and lack of sleep, both at work and with her family."[21]

One day, Lois came home and, sifting through the mail, found a letter from Annie Smith. Lois described the letter as warm and personal. "[Annie] told her what Bill's efforts meant to her and her family, how they had changed their lives. She said she would be honored if Lois could see her way clear to come for a visit so she could thank her in person."[22]

Bill was thrilled when Lois said yes. He knew Lois and Annie would become fast friends.

A little less than two months after Bill had arrived in Ohio, Lois boarded a bus to spend her one-week vacation in Ohio with Bill and the Smiths. It was late June, and the long, hot bus ride from New York to Akron gave Lois plenty of time to think. We don't know exactly what she thought about or how her reunion with Bill and first meeting with the Smiths went. We do know they quickly became very close friends and loyal partners in building what would become A.A.

The Oxford Group Connection

During that week, each morning began with Bill making coffee for the whole house. Annie had her coffee with her first cigarette of the day shortly after Bill had his. After a simple breakfast of toast and jelly or one of Annie's home-made pastries, Annie headed to her prayer chair, joined by Bob, Lois, and Bill.

There was no debate about quiet time. It happened every morning, and Lois loved it. In fact, Lois and Bill had begun practicing quiet time some mornings as a result of attending the Oxford Group in New York.

Annie usually picked the scripture reading. After the reading was done, the two couples sat in silence for twenty minutes and listened for guidance from God.

Given Annie's friendship with Henrietta Seiberling and her continued prayers for Bob's sobriety, it is likely Lois met Henrietta during her visit. Lois surely heard how Henrietta brought Bill and Dr. Bob together. And while she could not have fully understood the depth and mean-ing of this meeting, she could see that Bill was happy and his friendship with Dr. Bob was helping him stay sober.

In this way, the week unfolded: time for Bill and Lois to reconnect, daily prayer time, simple meals with lively discussions of life in 1930s America and helping drunks, important and helpful discussions with Henrietta, and, on

Wednesday and Thursday evenings, Oxford Group meetings.

Bob and Annie had been attending what was called West End Oxford Group meeting on Thursday nights since early 1933. Annie had convinced Bob to go. While Bob was, like Bill, skeptical of organized religion, he "realized these new friends had something he didn't." Before meeting Bill, Bob had this to say about attending the Oxford Group: "I at no time sensed that it might be an answer to my liquor problems." Through this experience, though, Bob began a lifelong study of spiritual literature.[23] (In fact, by the time of his death, Dr. Bob had amassed a vast and varied library encompassing spiritualism and Eastern religions, as well as Christianity.)

The Akron Oxford Group meetings were similar to the meetings Bill and Lois Wilson attended in New York after Bill had his spiritual awakening. In fact, some Oxford Group fundamentals can be seen in A.A. and Al-Anon beliefs and practices. Annie Smith, in her journal for the period 1933–1939, detailed the direct connections between Bible truths, Oxford Group principles, and the principles and practices found in early A.A., particularly in Akron.[24]

A typical Oxford Group gathering was called a "house party" or "meeting." Some were small and held in members' homes; others were larger, held in public meeting rooms and more like a combination retreat and prayer meeting. The West End meeting was held at the home of T. Henry and Clarace Williams. It might start with a new member who had a drinking problem going upstairs with a group of sober men and completing his "surrender." This required "absolute surrender to God" was considered a prerequisite to attending a meeting. For the man with a drinking problem, this meant ascribing to a belief that he could not overcome this problem by himself but needed to rely totally on God to stop drinking.

Sometimes the surrender occurred in a hospital before a drunk's release, kneeling beside the hospital bed with other members present as witnesses. There were occasions where the surrender took place after the meeting.

One wife described the process this way: "The men would all disappear upstairs and all of us women would be nervous and worried about what was going on. After about a half an hour or so, down would come the new man, shaking, white, serious, and grim."[25]

In New York, where members were more vocal about their opposition to requirements to believe in any particular "God," this process of a formal on-your-knees surrender was not practiced for long. However, this idea of surrender to a power greater than yourself became the essential Third Step of the Twelve Steps.

Once any surrender activity had occurred, all present gathered and held hands for an opening prayer. This was followed by a period of quiet time to seek guidance from God. Since what would become A.A. was initially based on typical Oxford Group practices, the quiet time was long, taking about half the meeting. However, quiet time at the Williamses was eventually shortened, adapting to the restlessness and lack of comfort with silence experienced by the men seeking sobriety.

Quiet time was followed by the leader for the evening introducing a reading from the Bible or other Christian literature. The leader would next speak and offer his witness for twenty minutes or so and then invite others to witness. Because the meeting was a mix of people with drinking problems and other Oxford Group members, much of the sharing had nothing to do with drinking. The meeting ended with recitation of the Lord's Prayer.[26]

Going to the Oxford Group meeting together further solidified the bond between the Wilsons and Smiths.

This shared interest and commitment to the Oxford Group practices and to helping men with drinking problems gave the two couples plenty to talk about. Annie and Lois might end their day with a chat and perhaps prayer or reading over a late-night snack and then head to bed. Dr. Bob and Bill often poured more coffee and stayed up until 1:00 a.m. or so, talking about all the ways their lives had changed. This might lead to a discussion about *Varieties of Religious Experience* by William James and what that meant to Bill as he tried to understand his sudden spiritual awakening and imagine how it might happen for others. Another night, it might be Dr. Bob sharing how reading Emmett Fox's book *The Sermon on the Mount* helped him make his faith practical.

Their conversations no doubt overflowed with gratitude for their wives, who had stuck with them, and hope for the man with a drinking problem they had visited that day.

On Saturday evening, Annie prepared a special farewell dinner for Lois: turkey with cranberries.

Lois' long bus ride home was quite different. She understood better what the Smiths meant to Bill and his sobriety. She was beginning to understand that she could not keep Bill sober any more than she had been able to get him sober. Her thoughts probably returned to their many conversations and her anxiety about when Bill would come home.

Bill wrote to Lois in early August, 1935: "Dear Lois: Business looks good. My lawyer friend came over this AM and we have spent the day with the company crowd who are now 100% for us.... Of course, this leaves me as mum in the dark as ever as to when I shall come but it really does seem as though the denouement is near and thus far the delay has played into our hands to perfection- I love you so much and am so elated- Bill."[27]

Despite Bill's optimism, his proxy fight failed, and his hope for a new career in an Akron company was crushed. It is unclear whether Bill was being overly optimistic in his August letters to Lois. On August 26, he was sufficiently convinced of his failure to return to New York.[28]

In the big picture and in ways Bill couldn't yet see or even imagine, his time in Akron with Dr. Bob was laying the groundwork for what would become Alcoholics Anonymous.

Fortunately, while there were ups and downs with helping other men, Bill and Bob were staying sober and launching something that would grow beyond their imaginations.

The Smiths' gift to Bill W. was keeping him sober during a time of business failure and welcoming him in their home to support the work to help other men. Together, these two couples were breaking new ground in developing the Twelve Step way of life.

The two couples also supported each other's spiritual journey. They each could look to one another for an encouraging act or a hopeful word when the disease tried to suck one of them under. "Bill was the promoter, Mom was the stabilizer and Dad was the rock," wrote Sue Smith. "Mom would have her quiet time and Bob and Bill would join her."[29]

Early Days of Working with Drunks in New York

Back in New York, Bill W. threw himself into working with other drunks. Having seen how important this work with others was to the sobriety of Bill and Bob, Lois threw herself into it completely as well. One historian describes Lois' renewal this way: "Her brief visit proved long enough to renew in her heart the first-married love and deep faith in her husband's abilities, the seeds of which had somehow survived the seventeen years of his destructive drinking. Certain more firmly than ever that Bill was a great man, she returned to Brooklyn's Clinton Street determined to cooperate in every way possible."[30]

Little did Lois know how much this faith in Bill would cost her. They attended Oxford Group meetings and started hosting a Tuesday meeting at their home, where men with drinking problems were welcome.

Learning from the Akron experience, Bill continued visiting Towns Hospital, where he had been treated, and the Calvary Mission, where his friend Ebby got sober. As in Akron, many of his attempts to offer sobriety didn't work, and Lois had to live through those failures. Like the Smiths, they invited men trying to get sober to live with them for a while. Consequently, their clothing was stolen, drying-out drunks had hallucinations, and one even committed suicide in their home. In effect, Lois Wilson and Annie Smith operated two of the first halfway houses in America.

Bill eventually found success with Hank Parkhurst and Fitz Mayo, two very different men. Hank was a lanky, red-headed salesman from New Jersey. He was quick with ideas and words and became a great thinking partner with Bill W. and collaborator for the book *Alcoholics Anonymous.*

Fitz Mayo was quiet, withdrawn, and lived almost two hundred miles away, south of Annapolis, Maryland. Fitz found his way to New York for treatment at Towns Hospital, and thus to Bill W. They become fast friends. In the words of one biographer: "Lois Wilson said Fitz was an impractical, lovable dreamer. His intellectual, scholarly qualities gave him common ground with Bill who—like Fitz—was also a dreamer.... The Wilsons and the Mayos became devoted friends, and visited one another often. Fitz frequently came up for the Tuesday night meeting at the Wilson home in Brooklyn."[31]

Hank and Fitz played important roles in the next growth phase of what would become A.A.: the development of the Twelve Steps and the writing of *Alcoholics Anonymous*, also known as the "Big Book." They were joined by the first woman to come to 182 Clinton Street to get sober, Florence R.

Florence was divorced from a Wall Street friend of Bill's. Bill and Lois visited her at Bellevue Hospital and invited her to live with them while she got sober. Despite facing the challenges of prejudices against women with drinking problems, both in society and within the meetings, Florence got sober and eventually moved to Washington, DC, where she worked with Fitz in starting a group there.

Like many early members, Florence could not stay sober. She returned to drinking, fell ill, and died. She was identified in the morgue by her friend Fitz Mayo.

Back then, as now, no one knew who would stay sober and who would not. Bill knew his primary purpose was to help the still-struggling alcoholic—and that effort would help him stay sober. Joined by Hank and Fitz, they moved forward with that mission.

And not even all those leading the way stayed sober.

CHAPTER 12

FUELING GROWTH: THE BIG BOOK, PUBLICITY, AND FREEDOM

"It must be so nice living in a house like this." We can picture Kathleen Parkhurst saying something like this as she climbed the steps of 182 Clinton Street in Brooklyn, New York.

"What do you mean?" Lois might have asked. Kathleen was the wife of Hank Parkhurst, who had become one of Bill's prime partners in working with other alcoholics. Lois and Kathleen held key things in common. These friends were each lively and tenacious women with salesmen husbands who had long histories of drinking too much.

"Didn't you say this is the house where you were born? With all our husbands are involved in, it must feel safe to have one steady place in your life."

Life for the Wilsons could indeed be precarious. Bill's work was episodic—a small project here or there. That left him plenty of time to continue looking for men with a drinking problem who were ready to ask for help.

The Wilson-Parkhurst Influence

Bill met Hank Parkhurst at Towns Hospital in the winter of 1935. Charlie Towns, the owner of the alcohol rehab hospital, and Dr. Silkworth, his lead physician, were amazed at the change in Bill since his miraculous spiritual experience at their hospital. So, they let him visit and tell his story to their patients. Towns Hospital served people with the money to afford the best treatment of the day.

Kathleen and Hank Parkhurst lived in Teaneck, New Jersey. Hank had a high-level management job at Standard Oil. He left that position, thinking he could do better on his own, but his drinking overcame his business sense. Like Bill, he was out of answers by the time he reached Towns Hospital.

As she welcomed Kathleen into her home for tea, Lois had no way of knowing what a big role Hank would play in working with Bill—or how the sweet relationship the four of them enjoyed would eventually change.

Hank became a regular at local Oxford Group meetings and at the weekly meetings at the Wilsons' Clinton Street home. Grateful for each other and their husbands' newfound sobriety, they shared some lighter moments such as this one, following an Oxford Group meeting.[1]

Hank loved to show off his car and drive fast at night in Manhattan, and Bill was equally up for some excitement. Off they went, the convertible top down. The faster Hank drove, the more all the passengers screamed—and laughed. At one point, Kathleen stood up in her seat and began howling at the moon. They were so happy to be sober and together. Like kids on a roller coaster for the first time, they all started howling.

Lois and a friend looking out the windows at 182 Clinton Street. (Permission required for use.)

Why shouldn't Lois and Kathleen be happy? Their men were sober and on fire with helping other men with drinking problems. They were elated to have their husbands back. And the roller coaster had not begun to pick up speed. It would—and soon.

The Wilsons and Parkhursts spent most weekends together. Bill and Hank understood each other. They were both big-idea guys with vision, determination, and a knack for selling.

Bill helped raise money to finance Hank's company, Honor Dealers. Hank had a plan to cooperatively sell gasoline, oil, tires, and a host of other automobile items, thus bypassing the big companies. Bill did this work out of Hank's offices in Newark, New Jersey.

The year 1937 was finally financially good for the Wilsons. Bill had a salaried position with Quaw and Foley, a Manhattan investment company. He even got two weeks' vacation. In late April, Bill learned that Ebby had relapsed and was in Towns Hospital. Bill dropped everything and visited his friend. The irony wasn't lost on Bill that he was now wanting to help the man who had helped *him* find sobriety.

When Ebby was discharged from Towns and came to live with Bill and Lois, Bill was ready to pay back Ebby. He invited Ebby to go with him to Vermont for some rest, the same medicine Lois had tried with Bill.

Bill used one week of his vacation for this trip with Ebby. Lois knew how much Ebby meant to Bill and reluctantly let go of her hopes for some time away with Bill for herself. This was the beginning of many ways Bill paid Ebby back through loyalty, financial help, and friendship.

Bill was busy with his day job at Quaw and Foley. Lois chronicled in her diary Bill's many work-related trips to the "West"—Detroit, Cleveland, Akron, and throughout New York state. Though Bill was busy, he and Lois made sure they attended Oxford Group meetings each week. Bill also regularly visited Towns Hospital and the Calvary Mission, looking for men with drinking problems to help.

The Akron Meeting

Bill was planning to use the second week of his vacation to visit Dr. Bob in Akron and talk about the future—specifically how they would help thousands of drunks. Bill's excitement about this trip was diminished by some more bad news. On Friday, October 8, 1937, the day before Lois and Bill planned to leave for Akron, he lost his job, effective immediately. Surprised, Bill rationalized it as a result of the 1937 recession. Lois told friends that Quaw and Foley had to let go of Bill and other employees to save the company. While Lois' diary mentions Bill exploring a number of job leads, his work for Quaw and Foley would be Bill's last salaried position.[2]

Unflagging in his zeal for helping drunks, and despite Lois' increased worry about paying the bills, Bill and Lois went ahead with their trip. They left for Akron with two other recovering couples. They took two cars and picked up Fitz Mayo on the way.

Lois was glad to have the others along for social reasons. Bill was glad to have three other New York members along to help him make his case about how to grow their impact with the Akron "Alcoholic Squad" (as the Akron members referred to themselves—or, more fully, the Akron Alcoholic Squad of the Oxford Group).

Bill, with Hank's encouragement, was far along in scheming about how to save thousands of drunks. Though Hank couldn't make the trip, he trusted Bill's sales ability, and he knew Bill could rely on Fitz Mayo, Bill R., and Sterling P. for reinforcement.

They were greeted warmly, like returning war heroes, by the Smiths. Akron member Paul S. hosted a dinner for them at his home on Sunday. Over dinner, the New York and Akron couples reveled in their newfound sobriety.

Discussions over the next two days started with Dr. Bob and then expanded to a meeting with him and the eighteen members of the Akron Alcoholic Squad, held after their regular Tuesday night meeting.

Bill had three ideas he hoped to sell to the Akron group members. He was convinced they needed: (1) hospitals where drunks could detox and get sober; (2) paid missionaries to visit men in hospitals and shelters to share their experience and the path to a spiritual experience; and (3) a book to explain exactly how to get and stay sober, based on their experiences.

The meeting was rocky. The details are unknown because Lois, who scrupulously kept a diary, tore out the pages from the diary for that trip. In surmising why Lois did this, one author offers this opinion: "After all else, Lois was a loyal wife."[3]

Some A.A. historians suggest that simmering tensions between Akron and New York had reached a peak because, in April or May of 1937, Bill and Lois and the early New

York members had separated entirely from the Oxford Group.

In New York, Bill and his prospects had found the Oxford Group to be increasingly unfriendly and not supportive. The upper-middle-class Oxford Group members knew they were supposed to be open to including people who were in trouble. However, they really did not like the people Bill brought to Oxford Group meetings. They dressed, talked, looked, and often smelled different than the well-dressed members. Bill found many of his prospects on the streets and brought them, as is, to the meetings.

This disdain had come to a head in the summer, when a young minister told Bill not to bring any more drunks to the Oxford Group meeting at Calvary Church. Oxford Group members looked down at Bill and Lois for having separate meetings in their home. Bill also resisted the Oxford Group's encouragement to focus on outreach to Wall Street friends rather than other alcoholics.

By August, Bill and Lois had had enough of the Oxford Group meetings and stopped going. Instead, they held what Lois called in her diary "seminars" at their home and, over time, in homes across the New York and New Jersey region.

This split with the Oxford Group meant Bill and the New York men had no formal program to follow. It was therefore urgent that they develop one. In contrast, the Akron men had a program adapted from the Oxford Group and were quite happy with it, despite some concerns raised by Clarence S. about clerical opposition to Catholics attending Oxford Group meetings. With all this in mind, Bill and his friends from New York made their pitch for why hospitals, missionaries, and a book were needed.

Objections from the Akron members came from all directions—opposition to raising money, fear of failure, and fear of changing a simple program that was saving their lives.

Some years later, Bill described his response to Akron resistance to his ideas this way: "I wasn't above getting personal when challenging the naysayers. I asked them: 'How can you people sleep at night when there are drunks in California who are dying right now because there is no way that they could ever hear about our solution?'"[4]

Eventually they took a vote, and Bill got approval for all three ideas by two votes. It is safe to believe that Dr. Bob was one of the positive votes. Without his quiet support at this meeting, the fledgling program could have splintered and possibly fallen apart.

But it didn't. The Wilsons and their friends from New York stayed in Akron all week. These couples and Fitz enjoyed being together and being sober. We can imagine Annie organizing them for some daily quiet time, spiritual reading, and prayer, followed by Lois suggesting a trip to the museum or the Perkins Woods Park. Still, the Wilsons arrived back in New York exhausted from the physical and emotional energy required for this trip.

Struggling to Fund the Vision

However, Bill and Lois didn't rest long. Bill and Hank began a feverish effort to begin raising the money to finance the dream. Over the next few weeks, Bill and Hank combined meetings with wealthy people they knew or had access to in New York with cold calls to major foundations.

What they found shocked them. It was the same story everywhere: There was absolutely no interest in funding anything to help drunks. One obstacle to their fundraising efforts was the fact that wealthy people wanted to prevent the problem through temperance and prohibition, not by helping people who were perceived to be hurting themselves.[5]

One advantage that Bill and Lois had as they worked to stay sober and help others was that they knew a lot of people of means. Neither of them was hesitant to ask friends, relatives, and associates for help. Among the Wilsons' contacts was Bill's sister Dorothy, who was married to New York doctor Leonard Strong. Dr. Strong had paid for two of Bill's trips to Towns Hospital to sober up.

Bill visited Dr. Strong in late October under the pretense of an ulcer attack (one of many recurring symptoms, which some say came from being a hypochondriac like his mother). He quickly shifted to bemoaning the lack of response to his efforts to raise money. He shared his incredulity that people with plenty of money could not see the potential in forty people miraculously recovering and staying sober.

Dr. Strong wanted to help. He recalled his relationship with Dr. Willard Richardson, whom he knew was connected to the Rockefellers. He called Dr. Richardson, shared the story of Bill's recovery, and asked him to meet Bill. Dr. Richardson agreed—not entirely out of altruism, but because the Rockefellers were adamantly opposed to drinking and interested in solutions.

This call and subsequent meetings shaped A.A. and its development, but not in the way Bill dreamed. From the earliest communications, Dr. Richardson stated that the Rockefellers were not interested in funding "any organization of this project" and "anything that tended to professionalize or institutionalize it."[6]

Bill, the optimist, while annoyed by this message, largely ignored it. He told Lois how excited he was to have gotten a meeting with key men associated with John D. Rockefeller Jr. Bill was sure this meeting was the answer to all their money problems.

However, Bill discovered that people with money move slowly and are careful. One meeting led to another. Eventually, Dr. Bob got involved and came to New York to meet with Dr. Richardson and three of Rockefeller's closest advisors.

Dr. Bob and Paul S. arrived in New York on a Saturday night. Lois hosted dinner, and the excitement grew.

Five New York members, the two Akron members, and their two doctor friends—Dr. Silkworth from Towns Hospital and Dr. Strong—joined them for the dinner meeting with four Rockefeller associates at Rockefeller Center. How exciting and intimidating this meeting must have been for a group of men who had each been near death just a few years earlier!

The meeting lasted five hours. Bill and his team told their stories of near death from excessive drinking and their recovery. Dr. Silkworth emphasized the idea of an allergy and that drinking too much is a disease. The Rockefeller team was moved. While they spoke glowingly of what these men had accomplished, each of the Rockefeller men, in different ways, stated their concern that money would corrupt this simple grassroots effort.

Seeing he was losing the big money argument, Bill shifted strategy. "How about we start with funding one hospital in Akron?"[7] Dr. Bob was in agreement. It would help him with his financial struggles. While not committing to it, Dr. Richardson and his colleagues seemed at least open to this new proposal. The meeting ended cordially with no commitment from the Rockefeller representatives.

The courtship of the Rockefeller people went on for several more months. It turns out, one of the Rockefeller men, Frank Amos, had two brothers with drinking problems. He approached Bill for help with another friend who drank too much. All this gave Hank and Bill some optimism, since Frank Amos was selected by Dr. Richardson to visit the Akron group.

Meanwhile, in February 1938, Hank proposed to Bill that they suggest to their group that members each pay monthly dues. Neither Bill nor Hank had steady incomes.

Lois' small income from her interior design business was feeding the men living with them, plus herself and Bill.

The wives heard about this idea and could not believe Hank and Bill thought they could afford to contribute. They were all as financially strapped as the Wilsons—or thought they were. Opposition from the wives shot this idea down for the moment.

Amos was positively moved by his meetings in Akron. His report included three options: (1) fund a new, small hospital as proposed; (2) fund services at an existing hospital; or (3) provide small monthly payments to Dr. Smith for two years to support his work there.

On St. Patrick's Day, 1938, John D. Rockefeller Jr. wrote to Dr. Richardson to render his decision on the proposal. Rockefeller restated his policy of not supporting organizations or institutions and agreed to make a personal exception outside his Foundation and contribute $5,000 to Riverside Church to be used over one, two, or three years to support Dr. Bob in Akron. He was clear he would not entertain additional requests.[8]

Bill and Hank were flabbergasted. They found it hard to believe that all the good feelings at the meeting and positive statements about their work had not translated into financial support.

Lois had to be both frustrated and scared. It was hard being the primary breadwinner for Bill and all those living with them. It was difficult to comprehend how those with so much would not want to help.

Despite their disappointment, Bill and the early members of A.A. came to see, over time, that Mr. Rockefeller helped save them from endless arguments about money. Ultimately, this rejection led to the decision that A.A. would be self-supporting through its members and accept no outside contributions—a decision that has served A.A. well for over eight decades.

Lois, meanwhile, struggled to feed and clean up after as many as five drunks who were trying to get sober in her family's Brooklyn Heights home. Drama and chaos were a certainty most days. With Bill out of the house and traveling out of town much of the time, Lois was left to deal with it as best she could.

One man came to stay and appeared to be getting sober. Bill even took him to a meeting about the Rockefellers. Two weeks later, he was drunk again and stole clothes from Bill and Lois to pawn for funds to drink.

A man named Russ came back drunk at 2:00 a.m. while Bill was away and decided it was a good time to be affectionate with Lois. Russ slurred his words, and Lois looked for cover. She didn't detail what came after his romantic words of love, writing only, "etc. etc. etc." There was no end to the "etceteras" Lois faced.

Given all this chaos, Lois needed a break, so she headed to Maryland, arriving at Fitz's home and staying there for twelve days.

Meanwhile, feeling down but not out, Hank, Bill, and others cooked up a new scheme. They decided to create an Alcoholic Fund and raise more money. This was the beginning of building the organizational structure of A.A., because Bill knew money needed oversight and accountability. After some initial thinking about how the Fund might operate, consultation with Rockefeller associates Frank Amos and Willard Richardson resulted in the decision to incorporate as the Alcoholic Foundation.

Bill proposed a board for the fund with three nonalcoholics and two former alcoholics, believing that would give nonalcoholic donors more confidence. This Foundation oversaw A.A. operations until it evolved into the later General Service Office and structure.

Having a foundation did not solve the money problems, however. Instead, Bill and Hank shifted to focus on the idea of the book. They talked endlessly about the book (now referred to as "the Big Book" or *Alcoholics Anonymous*) and what needed to be in it. Hank went so far as to develop a business plan for the book that estimated the potential market as three million readers. Giving up on a windfall from the wealthy, Hank and Bill put all their hopes in the success of the book.

Writing the Big Book

Bill knew intuitively that writing the book was his to do. Hank, as the lead promoter, realized they needed sample chapters to build interest in the book. Their fundraising efforts netted $500 from Towns Hospital owner Charlie Towns, then another $500, and finally an agreement to make five monthly payments of $200 to Bill to support his writing and $100 a month to support Ruth Hock for her work in typing the book. (Bill knew Ruth from his friendship with Hank, so Bill wrote the book in the Honor Dealers office.)

Bill began writing on Friday, May 20, 1938. Despite his enthusiasm for the project, Bill faced some big challenges: he wasn't a writer, and he wasn't sure what needed to be written. His larger fear, which he shared in a letter to Dr. Bob, was "the possibility that someone else garbled the situation before we had a chance to say anything."[9]

Bill decided to start by telling his own story of nearly dying from drinking and sharing his amazing spiritual transformation. He thought the reader needed something hopeful.

It took Bill three tries to get a draft of the chapter known today as "Bill's Story." His second draft introduced the idea

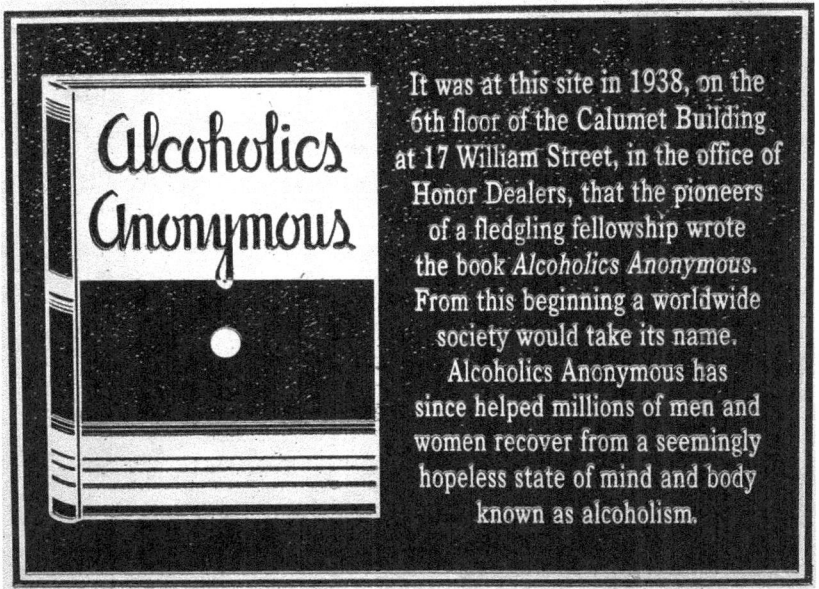

Plaque at site of Calumet Building, 17 William St., Newark, New Jersey, where much of the text for the Big Book of Alcoholics Anonymous was written in 1938. (CC-1.0 Public Domain)

of four steps, which became part of the ultimate Twelve Steps, and used the exact words "God as we understood him."[10] This is considered by many the most radical contribution Bill Wilson made to the Twelve Steps. Bill and others acknowledge that the Twelve Steps are largely a distillation of proven spiritual and religious beliefs passed down over the centuries. Bill also acknowledged the role played by Oxford Group leader the Rev. Shoemaker of Calvary Mission in helping shape the Twelve Steps. From 1935 until the New York members broke from the Oxford Group and the Big Book was ultimately published in April 1939, early recovery was based on the Oxford Group teachings and practices which were fully based in Christianity, including a belief in Jesus.

Through a gradual process, Bill moved from seeing religion as the key to sobriety to seeing a spiritual awakening as the path. That led him eventually to write about "God as we understood Him." Bill advocated for and stuck to this flexibility despite aggressive and loud objection from early members. One author sums up Bill's position this way: "It is, frankly, a radically pragmatic and amazingly democratic approach to the concept of religious beliefs; one that Bill Wilson carefully laid as a critical foundation stone in the creation of Alcoholics Anonymous."[11]

Bill's third draft, known simply as "Bill's Story," is very close to what is found today in Chapter 1 of *Alcoholics Anonymous*.

For Bill, writing the second chapter brought front and center a raging debate between a mostly Christian group that believed religion was the solution and a small and vocal group who saw moral psychology as the answer.

Bill had the courage and willingness to trust his vision in the face of strong and persistent opposition. He came down squarely on the side of "religion"—a progressive, open-minded faith in some power outside oneself—as the solution. This chapter was also Bill's opportunity to complete the break with the Oxford Group. Bill had come to see that striving for moral perfection, as outlined in their four absolutes, was both a distraction to men getting sober and, for some, led back to drinking. In this chapter of the Big Book, Bill provided a new spiritual and intellectual home for such early members as they moved away from Oxford Group affiliation.

Unfortunately for Bill, his number-one supporter and partner, Hank Parkhurst, was not happy with the two draft chapters and their emphasis on religion as the solution to alcoholic drinking. Imagine the scene for a moment. Hank is sharing his Honor Dealers office and secretary Ruth Hock with Bill as he does this writing. Bill's "writing" process is to make notes on a legal pad and then stand behind Ruth and dictate so she can type, and he can see it and make changes as they go. It's a small office, and Hank's desk is not far away. Hank probably took advantage of many opportunities to oppose Bill's direction on the "God" point.

The "God" argument continued for nearly a year and was not resolved until the final editing stage. At its core, the disagreement was about what comes first—personal change and then faith in some God or larger Being, or is belief in God the starting point?

Bill and Hank, unlike many strong-willed leaders, were able to set aside these differences and remain friends. In fact, Hank developed a twenty-five-chapter outline for the book, which Bill mostly followed.

In late June 1938, Hank and Bill mailed the first two chapters to doctors, ministers, and priests, looking for support and interest. Again, like their initial efforts to seek funding, there was little response or interest.

As tensions mounted between Hank and Bill, Bill found Lois less accepting and testier. On June 27, 1938, Lois reported in her diary, "Bill and I had a big fight and he stormed out saying he was going to get drunk. I was terrified. Instead, he went to NJ to see Hank and didn't drink."[12]

Bill focused that summer on organizing the structure for the Alcoholic Foundation and seeking testimonials for the book. Bill and Hank likely wanted to have the organizational structure in place to handle all the money they expected from the sales of the book. This structure served A.A. and its members well until Bill introduced a more expansive structure in 1950. Without these structures, it is unlikely A.A. would have survived its first decades.

The next controversy with the book caught Bill by surprise. Bill wrote the chapter entitled "To Wives" despite Lois offering to write it. Lois was clear on how she felt about it: "Bill wrote it, and I was mad. I wasn't so much mad as hurt. I still don't know why Bill wrote it. I've never really gotten into it—why he insisted upon writing it. I said to him, 'Well, do you want me to write it?' And he said no, he thought it should be in the same style as the rest of the book."[13]

Lois' partnership with Bill was teaching her about the effect of alcoholism on families and what it takes to rebound from its demoralizing impact. At the time the Big Book was written, early members were mostly men who were often accompanied to meetings by their wives. Women at that time had few rights and little voice. In addition, beliefs at the time about sexuality, promiscuity, or out-of-control sexual activity further complicated and delayed the acceptance of women as A.A. members.

Among the early (male) members getting sober, there was fear about women coming to meetings. Both men and their wives feared the possibility of sexual relationships between women with drinking problems and men trying to recover.

From an early age, Lois had been raised to be true to herself and make her own decisions. Her partnership with Bill was teaching her about how devastating alcoholism was to families and how these spiritual principles might also help families. But Bill remained adamant in his position that he would write the chapters "To Wives" and "The Family Afterward." Lois mentioned in her memoir her frustration that Bill wouldn't let her write "To Wives" and discounted her concerns by saying she was too busy to worry about it.

While there is not a lot written by Dr. Bob and the early Akron members commenting on the book, Dorothy S., the wife of Cleveland leader Clarence S., observed in her reflections: "I'll never forget the time the fifth chapter ['How It Works'] came out.... *Our* fifth chapter. I was staying all night with the Smiths, and Anne and I sat up, and we read the thing until four in the morning. And we thought, 'Now this is it. This is really going to bring people in.'"[14]

Chapter Five tells the reader he is hopeless if he, as an alcoholic, thinks he can stop drinking on his own. It makes clear how people with drinking problems have lost the choice of whether to drink. This chapter then introduces the Twelve Steps as the solution to the dilemma of compulsive drinking.

Bill and Hank agreed on the importance of including personal stories in the book. They both firmly believed in the power of one person with a history of the problem talking with the person who wants to stop drinking.

The personal stories were intended to show the wide variety of alcoholics' backgrounds—age, income, profession, marital status—and how different the drinking problems faced by early members were.

Bill codified the central belief of A.A. in his chapter "There Is a Solution": "But the ex-problem drinker who has found this solution, who is properly armed with facts about himself, can generally win the confidence of another alcoholic in a few hours. Until such an understanding is reached, little or nothing can be accomplished."[15]

Writing the stories introduced another controversy for Bill—suspicions and resentments about money. Not everyone in Ohio—in Akron or the newly forming Cleveland group—wanted their stories published. Rumors abounded that Bill Wilson was going to get rich on this book. Why should members contribute their story with no royalties?[16]

Bill offered several explanations about how the name Alcoholics Anonymous was selected. Hank asked Fitz, who lived near Washington, DC, to visit the Library of Congress and check on the two leading names: The Way Out and Alcoholics Anonymous. Fitz reported there were twenty-five books with the name The Way Out and none called Alcoholics Anonymous. Hank and Bill quickly embraced Alcoholics Anonymous as the name for the book and subsequently the organization.

As 1938 came to an end, a *Reader's Digest* editor promised a story on the book when it was published. (This excitement was wiped out the following spring when the editor had convenient amnesia and didn't inform Bill his editorial board had decided not to print the story.)

The Suggested Twelve Steps

The Twelve Steps might not have been so well received but for the resolution of one last fight before publication. Bill had sent a prepublication edition to a handful of doctors and people he trusted for review. A Dr. Howard responded, suggesting that it was a great book, but the tone was too preachy and prescriptive. There were too many "you should" statements. Dr. Howard suggested the tone would cause rebellion within the reader.

Therefore, Bill took a more tactful approach by writing, "Here are the steps we took, which are *suggested* as a program of recovery."[17]

It is unlikely that A.A. or any Twelve Step program would have been as successful without Bill giving up on his *musts* and *shoulds*. These changes—"God as we understood Him" and "suggested as a program of recovery"—are critical to the power and broad acceptance of Alcoholics Anonymous and the Twelve Step movement as it evolved. (See the Appendix for the Twelve Steps.)

While the Big Book was coming closer to publication, several crises continued to haunt the Wilsons. On the personal front, Hank's marriage was showing more signs of strain, as he and Kathleen lived sometimes together and sometimes apart.

As each of Hank's and Bill's schemes to raise money failed and the bills for the book piled up, Lois shared her financial worries with a friend: "I had difficulty sleeping at times. I would walk through the house late at night wondering what I would do if I ever lost the only real home I ever knew. It was frightful to think about. Bill kept assuring me things would work out. That soon the book would begin to sell. That it just had to."[18]

Despite Bill's assurances, finding the money for the printer became a crisis. Hank and Bill tried selling stock in the book, but that didn't raise much money. Bill visited Charlie Towns and asked him for money for the book. Towns contributed another $500.

In the end, Bill was still short of money for printing. He went to see Bert T., a tailor who had been coming to meetings with the New York group for a few months. The tailor put up his Fifth Avenue business as collateral to borrow $1,000 as part of the final funds needed to pay the publisher.[19]

The Big Book Published

Finally, on April 10, 1939, Cornwall Press printed 4,650 copies of *Alcoholics Anonymous*.

Ever the optimists and promoters, Hank and Bill had 20,000 postcards printed to send to influential people in medicine, education, the faith community, and the press, announcing the book and offering a prepublication copy. Included was a tear-off section to send book orders to a post office box. The daily trip to the post office changed from wild enthusiasm to disappointment to depression, as they received twenty returned postcards and only two book orders.

Slowly, Bill and Hank realized that immediate acceptance of the book was not going to end their financial problems or swell membership.

While first copies of *Alcoholics Anonymous* were quickly sent to key Rockefeller family connections Frank

Amos and Willard Richardson, Bill held on to the first copy and gave it to Lois as a Christmas gift with this inscription: "To Lois / One whose loving / care and fortitude in / our dark days together / made these pages possible. / So to her, this first/book of the first edition / is lovingly and / thankfully given. / Bill./ In memory of /'The Fifth Christmas'/12/25/39."[20]

Although Lois was probably delighted with this Christmas gift, we wonder if she felt sufficiently thanked and acknowledged when the printing occurred. Lois had little time for such musings, and her diary shows no inclination or desire to be recognized. Bill was her hero, and she was thrilled he was sober and this book he cared about so much was now published.

Yet, her hero had failed to protect her home.

In the midst of the book publication excitement, on April 26, 1939, the bank foreclosed on the Wilsons' home at 182 Clinton Street in Brooklyn Heights. Lois had to be devastated at losing her childhood home with all its security and comfort. However, she stoically reported in her diary entry that day: "1939 Wednesday April 26th Left 182 for good. Went to Parkhursts."[21]

CHAPTER 13

HOW A.A. SPREAD AND HANDLED ITS GROWING PAINS

Bill Wilson had a vision, but not a plan. He could see important things unfolding with the A.A. Fellowship. So could Lois. But alongside all the progress, there were serious problems, including having no place to live.

The Wilsons Embrace Sobriety and Homelessness

Once again, Lois was determined to stay positive, despite the confusion and chaos of being homeless for what became nearly two years. How did they manage this? As an example, one week in February 1940 included a Saturday night stay with Bill's sister Dot. On Sunday, Lois missed a ferry and waited three hours for her hostess for the night. She spent Tuesday with Chris in "town," Friday with Vy and Lois' sister Barbara when Bill was speaking in Greenwich meeting. Sunday, she unexpectedly met Bill at Grand

Central Station in Manhattan and traveled to a meeting in South Orange, New Jersey and an overnight with M ____s. Monday, she stayed in a more luxurious home offered on the way to Newark to look for a furnished room.[1]

> Lois termed it "living around." With one notable exception, she seems to have endured their two years of gypsy existence with her usual forbearance, good cheer, and extraordinary ability to find the positive.... The one exception to Lois' good cheer— or at least the one exception that survives in the histories of this period—took place as the Wilsons were (appropriately) walking through Grand Central Station. Lois suddenly found herself sitting down in the middle of a flight of stairs and weeping. Would they never have a home of their own? Would they never stop moving around?[2]

Bill sleeping on the grass in August 1940 at Joy Farm, a spiritual retreat center—later known as High Watch—in Kent, Connecticut. (Permission required for use.)

Bobbie B. Joins A.A. and the Wilsons

Amid all this uncertainty, Lois received an unexpected letter in March 1940 that greatly influenced how A.A. would grow. Just as Marty Mann had reached out to Lois when

Marty was hitting bottom with her alcoholism addiction, another woman, Bobbie B.,[3] decided the gateway to A.A. was through Lois Wilson.

After a successful career as a dancer and actress, performing throughout Europe and the United States, Bobbie's life soured as she was left widowed with two children after a brief three-and-a-half-year marriage. Her second marriage was volatile, and she left her career and began heavy use of alcohol and barbiturates. Three years before contacting Lois, she began frequent trips to sanitariums to stop drinking and regain her health. This approach proved unsuccessful.

Bobbie wrote to Lois: "My dear Lois Wilson, Your name was given to me by Dr. Allen of White Plains (Bloomingdale's). May I please attend your meeting on Tuesday, March 19 at Steinway Hall. I forgot to ask Dr. Allen at what time. I would like to attend with the hope of becoming a permanent member if I qualify."[4]

Bobbie began attending A.A. meetings, met Bill and Lois Wilson, and became a volunteer at the 24th Street Clubhouse, one of the first established places around the country where A.A. and other Twelve Step members met and held meetings. (Such Clubhouses are not affiliated with A.A.) This volunteer engagement resulted in her becoming the second National Secretary for A.A. two years later.

One of Bobbie's many roles was reporting on the bumpy road both Bill and A.A. faced in the 1940s. One such report is about one of Bill's early encounters with racism and the desire of some members to limit A.A. access to white people.

African Americans' First Experience with A.A.

In his zeal to invite anyone who thought they had a drinking problem to meetings, Bill ran into the limits of open membership and the prevalence of racism in 1940. Two prison inmates attended an institution meeting where Bill was speaking. The two men asked where they could attend a meeting when they got out. Bill told them the meeting location and enthusiastically invited them to attend. The two African Americans showed up at the meeting a few months later. To Bill's dismay, some members objected to African Americans attending the meeting.

Bobbie was present at the meeting and later described how the racial attitudes of members were apparent immediately. Some opposed African Americans attending, some were supportive, and some were on the fence. Bill sized up the dilemma immediately, realizing he had made a mistake by inviting African Americans to a meeting where they would not be welcomed by all. "So [Bill] asked those who objected if they would agree that Negroes had the right to A.A. just the same as any other human being. On the basic principle, there was complete agreement. So it was more or less decided then that Negroes should be invited to attend open or closed group meetings as visitors." Early A.A. history noted that this "compromise method of permitting blacks to come to meetings as 'observers' worked."[5]

While this solution may have "worked" for the white majority in A.A., it reinforced racial segregation and did not "work" for African Americans and other minorities. It took several more years for early Black meetings of A.A. to develop in St. Louis, Chicago, and Washington, DC. To say the visitor method "worked" is obviously a question of perspective.

The African Americans who began an A.A. meeting in St. Louis in January 1945 were so afraid of attacks from white racists that they chose not to publicly advertise their meeting time and location and eventually disbanded.[6] An early A.A. historian reported that the A.A. Central Office incorrectly named the Washington, DC, Cosmopolitan

Group founded in April 1945 as the first Black A.A. group. However, the St. Louis group began in January 1945 and was followed by the Evans Avenue Group (Chicago) in March 1945 and the Washington, DC, group in April 1945. Like many remaining differences of opinion in A.A., the Cosmopolitan Group in Washington, DC, continues to celebrate being the first Black A.A. group in the United States.

The history of the first Black A.A. group in Washington, DC, is well documented. A.A. reached Washington, DC, in 1939 because Fitz Mayo and Florence R., who were part of the early A.A. meetings in New York, started meetings for whites in Washington, DC. At the time, Washington, DC, was a legally segregated city. Like in much of the South, Blacks were not allowed to be in the same areas of restaurants, meeting spaces, churches, or buses with whites.

Dr. Jim S.'s story of the progression of his drinking is told in his own words in "Jim's Story" in the Big Book. Jim's father was an African American country doctor, and Jim grew up in Virginia. He got married early and describes in his story his need for his wife Vi, much like Bill needed Lois. Jim spent ten years trying to live sober at home with his wife and three children while traveling for work to keep up his drinking. After prescribing a drug in a blackout, he realized he needed to give up practicing medicine. He did some electrical work for a family friend, Ella G. She introduced him to Charlie G., a white member of A.A.

Charlie told Jim about his own experience with drinking, what it did to him, and how he was recovering through A.A. and the Twelve Steps. Jim later recalled the feeling he got about this unusual meeting in 1945 of a Black man and a white man sitting together and discussing how to stop drinking. In hearing Charlie's experience with getting sober, Jim realized Charlie had hope, something he had lost a long time ago.[7]

Jim and Charlie began meeting at Ella G.'s home. Slowly, other Black members joined. Charlie suggested the group find a meeting room in a church, a common practice for white A.A. groups. After being turned down by several white churches, Jim rented a room at the YMCA and began the meetings of Washington's first African American meeting.

Jim's wife Vi, like Lois, played a key role in Jim's sobriety and in the spread of A.A. among Black families in Washington, DC. Lois interviewed Vi about her experience and asked her about bringing men with drinking problems into the house. Vi explained to Lois her belief that

> There's no good [in] A.A. if I can't put it in practice when it's needed. So, owing to that fact then, if a fellow would get drunk and just about wear out everyone at his home, they'd call Jimmy to come in and he'd find out this fellow would be in bad shape and couldn't be left alone, so he'd ask me, "Vi, what about bringing this fellow home? I can't afford to put all my time at his house with him. If you're not afraid to have him in the home, then I could run out and do a little work and be back and forth and still look after him." So, I said, "It's certainly all right with me, I'm not afraid." So, he'd bring him on home and if they were very drunk, he'd put them to bed, or if not, we'd sit around and I could [talk] A.A., just like I was an A.A. to them, and do my talking."[8]

In her interview, Lois asked Vi how many men she estimated lived in their home, and Vi responded around one hundred! Lois talked with Vi about her experience with the wives and asked if Vi found that the A.A. program applied to her or other wives. Vi replied, "I think that was the main thing I recognized in this program when I read the story and some of the book. It's a new way of life for me as well as for him."

As the interview concluded, Lois observed:

> It helps the alcoholic tremendously, by the wife releasing him, just the way Jim's mother was possessing him and trying to correct his ways and almost live his life for him, so wives very often do. It keeps the alcoholic in a frustrated state of mind and when we realize that and try to not solve all his problems for him, give the problem over to God ourselves, and then live according to the A.A. program ourselves, then the alcoholic is free from this apron string that we wives have held on him, and it helps him tremendously as well as helping his wife. We can live a life of serenity and capability and joy that we wouldn't have, no matter what happened, which is really one of the main purposes of the Family groups.[9]

A Temporary Home and a New Friend

While Lois might have sensed some serenity in sobriety, the Wilsons were looking for a permanent home, even as they realized they could not afford one. An earlier Lois probably couldn't have imagined making do with an upstairs bedroom in the 24th Street Clubhouse that was used for A.A. meetings during the day and was home at night for a handful of problem drinkers trying to get sober. Hanging her clothes from a broom handle and listening to drunks snore was not Lois' vision of home.

Nevertheless, that became their residence in early November 1940. This room was also where an important spiritual anchor appeared for Bill. It was a windy, cool, and rainy Saturday night, as Bill recalled it later. The club janitor who answered the door figured the priest—rain-soaked, portly, and disheveled—was another drunk looking for help. The priest insisted he wanted to see Bill. Fr. Ed Dowling, a Jesuit from St. Louis, thus met with Bill Wilson in a small room alongside boxes doubling as dressers.[10]

This meeting was not Fr. Ed's first introduction to A.A. He ministered to people in need in St. Louis and was friends with a newspaperman in Chicago named Eddie who couldn't stop drinking. Fr. Ed invited Eddie and his wife Grace to St. Louis for a visit in January 1940. A month later, Fr. Ed went to Chicago to visit Eddie and his family.[11]

Fr. Ed was happy to find Eddie sober and surprised and "concern[ed] as Eddie told him that the very people who were helping him avoid drinking were themselves active drinkers until very recently."[12]

Like many who first heard of A.A., Fr. Ed described himself as "confused and apprehensive." He attended an A.A. meeting to look out for his friend. He described the men present for the meal as "some thirty to forty vapid and uninteresting people" and "just like the family entrance to skid row. Then the talks began. And so did my amazement. In the four years since that moment, I have been transfixed in the fascinating stories of Alcoholics Anonymous. The greatest drama in America today."[13]

From his first exposure to A.A., Fr. Ed realized that they, like others he served, had something to give him through the stories told at meetings. His biographer sums up Fr. Ed's relationship with A.A. this way: "To say that Father Ed was inspired by A.A. members' stories would be an understatement. He *thrived* on them."[14]

On that rainy night, after a few minutes of confusion and feeling each other out, Bill and Fr. Ed had a long conversation which laid the foundation for a friendship that lasted until Fr. Ed died twenty years later. He became Bill's spiritual advisor and confidante in the turbulent times that would lie ahead. One A.A. historian describes this meeting as Bill's first experience of taking A.A.'s Fifth Step ("Admitted to God, to ourselves, and to another human being the exact nature of our wrongs"). Fr. Ed reportedly showed his spiritual compassion to Bill by responding with a New Testament quote (Matthew 5:6): "Blessed are they who do hunger and thirst." The gentle and direct priest explained to Bill that "God's chosen were distinguished by their yearnings, their restlessness, their thirst."[15]

Bill and Lois both needed spiritual encouragement and hope at this point. Late 1939 and 1940 had been a disappointing and personally difficult time. Their troubles began with both Bill and Lois feeling their loyalties torn as the marriage of their close friends, Hank and Kathleen Parkhurst, began to disintegrate. And while she didn't admit it often or to many people, Lois was struggling with being married to a recovering alcoholic who wasn't very available to her.

Meanwhile, the book was not selling, and the Wilsons' poverty intensified. Despite no home and no income, Bill and Lois kept believing God would help them help more people with drinking problems.

There were a handful of members of the fledgling group in New York who wanted to help the couple that helped each of them get sober. Five minutes before one of the weekly meetings was about to close, one of the men suggested the group consider offering some financial support to Bill and Lois. Everyone nodded in agreement. They voted to start a Bill and Lois Improvement Fund. Lois commented in her memoir that she and Bill were unclear what the Improvement Fund was supposed to improve. She thought maybe their dispositions, as the money was $20 a month.[16]

Fortunately, Lois shared Bill's passion and did not give up easily. Despite being houseless, Lois mustered the energy to try writing as a way to increase their nonexistent income. Having sold an article on veneers to *House and Garden*, Lois submitted tales to *Romantic Stories* and some poetry. Nothing sold.

Help didn't come quickly, but it came. Fr. Ed Dowling walked with Bill through many low moments in the early 1940s. When Bill's depression returned with a vengeance in 1945, Fr. Ed stood with Bill and helped him deepen his understanding of depression and its spiritual challenges.

From the beginning of their relationship, Fr. Ed introduced Bill to the ideas of discernment and detachment. He pointed Bill back to his own Twelve Steps, particularly the Sixth and Seventh Steps, where the recovering alcoholic becomes willing to have God remove character defects or limiting habits or beliefs and humbly ask God (as the person understands God) for help. In a 1942 letter to Bill, Fr. Ed reminded Bill: "Most spiritual development seems to be not through development but through detachment. Detachment from the sensual gratification of alcohol brings the spiritual gifts of clear thinking and peace of mind."[17]

In May 1946, Bill replied to a letter from Fr. Ed and addressed his depression: "Little by little I seem to be getting out of the clutches of the Devil—or whatever it was had hold of me the last couple of years. The past few weeks have been the best yet."[18]

More on A.A.'s Early Growth

New members came to A.A. very slowly in New York and New Jersey. The publishing of *Alcoholics Anonymous* in April 1939 helped some, but growth from the Big Book publication was frustratingly slow for Bill.

Amazingly, momentum began to grow independent of Bill's efforts. While Bill and Lois were keeping the small New York and New Jersey groups going, back in Akron,

Dr. Bob and Annie were becoming the Midwest center for help for men with drinking problems. Unable to practice much medicine because of his damaged reputation, Dr. Bob gave himself entirely to working with men he called "drunks."

Annie and Dr. Bob had a consistent message for those they helped get sober. They offered unconditional love and a way, through surrender and the still-developing Twelve Steps, to find God and get sober. Two wives of new members repeated almost the same words in describing Annie's message to them: "People have been good to you here. Make sure you go out of your way to help the newcomer."[19]

By May 1939, Clarence S. was eager to start a meeting welcoming to all, including Catholics, in Cleveland. At the May 3 meeting in Akron, Clarence made his case to Dr. Bob and the others for why it was time to split from the Oxford Group. A week later, when it was obvious Dr. Bob disagreed and wanted to stay with the Oxford Group, Clarence announced he was starting a meeting in Cleveland that had nothing to do with the Oxford Group. It would be called Alcoholics Anonymous, like the book.

The Cleveland group benefited from an article in *Liberty Magazine*, a popular religious magazine published by Fulton Oursler, author of the well-known book *The Greatest Story Ever Told*. The article, "Alcoholics and God," resulted in eight hundred pain-filled letters of inquiry from people who themselves had drinking problems or had family members with drinking problems. Ruth Hock, as secretary to the Alcoholic Foundation, began what became standard procedure for responding to these letters. She sent the inquiries to recovering members in the three existing groups—New York, Akron, and now Cleveland—and asked members there to contact and visit the person making the inquiry. This approach became what is now known as Twelfth Step work for members: carrying the message to those still suffering from alcoholism.

Clarence's wife, Dorothy, did more for A.A. than demand her husband go see Dr. Bob. After Clarence was sober, she took ten copies of the prepublication edition of *Alcoholics Anonymous* to local doctors and ministers. One such minster, the Rev. Dilworth Lupton, was a prominent church leader in Cleveland who had been opposed to A.A. because it was too much like the Oxford Group. After reading *Alcoholics Anonymous*, he devoted a Sunday sermon entitled "Mr. X and Alcoholics Anonymous" to a positive review of the book and the work of A.A. His sermon resulted in *The Cleveland Plain Dealer*, the major local paper, printing a series of five articles on the editorial page. The sermon and the articles fueled an outpouring of interest in A.A. in Cleveland, making Cleveland larger than New York or Akron in the number of groups and membership for a while.

Men barely sober a few weeks themselves were enlisted to help respond to these new inquiries, fueling the growth in Cleveland and elsewhere.

Clarence S. also followed the lead of Bill and Dr. Bob in going to hospitals to visit patients with drinking problems. One such patient was Larry J. He was found coatless and near death on the street on a bitter winter day, weighing just one hundred pounds. He was taken to a local Cleveland hospital and diagnosed as having tuberculosis in addition to delirium tremens from his drinking. Clarence visited Larry regularly. It became clear Larry needed a warmer climate to recover his health. Clarence had a friend with the Houston newspaper and recommended Larry for a position.

Larry headed to Houston with no A.A. experience but his conversations with Clarence and a Big Book. Reading the Big Book on the train, he had a conversion. He convinced the newspaper editor to let him write a series on A.A. This was another major information breakthrough, as the Alcoholic Foundation office and Ruth Hock, now the full-time secretary at that office, reprinted the series and sent it to those inquiring for help.

Word was getting out through other channels as well. Judge Curtis Bok, one of the owners of the popular *Saturday Evening Post*, had heard positive things in late 1940 about A.A. from two Philadelphia friends. He assigned investigative reporter Jack Alexander to find out more about A.A.

Alexander took his time and was thorough in checking out the meetings and the people. He spent time in Akron with Dr. Bob and the Akron members and in New York with Bill and the New York and New Jersey members. To his own astonishment, these visits and meetings convinced him that the Twelve Steps and Alcoholics Anonymous worked. Men with terrible drinking problems were now sober and productive members of their community.

His article, "Alcoholics Anonymous," was published on March 1, 1941, and raised awareness of A.A. all over the United States. Because of the popularity of the *Saturday Evening Post*, the Alcoholic Foundation office in New York received six thousand inquiries in 1941.[20]

Ruth Hock, the only staff person at that point, with help from Bill, Lois, and other newly sober volunteers (including Bobbie B.), responded personally to every letter and telegram. Lois was actively involved in developing the plan with Ruth for responding to the letters and in writing letters herself.

The story of how A.A. grew from three or four communities to forty a year later and thousands more in a few years is taken for granted but is still a miracle that defies imagination. While Lois paid attention to those who were trying to recover and their wives, Bill continued to devote most of his energy to looking for respected publications to print information about A.A. and the Big Book and sought endorsements from leaders to give credibility to A.A.

Much of the effectiveness of A.A. appears serendipitous in hindsight. Bill had ideas, but he had absolutely no plan for how A.A. would grow. His spiritual awakening seemed to give him the gift of trusting the process and the power of the book *Alcoholics Anonymous*.

He didn't develop procedures for groups to apply for membership by filling out a form. There was no test. You were a member if you said you were a member. Bill and Lois encouraged anyone who wanted help to get it how they got it: talk to another person with the same problem and come together in meetings to form a community.

Bill described this growth period this way:

> This sudden growth ushered in a period of awful uncertainty. The big test of A.A.'s unity began in earnest. We were operating with only the benefit of casual contacts, travelers going from one place to another, letters from the office, one pamphlet, and one book. Could we, on that slender basis, form ourselves into groups that could function and hang together? We simply did not know.... We could only do our best, and leave the rest to God.[21]

This "chain effect"—the way Bill described the early growth of A.A.—and simple method of encouraging one member to respond to another person wanting to get sober fueled A.A.'s growth around the country and eventually the world. Through it all, Bill and Lois dealt with home-lessness, this chaotic and out-of-control growth, and their challenges as a couple.

A month after publication of the *Saturday Evening Post* article, another event changed the lives of Bill and Lois. Early members knew the Wilsons needed a home. Joan C., an early New York member, had a realtor friend, Helen Griffith. She also owned a home in Bedford, Westchester County, outside New York City, that she wanted to sell. Joan and Helen agreed this home would be perfect for the Wilsons.

Given their situation, it is likely that Bill and Lois looked at this possibility differently on different days. We can imagine that Bill may have been optimistic one day, while Lois would focus on the practical concerns about affording upkeep on a home, particularly in posh Westchester County. Alternatively, if Bill had been feeling down, flirting again with depression, he might have been dismissive of the idea, while Lois offered hope. Either way, it likely was not easy for the Wilsons to believe this dream might come true.

They had stayed with friends and strangers, primarily in New York, New Jersey, and Vermont, during their two years without a home. They were grateful for the hospitality. But to put down roots and put up pictures in a home of their own? We can imagine Lois feeling that would be lovely!

They both were clear they needed a house, and one was being offered. But without a precise plan, was that possibility enough?

CHAPTER 14

BUILDING A MOVEMENT, ESTABLISHING A HOME

Can you live in a house and build it at the same time? Perhaps you can if home is where the heart is. In many ways, that's how A.A. developed. The plan was being formulated simultaneously with its rollout.

In a similar way, the Wilsons finally found a home of their own. The blocks fell into place almost miraculously. They went from "no place to call home" to "no place like home."

Bill-Lo's Dream Becomes Real

On a sunny day in March with snow on the ground, as Lois recalled it, she and Bill were visiting friends and realized they weren't far from Helen Griffith's property. So, despite their doubts about the feasibility of owning it, they decided to stop and see it.

The home was about forty-three miles from Midtown Manhattan and the 24th Street Clubhouse where they were living. Lois described the visit this way: "We were charmed by its secluded location and wanted to see the interior. A window was unlocked, and we clambered in. Bill was crazy about the large living room with its huge stone fireplace. I, too, liked it all but had always pictured a little white cottage beside a brook. This house seemed too big and formal to me, and there was no brook, although the surrounding woods were lovely."[1]

Lois goes on to say that in reality it wasn't so big—seven rooms and the big fireplace offered "cheer and friendship and hominess." Griffith set up financing, which involved a $40-a-month payment on a $6,500 sales price (equivalent to $136,000 in 2024).

As the prospect of actually having a home became reality, Lois couldn't believe it. She was incredulous that she was actually talking to Bill about measuring windows for drapes in a home of her own. The seamstress in her was excited. The loyal wife, weary from being homeless, was ecstatic.

When the Wilsons first moved to their new home, they gratefully referred to it as "Bill-Lo's Break." Not long after moving there, they and others began referring to it as Stepping Stones. This name came from the fact that there were twelve stone steps going up the steep hill to their home, connecting it to A.A.'s Twelve Steps.

Lois Cruises, Bill Struggles

By April 1941, Lois was a busy lady. Besides responding to letters from the Jack Alexander article and moving into this new home, she had a planned six-week cruise to South America. Fran, the mother of a friend, had invited her to travel with her at no cost. While she hated to leave her new home after barely moving in, her love of travel made it impossible to say no.

Fran's brother was part owner of the Moore-McCormack Steamship Line. Lois recalled this about her amazing trip:

> We were the only passengers on the freighter, and the captain was an old friend of Fran's. He had a canvas swimming pool put up on deck. We had our meals at his table with the officers and played bridge with him at night. At various ports, while freight was being loaded and unloaded, he guided us on tours of the city. It was a great and wonderful experience; but I kept wondering what was happening at "Bill-Lo's Break." How was Bill getting on in the house alone? What spring flowers were out, and were there any birds around? After all these years, we now had a home of our own in the country, and I wasn't there to watch the drama of spring.[2]

Lois would have felt even worse if she knew that Bill was having a terrible time. The only heat in the house was the fireplace. Bill caught a wicked cold in his chest and began taking cough medicine for it. Lois later reported that, like any good alcoholic, Bill figured that if twice a day was the dosage, if he doubled it, he would get well quicker. Bill didn't realize the cough medicine had alcohol in it. He told Lois how his thoughts quickly went to whiskey. He confided to Lois when she got home how his crazy thinking took over. He figured Lois was away, no one knew where he was, and that a little whiskey would help him get over this cold more quickly—and no one would know he'd had a drink!

Fortunately for Bill and A.A., he quickly realized this was crazy thinking. Bill had failed to pay attention to the fact that there was alcohol in his medicine, and his craving was reactivated. From this event, Bill also learned the danger of isolating, particularly when he didn't feel well.

Upon her return, Lois had lots to do to make their new home warm and comfortable for them. Lois worked on painting and papering. She reflected in her memoir about the neck pain she developed painting a ceiling in the forty-three-foot-long upstairs library. Only an interior decorator and someone with an eye for detail could be so precise about the length of the ceiling![3]

Lois arranged the furniture and made their new home livable while Bill commuted to the New York office three or four days a week and worked at home on writing and organizing projects for A.A. Fortunately, Lois was a trained interior decorator and enjoyed organizing their home. And Bill, as Lois often observed, was oblivious to details, unless it was something he really cared about.

Bill did use his engineering ingenuity to solve the problem of how to get water to the second floor of their home, as the pump was insufficient to the task. Bill bought an open tank, used to provide water for cattle, and put it in the attic. He reinforced the attic floor so the heavy tank would not fall through the floor. Next, he designed a clever system that would ring a bell to signal when the tank was empty and when the pump had refilled it. Lois was impressed by Bill's ingenuity and his clever way of pumping water to the second floor with a bell that told them when the tank was full.[4]

As happens with many clever inventions, the Wilsons discovered an unexpected flaw in their water system. Lois described the "minor" problem this way:

> One day...Bill was afraid there wouldn't be enough water in the tank for company on the weekend. He turned on the pump "only for a short time." But friends unexpectedly invited us out for the evening, and we forgot all about the pump.
>
> On our return, we could hear the alarm bell ringing before we entered. Our hearts sank. Inside, water was cascading down the stairs.[5]

Lois ended her report on the incident there. Given her temper and the work she put into painting, carpeting, and decorating her new home, Bill likely had a rough evening.

The Smiths Visit the Wilsons' New Home

Nineteen forty-one continued to be a year of change and stress. On December 7, Pearl Harbor was bombed. Bill decided, both out of civic responsibility and a desire for financial stability, to enlist in the Army. Fortunately for A.A., he was not eligible due to health issues.

As Lois made progress in giving their new home the look and feel she wanted, she and Bill began to welcome guests. Dr. Bob and Annie came often, usually on their trips to Vermont to see his parents. While they didn't stay long, the two cofounders and their wives, who were essential partners, enjoyed one another's company and talked over the different growth challenges arising for A.A. Lois also received encouragement from Annie about her loneliness and accepting Bill's many absences to do A.A. work.

Annie and Dr. Bob Smith. (Courtesy of Dr. Bob's Home.)

Having gotten through the early controversies around the writing of the Big Book, Dr. Bob was content to be a "worker among workers," spending all his time trying to help people with drinking problems. He was glad Bill was willing to take on the administrative and policy questions. There were now hospitals—St. Thomas in Akron and Knickerbocker in New York—with units devoted to the care of people with drinking problems. These were great sources of new members.

"Bill, you keep doing what you're doing. I am happy to work with Sr. Ignatia at St. Thomas and bring more men into our group," Dr. Bob likely assured him. Sr. Ignatia was a small woman and member of the Catholic Sisters of Charity. She was a former music teacher who was still recovering from a nervous breakdown two years earlier that had ended her work in music and teaching.

Perhaps because of this life-changing experience, she was able to relate to and communicate with men who had drinking problems. From a tentative beginning assisting Dr. Bob in finding private rooms for men needing to detox, Sr. Ignatia went on to provide care to alcoholics, over fifteen thousand of whom overcame their addiction. She also facilitated reconciliations between estranged husbands and wives. She gave each husband a badge with a picture of the Sacred Heart and told him to give it back to her before he took the first drink. She gave the same badge to each wife and told her she could keep the badge as long as she didn't bring up the past.[6]

Her biographer sums up this commitment to marriage this way: "Preserving family unity and encouraging husband and wife to work out their difficulties rather than separate were second in importance only to recovery."[7] Appreciating Annie Smith's commitment to the wives and families, Sr. Ignatia frequently shared a quote from Annie Smith: "The real test of a surrendered life is that we are nice to live with. Surrender takes away shams and gives us real life."[8]

More Growth and Money Tensions

In Cleveland, Clarence S. began accusing Bill and Dr. Bob of taking royalties from the sale of the Big Book. (Some say Clarence did this with encouragement from an angry and drinking Hank Parkhurst.)

Bill and Bob went to Cleveland, bringing a certified audit of the finances from the beginning of the Foundation that made clear they were not getting rich off A.A. or the book sales. After the attacks on their integrity and finances, Bill and Dr. Bob struggled to find a way to support their families. They did not want to be paid for direct service to alcoholics, as one of the keys to A.A.'s success was the unconditional love being offered to people with drinking problems.

Perplexed and unsure how to give A.A. the full-time attention he believed it needed and support himself, Bill discussed his dilemma with Fr. Ed in 1941. Fr. Ed said: "Well, Bill, if you were the only one concerned, you could certainly start wearing a hair shirt and take nothing. But what about Lois? Once upon a time, you made a marriage contract to support her. Suppose you put her on the charity of friends so that you can do a service organization job for A.A. free. Would that be the kind of support your marriage contract called for? I should think the royalties would be the best bet."[9]

With this and other counsel and discussion, Bill, Dr. Bob, and the Foundation Board concluded that royalties from written publications would be how Bill and Dr. Bob would support their families.

The Foundation Board wrote a letter in March 1943 to all A.A. groups, explaining how the proceeds of the Big Book were used and that Bob and Bill received no salary for their nearly full-time work for A.A. and instead received book royalties to support their families.

Despite his concerns with (some would say jealousy of) Bill Wilson, Clarence S. was an early A.A. innovator. He and Abby G. in Cleveland opened a local office, which they called the "Central Office," to handle inquiries so they didn't have to go to New York. Clarence S. revised the original pamphlet on sponsorship in 1944, removing the religious language found in the original Akron pamphlet.

A.A.'s growth continued at a staggering rate. At the end of 1940, the estimated census reported approximately twenty-two groups and 1,400 members. By the end of June 1941, Ruth Hock sent her A.A. Bulletin to 116 cities.

At the end of this bulletin, Ruth shared a prayer she had received from a New York member who found it in the *New York Herald Tribune.* The prayer, later attributed to Reinhold Niebuhr, was well received by A.A. members. One of the New York members got it printed on small cards and distributed it at meetings. This practice continues today. The prayer, known as the Serenity Prayer, states, "God, grant me the serenity to accept the things I cannot change, the courage to change the things I can, and the wisdom to know the difference."[10]

Lois wrote in her diary about all the people who remembered her birthday in March 1941, including lunch with her sisters, Barbara (whom she reported was still not drinking and impressed by the Alexander article) and Kitty (who was having financial difficulty). Bill bought her a large suitcase for her birthday, and they had dinner out alone.[11]

By the end of 1941, A.A. census reported 169 groups and 5,500 members. But Bill got a shock in December. Ruth informed Bill she was in love and engaged to be married. More troubling for Bill, Ruth's fiancé's work was in another city, so she would be leaving Bill and A.A.

Farewell to Ruth Hock, Welcome Bobbie B.

Bill, rarely speechless, may not have known what to say. He likely forced a smile and congratulated Ruth enthusiastically. But with his history of losses of important relationships and Ruth's vital service to both A.A. and Bill, this likely hit Bill hard. Later, he expressed his gratitude by writing a letter to Ruth, inviting her and her husband to the 1955 International Convention in St. Louis as his guest. Ruth was unable to attend.[12]

Prior to Ruth's resignation, Bill had intensified his efforts to recruit more volunteers for the New York office and to hire more staff. Bill had met Bobbie B. at an A.A. meeting, and she became an active volunteer in responding to letters generated by the *Saturday Evening Post* article.

Bill hired Bobbie B. to become the second National Secretary in 1941 or 1942. Bobbie was the first member of A.A. to be hired and quickly won broad support from A.A. members around the United States and the world, due to her deep caring for those suffering from alcoholism and her amazing skills as a communicator.

While Bobbie and the volunteers kept responding to the letters and telegrams that poured in, Bill split his attention between overseeing the office and dealing with the many questions and brush fires that came up.

The Cleveland group had so many meetings that the leaders there decided to print a monthly bulletin that went to all registered groups. This innovation was copied eventually by major communities and regions around the country and the world. Besides news about new meetings and events, each bulletin listed the members celebrating a sobriety anniversary that month, a date that was, for many, equal to or more important than their biological birthday. Two years later, six New York members developed a newsletter for New York City A.A. members which became the *AA Grapevine*, now A.A.'s national member publication.[13]

One letter that Bobbie responded to launched a whole new way to bring hope and help to people with drinking problems. Ricardo M. was incarcerated at San Quentin Prison.[14] He found a copy of the book *Alcoholics Anonymous* in the prison library because A.A. member Archie L. convinced the prison warden to put it there. Bobbie and Ricardo began to write back and forth.

The first prison A.A. meeting was held at San Quentin on September 27, 1942. A.A. members from San Francisco attended the meetings and taught Ricardo and others how to lead meetings. This meeting led other jails and prisons to begin allowing local A.A. members to bring meetings to people in the prison. The following year, when Bill and Lois began traveling the country together to visit A.A. groups, Bill attended the San Quentin meeting. Unlike many other places where Lois also went to the A.A. meetings or met with the families, Lois was not invited to the prison meeting.

Besides her letters to San Quentin inmates, Bobbie B. began regular communication with A.A. members who were in Europe fighting in World War II. In 1942 and 1943, she was writing to three hundred members of the armed services.

Marty Mann Launches NCEA and a Recovery Movement

Bill and one of the first women to become sober, Marty Mann, were invited to give talks at Yale University in 1943 as part of the Yale University School of Alcohol Studies. Bill and Marty were launching what would become a decades-long campaign to educate professionals and the public about alcoholism. After the second Summer School of Alcohol Studies in 1944, Yale decided to serve as a short-term home for Marty's new organization, the National Committee for Education on Alcoholism (NCEA).

Bill and Lois were totally supportive of Marty's work around the country educating health professionals, business leaders, and citizens that alcoholism is a disease. In countless speeches and press conferences, Marty repeated these three basic messages:

1. Alcoholism is a disease, and the alcoholic is a sick person.

2. The alcoholic can be helped and is worth helping.
3. This is a public health problem and therefore a public responsibility.[15]

Marty's role in advancing acceptance of alcoholism as a disease was history making. Given the limited role of women and their lack of access to leadership positions at that time, it is incredible how effective she was. Marty was also a lesbian. She met her partner, Priscilla Peck, while they both were working at Macy's. Marty and Priscilla bought property on Fire Island and were able to live there openly as gays and recovering alcoholics in a period hostile to gays.

Bill and Lois remained very close friends to Marty and Priscilla for their respective lifetimes. Priscilla also struggled from a drinking problem, was introduced to A.A. by Marty, and was hired by Bill as an editor for the *AA Grapevine*.[16]

In her memoir, Lois told how she and Bill attended the summer school annually and spoke on the last day of what became a four-week course. After Bill spoke, Lois "usually spoke briefly about my reactions and the need for families not only to understand as much as possible about alcoholism, but also to live the A.A. principle of recovery."[17]

Visiting A.A. Groups Across the United States

Bill knew how much Lois disliked being alone when he traveled, though she rarely complained about it. So it's hard to overestimate Lois' enthusiasm when Bill began discussing a joint road trip to visit some of the rapidly growing A.A. groups. Bill liked to see and be seen. Answering letters and sending out Big Books was not enough for him.

On a crisp New York October morning in 1943, Lois and Bill headed to Grand Central Station to board the 20th Century Limited, the premier train from New York to

Chicago. Bill likely smiled his widest little-boy grin as he led Lois into the club car for a cup of coffee. It's not unlikely that such a moment would remind him he would have been dead without Lois, his spiritual awakening, and his resultant sobriety. He may even have taken the opportunity to thank Lois one more time for believing in him.

Courtesy Stepping Stones

Bill and Lois Wilson walking at Hampton Court, June 1948. (Permission required for use.)

Earl T., a leader in getting A.A. started in Chicago, greeted the train at LaSalle Street Station in downtown Chicago. Lois and Earl's wife Katie became fast friends. Earl took Bill and Lois to a different A.A. meeting every day. Katie and Earl both held back tears when they dropped the Wilsons back at the train station.

The Chicago and Northwest train took them next to Omaha, Nebraska. Jim C. beamed as he welcomed the Wilsons off the train. Jim and his wife took Bill and Lois to the Hotel Regis A.A. meeting in Omaha. Again, they were met with love and gratitude.

Each visit brought them face to face with new people who all had the same emotion—being thrilled to meet the couple who saved their lives. And, in each city, Bill and Lois met with men and their wives who also knew they owed their lives to this new way of life.

Bill spoke to a banquet with two hundred people attending in Denver. He and Lois then took a side trip to meet some members in Colorado Springs. Next, the Wilsons treated themselves to a stop at the Grand Canyon. Lois recalled how she and Bill experienced seeing the Grand Canyon differently. Looking down the mile-long hole made Bill squeamish, while Lois savored and enjoyed the view. But when it came to the eight-mile ride into the canyon on an Army mule, Lois was the one full of fear, especially on the tight turns near the edge of the path, while Bill seemed completely relaxed.[18]

Next, the Wilsons took a train to Los Angeles, where they were warmly greeted and led to what Lois described as "a Townhouse with a lovely suite." Friday, November 5, was a full day which included a call from Bill's mother telling them that she would join them later than expected due to a minor injury, and a lunch at the famous and packed Brown Derby, where they saw TV stars Joan Crawford, Jimmy Durante, and Jack Oakie. The next day included a visit to Universal Studios and other movie sets and a short stop "home" at the townhouse, where Lois was surprised to receive an orchid from the "non-alkies" before they both headed to an A.A. meeting where Bill spoke for two hours to eight hundred people.

Lois commented in her diary on November 9 that Bill had called his mother and she was coming "next week" as the accident had affected her nervous system. Lois wrote one other time about spending the day with Bill's mother. She was with them for over a week. While Bill struggled to have a relationship with his mother, he was quite loyal to her. He visited her, and she was their guest at Bedford Hills a number of times.

Lois details this trip in her memoir. Bill and Lois then rented a car to travel up the west coast to San Francisco, Portland, and Seattle. In Seattle, Lois was to meet separately with the wives. Seven years before the formal birth of Al-Anon Family Groups, there were gatherings of family members of alcoholics in Seattle, and Lois shared her story with the Seattle wives.

The Wilsons then returned to Los Angeles. After a couple days of rest, a member from Palo Alto introduced the Wilsons to Gerald Heard, whom Lois described as "a non-alcoholic who was a great philosopher, writer, and student of both Eastern and Western religions. He became a lifelong friend and soon introduced us to the famous writer Aldous Huxley, who became another lifelong friend and admirer of A.A. It was Huxley who wrote that Bill was 'the greatest social architect of the century.'"[19]

Over these three months of visiting A.A. groups, Lois and Bill were connecting with people all over America. These visits expanded the seeds of trust and love for Bill and Lois that allowed them to lead the growth of A.A. and Al-Anon. They met hundreds of A.A. members in over a dozen communities and had time to relax, be tourists, and enjoy one another. Bobbie B. mentioned in a November 1943 letter that Bill even quit smoking for a month during the trip.[20]

Lois and Bill returned to New York both thrilled by what they had seen and concerned about the effort needed to sustain such growth. They were also exhausted. Lois went back to work on her new home. During the week, she made progress on projects she could do herself, like stripping wallpaper and painting. On weekends, Bill used his engineering acumen and "can do" attitude to put in a new coal furnace and to design yet another water system. Finally, Bill's big vision and big picture for a home and A.A. were coming into focus.

Bill's Battle with Depression

Sadly, for Bill and for Lois, the conclusion of this fruitful trip coincided with the return of Bill's battle with depression. In A.A.'s official story of Bill, '*Pass It On*,' the onset is described this way: "Hardly had they returned home when

Bill was plunged into a depression so black that its effect on him was more debilitating than a physical assault."[21]

Bill's slide back into a deep depression began in 1944 and became worse in 1945 and 1946. In April of 1944, Lois wrote of normal times that included planting apple trees with her siter Kitty, spending a cold and rainy day reading *Hypnotism* by Easterbrook out loud to Bill most of the day, Bill traveling to Greenwich to visit a spiritual medium, and an overnight visit from Henrietta Seiberling.

In May, her spirits were even higher as she wrote of a mid-month visit from Dr. Bob and Annie Smith; a day at home with Bill, cleaning house and reading aloud; and Bill surprising her by coming home early one day when they then "played in the evening." On May 20, she reported: "Wonderful day. Bill and I transplanted from cold frame to garden. May 21 Another perfect day. Got up at 6:30 am to get ourselves collected and went to Binghams' for 9 o'clock breakfast."[22]

From May 22 to June 2, Bill and Lois were on the road, this time to Florida and the southeast United States to visit groups. On June 17, Lois wrote: "It is certainly grand to be home. The vegs look fine...Bill seems fine but slightly tired. Bill and I read out loud from *The Life of the Medium*." Ten days later, Lois wrote: "Bill reports that Leonard [her brother-in-law and doctor] says he must get away. Bill has been a bit exhausted lately."[23]

On July 1, Bill left for an eighteen-day respite on a Vermont farm. Lois followed him in a few days, reporting he "seems fine and has done a good job of housekeeping." On July 6, Lois wrote: "Bill got up about 8 and brought me some coffee and then we had breakfast of about 1 dozen small trout which he had caught the day before."[24]

Lois wrote of more reading together and a walk to their old camping ground, where they "reminisced over the tremendous changes that had happened to us during those ten years. From being worse than nothing, we now have so much to be thankful for. When returning we took a swim in the pool Bill had dug out some 10 years ago."[25]

Bill came home on July 18, worked on the house and leveling the gravel in the driveway in July, went to the office on August 16 for the first time in a while, and then took off in mid-August for two weeks with friends in Martha's Vineyard.

Lois noted that Bill was back in the office in September, working on a pamphlet "To the Wives," taken from the Big Book. This time, she didn't comment about Bill not accepting her invitation to help write this chapter. Nor was Lois as clear in her diary about Bill's lack of energy and eventual depression as Bobbie B. would be in her letters.[26]

Bobbie commented on Bill's long absences from the A.A. office, which left A.A. relying on Bobbie to handle correspondence and, in effect, make day-to-day decisions. By April and May of 1945, Bobbie B. began to be more direct about Bill's absence from the office. On May 3, she wrote: "Bill is taking a long leave from active work in this office due to his health. For a year now he has been trying to come in part time but finds it hard to stick to this schedule."[27] The day prior to this letter, Bill had written a long letter to Leonard Harrison, chair of the Alcoholic Foundation Board, explaining the pressure on staff, the need for continuity beyond him and Dr. Bob, and the critical role Bobbie B. was playing as National Secretary. He also raised the possibility of his resigning.[28]

By early 1946, Bobbie was explaining in letters that Bill had delegated the opening of his mail to her and she was handling routine business herself. On February 26, 1946, she acknowledged Bill's depression, saying, "Bill must get away from all A.A. activity for a while—his doctors say so.

He is definitely not well. About the best name we can give his condition is mental exhaustion, but it takes the form of depression."[29]

Bill's relentless energy and persistence masked the pain and cost of his depression. Bill described his depression as neurotic, persisting for over a decade (from 1943–1955). Amazingly, despite admitting to being suicidal for three of these twelve years, his psychic or spiritual change was so profound that he was never tempted to drink, no matter how depressed he was.[30]

Marty Mann, his friend and partner in alcoholism education, had this to say: "It was awful. There were long periods of time when he couldn't get out of bed. He just stayed in bed, and Lois would see that he ate. An awful lot of people believed he was drinking. That was one of the worst rumors we had within A.A."[31]

Bill began twice-weekly sessions with psychiatrist Dr. Harry Tiebout, a friend of Bill's and an A.A. advocate, in mid-1944. Bill later began seeing Dr. Frances Weekes, and these sessions lasted until 1949.[32]

Lois didn't know what to do with Bill's new challenge. Having survived the drinking years, the homeless years, and the painful process of getting the first members of A.A. sober, Lois had a hard time responding compassionately to Bill's depression. "It was awfully hard for me to understand. I wasn't too sympathetic, actually. Or I didn't know how to be sympathetic, exactly. Or what to do differently."[33]

Bill Develops and Introduces the Traditions

Despite his battle with depression, Bill laid the foundation for A.A.'s successful structure through his writing and outreach during this period. In the foreword to the first edition of the Big Book, Bill addressed the importance of anonymity, being self-supporting, not being allied with any religion or faith, and having no membership requirement beyond the desire to stay sober. Without some guidelines, he and Dr. Bob both feared A.A. would implode from disagreements among members.

These concerns were not abstract theory for Bill. There were numerous threats to A.A.'s future, including violations of the anonymity principle. He had seen groups refuse to allow Black or gay people to attend. His experience with the Rockefellers showed him the seduction of outside money and the need to be self-supporting. During one trip, he heard about A.A. groups that required potential members to attend a pre-A.A. meeting before being admitted to A.A., creating unnecessary barriers and judgments about who could get help. The tradition that Bill wrote in response says, "The only requirement for membership is a desire to stop drinking."

In 1945, Bill began introducing individual traditions through a series of articles in the *AA Grapevine*. In April 1946, Bill outlined for all A.A. members his suggestions for the Twelve Traditions in an article "Twelve Suggested Points for AA Tradition," which were called "Twelve Points to Assure Our Future" in an A.A. pamphlet sent to all groups and members in 1947.

Bill summed up the dilemma for A.A. and its future by outlining what he thought most members of A.A. knew: The problems in A.A. groups had to do with relationships between group members and with the world outside A.A. He asked very simply if members could agree on a set of principles to guide these relationships. He suggested these principles could grow into Traditions.[34]

Bill traveled, wrote, and pleaded for attention to the Twelve Traditions for five years, from 1945–1950, despite his depression. His drive to get the Traditions adopted was intensified by Dr. Bob's diagnosis of terminal cancer on June 1, 1948. Sadly, while facing this cancer death sentence, Dr. Bob also had to face the loss of his lifelong partner and wife. Annie died on June 1, 1949.

Given the friendship both Bill and Lois enjoyed with Annie, her loss was a gut punch for them too. On behalf of the thousands who knew and were encouraged by Annie, Bill wrote a memorial article in the July 1949 *AA Grapevine* that made clear how important he considered Annie Smith to be for the growth and success of A.A. He acknowledged her role as the "mother" of the first A.A. group. He recognized how vital her support and work, side by side with Dr. Bob, was to his work with alcoholics and the birth and growth of A.A. He concluded his loving testimonial by calling Annie Smith one of the cofounders of Alcoholics Anonymous.[35]

As 1950 approached, Clarence S. and the Cleveland A.A. leaders began recommending a large public gathering of A.A. members. Bill's response was that "an international" A.A. convention made sense and suggested two reasons: to have one more opportunity for the Fellowship to hear from Dr. Bob and to formally vote on the proposed Twelve Traditions.

The months before the Wilsons left for Cleveland for the Convention in July were not easy on the marriage. Bill was actively exploring help on several fronts. He was meeting with Monsignor Fulton J. Sheen to receive instructions in the Catholic faith and continuing his weekly therapy sessions. Bill stopped the instructions and did not become a Catholic. He acknowledged in a letter to a friend how the therapist was helping him see how "my position in A.A. has become quite inconsistent with my needs as an individual." Bill described vividly how the demands of A.A. and its members had taken over his life and resulted in his inability to focus on what was primary. He concluded, "So we have the person of Mr. Anonymous in conflict with Bill Wilson."[36]

Bill's willingness to publicly admit his need for outside help was highly unusual for the times, especially in light of the pedestal on which members of A.A. had put him.

Lois, for her part, wrote in her diary about the stress on Bill (and perhaps, although unspoken, on her). As Bill left home for a train trip to Manhattan with his half-sister Helen (daughter of Gilly's second wife, Christine), who was living with them and working for the *AA Grapevine*, Bill voiced his frustration to Lois. As she recalled it: "Bill left saying that if anyone came to him with another problem, he'd scream."[37]

Visiting A.A. in Europe and the First International Convention

Despite these daily pressures and the upcoming Convention, the Wilsons left on May 11, 1950, to visit the many emerging A.A. groups in Europe. This seven-week trip included visits with A.A. groups in "four cities in Norway, three in Sweden, one in Denmark, two in Holland, as well as Paris, London, and now Dublin, Ireland."[38]

Bill wrote to Dr. Bob, regretting Bob wasn't with them and sharing what he saw: "We need not tell you that A.A. has come to Europe to stay. With its usual ease, it is breaking down all barriers of race, creed, language, and tradition."[39]

Lois described the exciting and at times humorous experience of seeing how A.A. was unfolding in Europe. She observed how the British stayed "very anonymous" and avoided any mention of God. A.A. grew much more rapidly in Ireland.

Lois and Bill joined three thousand members in Cleveland for the Convention at the end of July. For Lois, the Convention was an opportunity to reconnect with the wives of members she had met in her travels or through correspondence.

Beyond the excitement and energy of attendees being in a room with others who had overcome an addiction to alcohol, three things happened that continue to influence and shape A.A. and the Twelve Step movement: the adoption of the Twelve Traditions, Dr. Bob's farewell talk, and approval to test the General Service Conference plan.

After Bill reviewed the Traditions and why he considered each so important, he asked for comments or questions. To his amazement, there were none. Bill had convinced them that their lives and the future of A.A. were at stake. The Twelve Traditions, as read at A.A. meetings around the world, have been adopted by hundreds of other Twelve Step Fellowships. They are listed in the Appendix.

Dr. Bob's Last Message

While adopting the Twelve Traditions put in place much-needed guardrails for this evolving Fellowship of recovering alcoholics, Dr. Bob's last remarks on Sunday morning were undoubtedly the emotional peak of this gathering.

Most present likely knew of Annie's death thirteen months earlier and of Dr. Bob's cancer diagnosis. Al S., a member from New York and the *AA Grapevine* editor, drove Dr. Bob from Akron to Cleveland. When Dr. Bob came on the stage Sunday morning, his declining physical condition was apparent.

Greeted with thunderous applause that went on way longer than he would have liked, Dr. Bob gave a speech that can be found excerpted today on A.A. clubhouse walls and meeting rooms around the world. The speech remains a guide because Dr. Bob stated in a few words two principles that are fundamental to Twelve Step recovery:

> There are two or three things that flashed into my
> mind on which it would be fitting to lay a little

emphasis. One is the simplicity of our program. Let's not louse it all up with Freudian complexes and things that are interesting to the scientific mind, but have very little to do with our actual A.A. work. Our Twelve Steps, when simmered down to the last, resolve themselves into the words "love" and "service." We understand what love is, and we understand what service is. So let's bear those two things in mind.[40]

Bill W. and Dr. Bob's Last Meeting

Just weeks before Dr. Bob died in November, Bill traveled to Akron to ask for Dr. Bob's support for his proposal for a new governance structure for A.A. Dr. Bob agreed with convening on a trial basis what has become known as the General Service Conference Board, based on the structure of group representation. He stated, "Bill, it *has* to be A.A.'s decision, not ours."

Dr. Bob died a week later on November 16, 1950. Bill moved forward with implementing A.A.'s experimental General Service Conference. Lois also took action to convene members of the emerging Family Groups to form what became Al-Anon Family Groups. A.A.'s example would influence the architecture of the organization she would help establish.

Part Four

Expanding the Recovery Movement

1951–Today

CHAPTER 15

LOIS BRINGS FAMILY GROUPS TOGETHER TO FORM AL-ANON

April of 1951 was a milestone month for both Bill and Lois. For Bill, it was the first meeting of the five-year experiment with a General Service Conference to take over from the cofounders and Foundation Board and guide A.A. Thirty-seven delegates from the US and Canada attended, half the number allowed by Bill's formula for representation. The Vermont values of democracy and inclusion were present as fifteen trustees (Foundation Board members) and ten staff members from the New York office and the *AA Grapevine* also attended as voting members.

The theme of this first meeting was "Not to Govern— But to Serve." Four committees were formed, and an expression of gratitude to Bobbie B. for her service was approved, along with an increase in Bill's book royalty percentage from 10 to 15 percent, given Dr. Bob's death. Lois would be eligible for the royalties after Bill passed.

This realization of Bill's vision of a General Service Conference had to be exciting for both him and Lois. The knowledge that their hand-to-mouth survival days were ending was also reassuring and perhaps comforting.

Al-Anon Family Groups Is Born

But for Lois and Bill both, the icing on the cake on this April weekend was the meeting of the wives of the A.A. members attending the General Service Conference. Almost all of them attended Family Groups back home. These Family Group leaders came together with wives from local Family Groups in a meeting with Lois at Stepping Stones on Sunday, April 22, 1951. This landmark meeting became the founding of Al-Anon. This meeting, along with the actions taken by Lois and Anne Bingham to form Al-Anon, completed the transition from the early unstructured gatherings of wives while husbands went to Oxford Group/A.A. meetings to these early pioneer Family Groups, called by different names in different places, to the official Al-Anon Family Groups.

Lois and her friend and neighbor Anne Bingham[1] convened this luncheon meeting. The spouses knew they needed each other and the Twelve Steps just like their husbands needed A.A. Lois summed up the meeting this way: "It was then that I decided to open our own service office. This was three years after the death of Annie S."[2]

The roots of this founding moment extended back nearly fifteen years. Lois Wilson and Annie Smith were the first to realize that alcoholism hurt the whole family. The whole family needed to grow spiritually through the Twelve Steps and to be aided in this growth by the support of others. Both women told all newcomers about the pain of being alone with a drinking alcoholic and emphasized that they needed each other.

Annie Smith found this support in her friend Henrietta Seiberling and the members of the Oxford Group in Akron. Her surrender to her powerlessness over her husband's drinking came through her Oxford Group attendance and her deep faith. She was the first person most newcomers to Akron meetings met. Her welcome is legendary in Al-Anon: "Come in, my dear. Welcome home."

From Lois' first visit to the Smiths' home in the summer of 1935, Lois and Annie were connected by a bond no one and nothing could break. Like their husbands, they quickly realized they needed each other to survive.

Lois frequently shared the story of the painful day she realized she couldn't change Bill. This story is still repeated regularly in Al-Anon meetings around the world. Here's how Lois recounted the incident in 1935:

> One Sunday, Bill casually said to me, "We'll have to hurry or we'll be late for the Oxford Group meeting."
>
> I had a shoe in my hand and before I knew what was happening, I had thrown it at him and said, "Damn your old meetings."[3]

As we might expect, Bill was surprised by Lois' anger. But Lois detailed in her memoir how shocked and appalled she was at her own actions. In fact, her reflections on this incident make clear that it was the beginning for her of what Twelve Step people call hitting bottom.

Her outburst caused Lois to reflect. "I might have had an excuse for losing my temper during his drinking years. But why now, when everything was fine, had I reacted so violently to his very natural remark? ... A friend [at the Oxford Group meeting] helped me to realize that, although

I had been in the group for nearly two years trying to help others, I had never put my reliance wholly on God but had been trying to do it all by myself. That day I began looking at myself analytically for the first time."[4]

What Lois came to realize was that she had been focused for two years on Bill, his problems, and the problems of other alcoholics. She was confident that because she didn't drink and had always believed in God, she was someone who knew what was right, best, and good, especially for her spouse.

But that attitude wasn't confidence. It was arrogance. Lois freely admitted that, despite her faith in her ability to stop Bill's drinking, neither her willpower nor her personality worked.

Then, when Bill *did* recover, she realized that he didn't have to lean on her the way he once had. It made her feel unneeded and neglected. Covering for Bill's bad behavior, being the breadwinner, consoling him when he was depressed, advising him, or even scolding him when he acted out—now, none of that was necessary, and that made her feel unnecessary. It had made her feel important to be in charge. In a way, she got to play the role of mother by being in control of her husband.

This early shoe-throwing incident became Lois' first surrender. She acknowledged that it took her many years to fully understand the unhealthy aspects of her personality and her relationship with Bill. Like many who are caretaking a sick person, she assumed she was well and needed no help. She concluded her reaction to the shoe-throwing incident with this powerful admission: "I have come to see that even well-intentioned good deeds often fail of their desired purpose when they are done from our own power alone; that the only real good is accomplished by finding

God's plan and then using all of whatever ability He has given us to carry out that plan."[5]

After the shoe-throwing incident, Lois wrote in her biography how she began taking a daily inventory of her behavior. She acknowledged how easy it is to deceive oneself. The daily inventory helped her come to understand herself better over time.

Without this humiliating experience and Lois' openness to seeing her own character limitations (called "character defects" by Bill and Twelve Step authors), Al-Anon might not have developed as the spiritually based recovery program for families that it has.

Lois' relationship with Bill made her realize the need for Al-Anon. However, it was Lois' relationship with Annie Smith that laid the foundation for Al-Anon. She acknowledged Annie's role often: "Annie's part in the formation of A.A. and consequently in the foundation of Al-Anon should never be forgotten."[6]

Bill and Lois at Jacksonville Conference, February 1951. (Permission required for use.)

For example, Dr. Bob and Annie Smith's life in sobriety was shaken by the marriage in September 1941 of their adopted daughter Sue to Ernie G., a man twice her age, who had difficulty staying sober. The Smiths opposed the marriage—to no avail. This opposition was complicated by the fact that Dr. Bob had encouraged Ernie's interest in Sue when Ernie was first sober. Ernie turned out to be an unreliable and reportedly abusive husband. Sue and Ernie had two children, Mickey and Bonna. Bonna suffered from mental illness and fought most of her short life with alcohol and drug addiction. On June 11, 1969, she tragically took her own life after taking the life of her six-year-old daughter. Fortunately, Dr. Bob and Annie were not alive to experience this soul-shattering devastation from the family disease of alcoholism.[7]

Lois Wilson and Annie Smith were not the only wives of alcoholics coming to realize this need. Lois put it this way: "In the beginning, AA was a family affair. Many of the wives tried to live by the program themselves and made much progress but that was in a general way only. There was nothing to help them understand their own reactions. There was little sharing of experience. The later formation of the Family Groups filled this gap."[8]

Practical help coupled with spiritual reflection was the formula for success in confronting the ravages of addiction for both the addict and their family.

In 1942, Lois had met Anne Bingham, who lived not far from Stepping Stones and whose husband's drinking was driving her crazy. Anne's husband, Devoe, was a car dealer, and his journey into alcoholism was sudden and severe. One day, when he was around thirty, for no apparent reason, he decided to go to a bar and order a drink. One drink became two—then way too many. He got so drunk that he didn't make it home until the next morning.

Things quickly got bad: frequent lying, missed appointments, broken promises, public embarrassments, mismanaged money. Anne Bingham experienced all the despair and distress that Lois and most family members face. Anne had to take over running the garage Devoe owned. In her case, Devoe was an episodic drinker. That meant he could go for stretches of time without drinking, but then he'd succumb and get extremely drunk.

A.A. member Wilbur S. gave them a pamphlet about the program. Reading the pamphlet brought tears to Devoe's eyes. He knew he had to change. As Devoe began attending A.A., Anne Bingham began to meet the wives of other A.A. members. She and Lois lived a few towns apart and quickly became friends. Anne and Lois together started the first family group in Westchester.

As the size of A.A. meetings grew, wives typically began to congregate by themselves. These gatherings at first had many different purposes—some were purely social, while others were focused on how to support the alcoholic in his recovery. Comments such as, "Me, too!" "What can I do?" and "I understand" were frequently heard. In talking to one another, they found support, even when their husbands failed to get sober.

As the spouses of alcoholics unloaded their frustrations and began to trust one another, they started talking about how the principles of A.A. might help them, even though they weren't alcoholics. Like Lois, some spouses were beginning to realize the necessity of applying the Twelve Steps to their personal lives. The spiritual foundation of A.A. could help them cope and recover from the ways that alcoholism had affected them and other family members.

In 1945, a family group in Long Beach, California, became the first to register with the Alcoholic Foundation. Since there was no Al-Anon yet, they registered as an A.A. group with A.A. headquarters. They were quite serious about recovery and developed their own pamphlet, "The Aims and Purposes of the Non-Alcoholic Group."[9]

As early as February 1948, an A.A. Auxiliary was operating in Canada in the Winnipeg region of Manitoba. Lelah J., a member there, wrote: "Our big day arrived and passed but we in Winnipeg are still in the clouds. Bill and Lois came.... There is no yardstick that can measure the tremendous good gained spiritually. Grettir [her husband] was so overwhelmed with the grace, love and humility shown by Lois."[10]

In San Francisco, Ruth G. saw a need for A.A. family members to have a publication similar to the *AA Grapevine*. Her group, called the San Francisco Family Club, issued the first newsletter for family members in July 1950, calling it *The San Francisco Family Club Chronicle*.

A month before the founding meeting of Al-Anon in 1951, Lois traveled to Toronto, Canada, to chair a workshop on Right Relationships for A.A. wives at an A.A. regional conference. The speakers for her two-hour workshop included two women from Toronto and two from New York.

After one A.A. trip, Bill came home with an exciting idea, which Lois later explained this way.

> In 1950, Bill went by himself to the AA groups through the States and Canada to find out their feelings about establishing a General Service Conference for AA. He was surprised to run into so many Family Groups.
>
> Returning home, he told me about this budding Fellowship and suggested I open a service office in New York where these groups could register, receive helpful literature and become more unified. It would also be a place to which any distracted wife

could cry out for help and from which information could be spread to the public.[11]

Bill was also trying to solve a growing practical problem at A.A. Headquarters. Family groups that had sprung up spontaneously before 1951 were writing to the Central Office, sending donations, and asking to be registered in the A.A. directory.

This was a problem for Bill and A.A. because A.A. only accepted donations from alcoholics and A.A. groups. Bill turned to Lois for help, both to support families and to resolve this organizational dilemma.

Lois admitted to being initially unenthusiastic about Bill's suggestion. She and Bill finally had a place of their own. She loved gardening, being in nature, sewing, and interior decorating. She was looking forward to being a housewife and taking care of the various A.A. members who were always dropping by. That was a full-time job in itself.

But Bill saw a bigger job that needed doing. There were not just men suffering from alcoholism. Their wives and children, friends and siblings were suffering and could find healing if only the principles of the program were provided to them. Bill believed that Lois was the one who could lead this effort.

Reluctant at first, Lois eventually agreed that Bill was right, and his vision was worth supporting.

First Steps for Al-Anon Family Groups

After the April meeting, Lois and Anne Bingham wrote to the eighty-seven Family Groups already registered with the Alcoholic Foundation, asking if they were interested in being part of an official group that followed the A.A. Twelve Steps. "Forty-eight groups responded. The movement was beginning to speak with a common voice. Conscientiously,

Lois and Anne recorded information received on three-by-five cards. An overwhelming proportion responded favorably to adopting the Twelve Steps of A.A."[12]

An article about the Family Groups in the June 1951 *AA Grapevine* helped increase the registered groups to 145, with 39 states represented. Lois and Anne Bingham saw quickly the need for literature. "Together they wrote a pamphlet called 'Purposes and Suggestions for Al-Anon Family Groups' which included the development of a new principle—focus on oneself, rather than the alcoholic."[13] This principle, which builds on Lois' spiritual awakening after throwing a shoe at Bill, remains the bedrock principle of Al-Anon today. As Anne Bingham so wisely noted, the "miracle" of Al-Anon is that family members can find serenity even if their spouses don't stop drinking. This simple and profound description of the power of Al-Anon Family Groups is repeated daily around the world.

While other names were initially used around the country—"Triple A," "Non A.A.," "A.A. Helpmates"—these family groups became known as Al-Anon Family Groups. Over time, the conflation of the Alcoholics Anonymous name—Al-Anon—became commonly accepted and adopted.

Lois and Anne Bingham set up an office at Stepping Stones to handle correspondence with the groups and to respond to inquiries. They recruited volunteers to help, and each committed two days a week to this effort.

By November 1951, Lois and Anne could see the need was quickly outstripping what they could do as volunteers. Lois organized a meeting of local members on November 17 at Stepping Stones, where she asked for more volunteers and organized a service committee to advise on policy.

This meeting marked the establishment of the Clearing House, the initial name for Al-Anon's service organization.

By January 1952, the rapidly growing group had moved to an office shared with A.A. in the old 24th Street Clubhouse in New York. It had two officers: Lois as Chairman and Anne Bingham as Secretary.

Lois was quick to adapt the proven A.A. Twelve Steps and Twelve Traditions to Al-Anon. The only change in Al-Anon Twelve Steps is in the Twelfth Step, which is to "carry the message to others" rather than to "alcoholics."

When the editing and member input process was done, Al-Anon changed Tradition Three, which defines who can be a member, to "the relatives of alcoholics." Tradition Five, about primary purpose, is explicit that the common purpose of Al-Anon is helping families of alcoholics. Tradition Six shows the importance to Lois and the Al-Anon founders of cooperation with A.A. by adding this sentence: "Although a separate entity, we should always co-operate with Alcoholics Anonymous." A.A. did not add cooperation with Al-Anon to its Traditions.

As early as 1953, the idea of alcoholism as a family disease was introduced. An Al-Anon Family Group in Prestonsburg, Kentucky, had partnered with a nonmember to produce *Alcoholism: The Family Disease*. Lois, Anne, and the Clearing House purchased 275 copies of the booklet and distributed them. Lois articulated the family disease idea and its importance in a memorandum she wrote to the first A.A. General Service Conference in April 1951, before the launch of Al-Anon. Her headline was "Estimated Value of the Family Group to A.A." She wrote:

> A.A. now recognizes that alcoholism is a family problem and that recovery can be greatly hastened by family understanding. There are many adjustments to be made, relationships to be changed. Bill and I were heart-sick and puzzled that after the alcoholic had recovered..., so many family relationships were

still strained. In my own case, I now feel that if I had had a Family Group to turn to I would have been spared three or four years of confusion and perplexity, which on one occasion almost caused Bill to get drunk. Only the thought of those he would let down made him turn back at the door of the saloon. It wasn't until I actually practiced the 12 Steps that our home life became really happy.[14]

Funds for the purchase of *Alcoholism: The Family Disease*, the hiring of the first part-time employee, and the publication of a monthly newsletter were possible because of a request that each group contribute $1 twice a year and from the sale of each publication.

In the December 1953 newsletter, Lois and Anne Bingham welcomed a family group from Finland, one of the first groups outside North America. Al-Anon growth clearly benefited from the rapid growth of A.A. around the world.

All this work was legally formalized with the incorporation of the Clearing House as Al-Anon Family Group Headquarters on October 26, 1954. Paralleling A.A., Lois and Anne Bingham initially hired a part-time secretary and over time added an executive and more staff to keep pace with growth.

Today, Al-Anon provides a welcoming place for anyone concerned about a person's drinking through both in-person and electronic meetings. According to the 2023 World Service Office Annual Report, there are now over 22,000 Al-Anon Family Groups and 1,174 Alateen groups meeting every week in the United States, Canada, and over one hundred other countries around the world.[15]

Chapter 16

Bill and Lois Build a Movement: Love, Pain, and Letting Go

It's uncanny how sometimes the thing we want most comes in an unconventional way. One of the unpleasant truths in life is that sometimes it takes pain to bring growth.

The Wilsons' Midlife Wakeup Call

It's unlikely that Bill thought he was being prophetic as he composed the sentiment in the card he prepared for Lois to mark their thirty-sixth wedding anniversary in 1954: "Come any peril, we know we are safe in each other's arms because we are in God's."[1]

Two days before their anniversary, Lois was running errands and felt pain. Her diary entry for January 22, 1954, explains:

(Permission is required from the Stepping Stones Foundation for any further use, display, or duplication of the following material from its archive.)

I had bad pain in my chest which continued for about ½ hour, while I did other shopping. After a bite of lunch I went to see "The Living Desert" movie at Sutton Theatre. Pain again and down left arm and when very bad down right arm. Sat till end of picture thinking pain would leave but it continued. Took taxi to Bedford Hotel where there was a message in our room box which I thought was for me and I called several places trying to find Bill and getting weaker and weaker. Did phoning in lobby, AA office finally told me Bill was at hotel and going up found him and Earle Treat. Bill put me to bed and called Leonard who arrived in about half hour. He called Doctor Reynikoff of N.Y. Hospital and an ambulance. About the time Leonard arrived, my pain stopped. When ambulance arrived they would not let me even go to the bathroom but carried me on stretcher into private room at N.Y. Hospital. So all following dates were canceled.[2]

On their wedding anniversary, two days later, the doctors confirmed Lois had had a heart attack, and her journal entry stated simply "heart attack." Bill picked up Lois and all her plants from the hospital on February 15 and took her home to care for her.

The prescription was rest—lots of it—for the near term and no strenuous activity for the long term.

In an unwanted way, Lois got what she had desired for so long: a great expanse of time to be at home and read books, sit by the window, observe nature, and have her dear Bill beside her. Bill sharply curtailed his commitments so that he could be by her side. "The time off gave her a chance to be with Bill again, to be close to him and spend time talking about things they had just let drift by in their constant busyness."[3]

During the year of her recuperation, Lois came to appreciate the heart attack, much in the same way recovering alcoholics come to appreciate their alcoholism. As she confided to a close friend, "I know it may sound kind of silly, but I believe that a heart attack can sometimes be good for the soul. I know in my case it was. It helped me to realize again just how fragile life is, just how fleeting. There were no more days to be wasted. I had to focus on what was really important, like how dear Bill was to me and how much God had given us both through this terrible disease of alcoholism and this wonderful gift of recovery."[4]

As Lois got stronger, she and Bill returned to building and serving A.A. and Al-Anon. They recognized their commitment to service and the A.A. mission made it difficult to keep their lives in balance. They rented a small building a few miles from Stepping Stones as an occasional escape from the busyness and frequent visitors to Stepping Stones. Their lives returned to times of intense activity and service, followed by vacations and social times with friends.

Lois' Love for Alateen

Lois was clear to everyone about the service that brought her the most joy. Anything she could do to make Alateen more accessible to young people in families with one or more alcoholic parents gave her delight. Lois was a passionate advocate for Alateen and for young people being part of the A.A., Al-Anon, and Alateen family from the outset.

Her awareness of the needs of teens came from her travels around the United States with Bill and the letters she and Anne Bingham received at the Al-Anon Clearinghouse. By 1955, she convinced the A.A. Convention planners to add a session for teens to the program. In 1957, she learned about Robert, a seventeen-year-old in Pasadena,

California who had started a meeting for teens using the Twelve Steps. Robert wrote:

> My father has been in A.A. for some time. My mother goes to Al-Anon. I went with her several times. There were other teenagers there too. I wanted to talk over my problems but I didn't think the adults would understand, so we started an Al-Anon group for teenagers. We call it Alateen. I have made more real friends than I ever had before. We understand each other and can help by talking out our problems.
>
> We learn that alcoholism is a disease and that they [alcoholics] are sick people, not bad. They can't help what they do and say.
>
> We learn to get over our resentments and self-pity. When we plan on going somewhere or doing something and something happens and we can't…. Well, instead of feeling bad or getting mad, we get busy and call our friends and try to do something nice for someone else. Also we try to look at the other person's side and take our own inventory.
>
> Alateen has helped me to get along better and understand people and get better grades in school. I'm a lot happier, too. It's a good deal! [5]

With Lois and others as champions, Alateen grew quickly. Columnists Ann Landers and Dear Abby encouraged families and teens to consider Alateen. By the 1960 Conference, there were one hundred Alateen groups around the country.

Lois provided leadership in solving one of the biggest challenges to Alateen growth and impact—finding adult sponsors for the Alateen groups. Lois explained the sensitivity required in finding an adult who could meet with the teens without dominating or taking sides. A teen's parent, who might be in A.A. or Al-Anon, would be too close. Some parents would be afraid of what the teens might say and afraid of damage to their reputation. Lois worked at encouraging Al-Anon groups to find and train Alateen sponsors, and she recruited Alateen sponsors for her Westchester community.

Writers, Builders, and Planners

As with Bill, Lois' work also included responding to worldwide correspondence, writing for and editing the newsletter, and working on the publications needed to bring the Al-Anon message to members.

Lois, with Bill's help, worked from 1953–1955 on Al-Anon's first written publication. Like the A.A. Big Book, it was intended to be a basic text for new and existing members of Al-Anon. Lois credited Margaret D., Trudy M., and Ralph B. (an A.A. writer) with forming the writing and editing team along with her and Bill. Referred to as the "Handbook" and titled simply *The Al-Anon Family Groups*, this book served Al-Anon into the 1980s, with Lois being involved in various edits to make it timelier over the years.

Given that A.A. was sixteen years older than Al-Anon, Bill's organizational work was different than Lois' but still intense. With the leadership and support of A.A. Foundation Board member Bernard Smith (a nonalcoholic member), Bill guided A.A. through the implementation of a temporary new structure called the General Service Board. The United States and Canada were divided into areas from which conference delegates were elected by A.A. groups.

As a visionary leader and a student of the history of failed efforts to overcome alcoholism, Bill was very clear on the need to prepare A.A. for a new type of leadership structure. He knew putting A.A. in the hands of individuals was too risky. Bill was convinced that the groups would be the best long-term guides for the future of A.A.

So he proposed a structure that began at the grassroots level with individual groups, comprised simply of people who came together because of a shared desire to stay sober. Bill's structure had each group electing rotating representatives to a district and district representatives coming together as an Area Assembly, which elected Area Delegates who came together annually as the General Service Conference each April.[6]

The initial meeting in 1950 was poorly attended. Over the four-year trial period, attendance improved, and this unusual structure and decision-making process were refined and eventually unanimously adopted. This same organizational model is still used today.

In 1950, Bill also began drafting what would become the Twelve Concepts, a critical companion to the Twelve Steps and Twelve Traditions (see Appendix). Described as an interpretation of A.A.'s world service structure as it emerged through the program's early history and experience, these operational guidelines are used today by A.A. and were adopted by Al-Anon and other Twelve Step fellowships.

Bill's primary focus between 1950 and 1955 was introducing the Twelve Traditions through a series of articles in the *AA Grapevine* and frequent travels to explain their importance to A.A. groups around the country.

Family Loyalty

For Bill, being sober and growing emotionally and spiritually meant that he paid attention to family and other relationships. In the case of his father, this meant support for Gilly and Bill's stepmom Christine as they aged. Following the 1950 A.A. Convention in Cleveland, Bill exchanged letters with an A.A. member he met at the conference who lived near his father in British Columbia. The letters make clear that Bill had asked this new friend to keep an eye on his father. Letters to other family members from Bill indicate his role in contributing and soliciting money to support his father and stepmom.

Christine was the communication bridge between Bill and his father. She wrote to thank him for Christmas gifts and money. In January 1954, she acknowledged that, though coherent most of the time, his father's speech was garbled, and he was somewhat confused. A month later, Gilly Wilson died. He was cremated, and the remains were sent to Bill for burial in East Dorset. The program for the service indicates a Christian burial, opening with the hymn "The Old Rugged Cross."

In a letter to a friend in March 1954, Bill commented on the impact of Lois' recent heart attack and his father's death:

> I suppose we ought to take this as a warning, perhaps the both of us [Lois and Bill], that we should find more detachment and less activity of an emotionally wearing kind. I guess we aren't quite as young as we used to be, a fact further driven home by the death of my father in British Columbia recently. He was pushing 84 and had never been sick in his life that I can remember. I regret that I have seen him scarcely a dozen times since I was ten years old when he and mother parted. Happily, though, he did pay us a visit down here last fall, something for which I am most grateful now.[7]

International Growth

A.A.'s international growth quickly expanded from the first international groups begun in 1943 and 1944 in Toronto and Quebec. Bobbie B., in her role as the "great communicator," was instrumental in helping a nonalcoholic psychiatric nurse in Sydney, Australia, bring A.A. there in 1945. A Bermuda group started when an early Trenton member moved to Hamilton in 1945. A Philadelphia A.A member, visiting Ireland, sowed the seeds that resulted in the first Ireland meeting in Dublin in 1946. Another traveling American helped A.A get started in London in 1948.[8]

Similar to the growth in the United States and Canada, growth around the world was spontaneous, unplanned, and unmanaged. People like Captain Jack S., chief officer of a merchant marine oil tanker from the Boston region, was so grateful to get sober he ended up helping the A.A. headquarters launch what was called the *Internationalist Bulletin* and outreach.[9]

In 1950, Bill wrote in *The Million Who Still Don't Know the AA Message* about a new group in Durban, South Africa, describing Captain Jack's report on his approach and how he visited all the doctors and sky pilots in Durban and gave them a supply of Big Books and pamphlets.

Captain Jack contributed to international growth in two ways: by being part of the development of A.A.'s service to Loners (those unable to attend meetings because none are nearby) and Homers (those unable to physically get to a meeting) and by starting and supporting meetings around the world. By 1958, A.A.'s Internationalist Bulletin contained four pages of contacts with over 120 names and contact information around the world.[10]

Al-Anon's international growth built on A.A.'s growth as wives of newly recovering A.A. members around the world began coming together. A 1949 letter from Cape Town, South Africa, tells of the start of a "Non-Alcoholic Group" for wives of A.A. members. Al-Anon's records include letters to and from Lois and the Al-Anon staff from members starting Al-Anon groups in Sydney, Australia; Dunedin, New Zealand; Belfast, Northern Ireland; and London, England, among other places.

International growth spurred the translation of the A.A. Big Book and other A.A. and Al-Anon literature into other languages. Cleveland A.A. member Ricardo P. initiated the first Spanish translation of the Big Book in 1946 to send to his home country of Mexico. In the early 1950s, Frank M., a member of the Hispano Group of New York (comprised largely of people of Puerto Rican descent), completed a second translation which was acknowledged by Bill and A.A. Headquarters and used in Mexico, Puerto Rico, New York, El Salvador, Colombia, and Spain to support A.A. groups.[11]

Music and Travel – The Wilsons' Downtime

Bill and Lois traveling with violin. (Permission required for use.)

Saving men and women from the depths of despair and pulling them away from death's door is serious work. But not everything was grave between Lois and Bill. They balanced gravity with levity through their love of music.

Lois found those hours precious when she and Bill could spend time together. After the evening meal, they'd turn to music. An evening might be spent listening to Mozart on WQXR, but they were also musicians, not just music lovers. Bill played violin, Lois piano. When they moved to Stepping Stones, they were finally able to get her piano out of storage. Bill had not only taught himself to play the violin and cello, but his first violin was one he had made himself by refurbishing his Uncle Clarence's old instrument.[12]

Travel was an annual relief from stress which was an important way for Bill and Lois to reconnect with each other and their friends. In March of 1953, they took a ten-day trip that included visits to the historic cities of Charleston, South Carolina, and Williamsburg, and Fort Monroe in Virginia. The Christmas and New Year holidays of 1953–1954 were spent on a freighter cruise through the Panama Canal that took just short of a month. Before heading off to St. Louis for the second A.A. International Convention in June 1955, Bill and Lois spent a refreshing five days at Capon Springs, a resort in West Virginia, with Gene Exman, a friend and the religion editor for Harper's Publishers.

Courtesy Stepping Stones

A tender moment while traveling. (Permission required for use.)

Lois and Bill also made new friends through travel. Lois reported on meeting Robert Oppenheimer during a 1957 trip to St. John in US Virgin Islands. As they became friends, Bill explored with Oppenheimer his theories about depression and neuroticism. Oppenheimer invited Bill to come work with him on this idea at the Princeton Institute of Advanced Studies, but Bill declined the offer.[13]

Despite this peacefulness—which had been a long time coming—Bill still had other demons. Although he had conquered his addiction to alcohol—one day at a time—he was still chained to cigarettes. And the disease that had gripped him since adolescence, depression, plagued him off and on. He also worried about A.A., its future, and how to hand it off successfully.

New Freedom for Bill and Lois

With this last issue in mind, Bill knew that the second A.A. International Convention would be a critical one. Lois was excited about celebrating A.A.'s twentieth anniversary in St. Louis. Lois and her many new Al-Anon friends were very much a part of the Convention. Al-Anon hosted five workshops, one of which, for children of alcoholics, would become especially precious to Lois. Continuing to learn from A.A., Lois and the early Al-Anon leaders had published *The Al-Anon Family Groups*, and it was being sold for the first time at the Convention.

As excited as Lois was about making the Twelve Steps available to the families of alcoholics, she was thrilled beyond belief at what was happening within A.A. at this Convention. A.A. was "coming of age." Through the General Service Conference, A.A. members themselves were becoming "the guardian of the Traditions of Alcoholics Anonymous, the perpetuator of the World Services of our Society, the voice of the group conscience of our entire Fellowship, and the sole successors to its cofounders, Dr. Bob and Bill."[14] As thrilling as this was for A.A., it meant for Lois that Bill would no longer be responsible for guiding and leading the organization.

It was four o'clock on Sunday afternoon, July 3, 1955. Around 3,500 A.A. members and families gathered in St. Louis. Bernard Smith, Chairman of A.A.'s Board of Trustees, opened the session, explained the agenda, and asked Bill W. to read the resolution handing over leadership of A.A. to the members acting democratically through a General Service Conference.

Bill opened the resolution dramatically: "We stand on the brink of a momentous decision. It is one of the most solemn hours in which this society will ever live, for we are about to confirm its permanent structure."[15]

Bill explained how this decision had evolved and why it made sense. He concluded by offering language for the resolution: "We...declare our belief that our Fellowship has now come of age and is entirely ready to assume full and permanent possession of the Three Legacies of our A.A. Inheritance—the Legacies of Recovery, Unity, and Service.... A.A.'s General Service Conference...should now become the permanent successor to the founders of Alcoholics Anonymous...thus avoiding in future time all possible strivings for individual prestige or personal power, and also providing our society with the means of functioning on a permanent basis."[16]

The conference members unanimously and enthusiastically adopted this resolution.

After the resolution was approved, Bernard Smith introduced Lois: "In the lives of men who have made a powerful impact on human society there is not infrequently a great woman, the wife and partner...without which support the man's impact might never have been made. To us, Lois is not only such a woman as the wife of Bill but is, indeed, a symbol to all of us of the A.A. wife."

Lois spoke from the heart about her faith and gratitude for A.A. and the Twelve Steps: "I want to express here before you all my gratitude for this great occasion, and my thanks for being allowed to share in it. It is this sharing that makes A.A. the power for good that it is.... I believe all these miracles have come about because the principles of A.A. coincide with the highest precepts we know, with the fundamental laws of the universe. These principles teach us to step aside so that God can act through us."[17]

The Wilsons returned from St. Louis grateful for the change in Bill's responsibilities and heading into a new chapter in their marriage. As important as this hand off of responsibility was for Bill and Lois, it was not easy. Bill was sixty, and Lois was sixty-five. The average life expectancy in 1955 was 66.7 years. While some people might use this enormous milestone to rest, that was not the nature of Bill and Lois Wilson.

Their lives did indeed change, but doing little or nothing was not in their nature. Lois continued to show more balance than Bill in her ability to take time off. Three months after the St. Louis Convention, she headed to Nantucket, Massachusetts, to spend time with a friend.

After their annual New Year's gathering, Bill and Lois headed to Florida for some rest and warmer weather. The following year, their winter break trip was to the Virgin Islands. With somewhat reduced responsibilities and steady income from growing royalties, the Wilsons were freer to travel for vacation, and they did.

The Twelve Concepts

Bill continued to think about what could be done to ensure that A.A. survived and thrived. While the Twelve Traditions gave guidance to the groups and their relations with one another, there were some more nitty-gritty operating guidelines and values Bill considered important to pass on. In 1956, he gave a talk to the sixth General Service Conference, where he outlined four principles to guide operations. Over the next years, these were refined and became the Twelve Concepts, adopted by A.A.'s General Service Board in 1963.[18]

Lois led Al-Anon through similar discussions in her own style. She presented a draft Conference Charter to the 1963 Al-Anon World Service Conference, not for a vote, but "for a year of study and discussion before bringing the issue to the 1964 Conference."[19] This charter was adopted the following year, reorganizing the Board of Trustees and creating a seven-person Executive Committee.

How much Lois and Bill collaborated in their respective work as organizational architects for A.A. and Al-Anon is unclear. Lois paid attention to the evolution of A.A.'s organizational structure and benefited from it. Their writings are silent on whether or how Lois may have influenced Bill and his positions.

Exploring New Frontiers

Bill described people with drinking problems as "restless." As he came out of his depression around 1955 and stepped back somewhat from his leadership of A.A., Bill had time and energy for ideas he considered important. His restlessness found release in a number of directions in addition to continued involvement with A.A. and traveling and enjoying time with Lois.

Bill's interest in psychic phenomena and spiritualism started early in his recovery and was part of "his conviction that our lifetimes on earth constitute what he liked to call 'a mere day in school'; that we are all pupils in a 'spiritual kindergarten'; and that life after life is a matter of fact as well as faith. This belief led to his attempts to get in touch with other lives in other lifetimes."[20]

Bill was not alone in exploring communications with spirits from the afterlife. Dr. Bob and Annie Smith shared this interest and had participated with Bill and others in seances. Bill would tell stories of communications with military leaders from the past with names that were accurate and about whom he had no prior knowledge.

After they got settled at Stepping Stones, Bill and Lois began hosting seances with friends, including Anne Bingham and her husband Devoe, Tom P. (a friend of Bill's who edited A.A.'s *Twelve Steps and Twelve Traditions*) and his wife Ginny, among others. Lois and other friends began referring to the room where these sessions were held as the "spook room."

Also related to his desire to grow spiritually was Bill's exploration of whether the hallucinogenic drug Lysergic acid diethylamide (LSD) could aid with the spiritual awakening needed to achieve sobriety. This was in the early and more serious period of LSD research before it became associated with the rebellious spirit of the 1960s.

One biographer suggests Bill was tired of being looked to as a leader and was searching for new sources of guidance himself. Aldous Huxley and Gerald Heard, a philosopher who founded Trabuco College, introduced Bill and Lois to two doctors, Abram Hoffer and Humphrey Osmond, who were conducting experiments in Canada with LSD.[21]

Bill continued to hunger for treatments for alcoholics and for depression and thought this form of spiritual exploration might have possibilities. At the encouragement of these two psychiatrists, Bill tried LSD in August 1956 under a doctor's supervision and was thrilled with the peace and tranquility it offered him. He encouraged Lois, Nell Wing, and others to try it, which they did. Neither Lois nor Nell reported any impact from the drug. For a short time, Bill continued to be an enthusiastic proponent of LSD treatments.

The General Service Board of A.A. was appalled and reminded Bill it was impossible to disassociate his activities from A.A. Consequently, "by the end of 1959, he had stopped exhorting friends to take LSD and had stopped himself."[22]

Nell Wing got to observe Bill's moods up close. She worked for A.A. as an assistant and executive secretary, but she grew to become just like family. The Wilsons regarded Nell as the daughter they never had. She noted that depression "was such a huge part of his life from his school days on. It was particularly troublesome during the decade 1945-55. Paradoxically, this was also one of the most productive decades of his life.... It always puzzled him why he had to endure this suffering since, as he often said, he was so fortunate and had so much to live for.... His most crippling depressions followed periods of intense emotional and physical activity, when he was expending enormous amounts of psychic and spiritual energy."[23]

One biographer cites four periods of major depression for Bill: as a child (when his parents divorced), as a teen (when Bertha died), during his drinking years (when he felt hopeless), and from 1944–1955 (as he struggled to find balance in sobriety).[24]

One thing Bill thought might ease his suffering was vitamins. The same psychiatrists, Humphrey Osmond and Abram Hoffer, were experimenting with vitamin B3, or niacin, to treat depression. Bill tried niacin and found it effective.

From his experience with the vitamin supplement, Bill became convinced that niacin could help alcoholics with alcoholic withdrawal.[25] He wrote papers promoting niacin and became involved in schemes to increase its marketing.

Lois explained Bill's enthusiasm this way: "I think the problem was that with most things Bill got interested in, he became overenthusiastic. Wherever he went, he was telling people to take niacin. He even had me taking it and I must admit it seemed to help. In fact, I still take it."[26]

In his zeal to explore the benefits of niacin, Bill became close to a fellow sufferer of depression who also was interested in alternative treatments. Helen Wynn was an attractive, charismatic, and divorced actress. When Bill and Helen met, he was about sixty. She was around forty-two, newly sober, and had been hired to work for the *AA Grapevine*.

Over time, they became close friends, soulmates in their battle with depression, and maybe lovers, depending on whom you ask. Their friendship lasted fifteen years.

Biographers of the Wilsons and those who knew them hold strong and differing positions about Bill's inclination to be what today we would call a "womanizer." While there are lots of hearsay stories about Bill's flirting and being involved with other women, they remain part of the Bill Wilson folklore.[27] His relationship with Helen Wynn was different.

Charges of misuse of funds, mismanagement, and womanizing were seen as part of a pattern of vicious attacks on Bill's character by those who were angry with him. Some were sober and disappointed in Bill or had major disagreements. Others had relapsed into drinking and, in that process, launched campaigns against Bill and A.A. These writers look to the source and discount or dismiss many of the allegations.

There is, however, compelling evidence that Bill and Helen Wynn had a deep and enduring relationship. They spent time together, traveled together, and worked on projects together. Bill went to battle with the A.A. Board of Trustees to have 10 percent of his book royalties left to her upon his death. Lois received the other 90 percent.[28] The exact nature of the relationship Bill had with Helen Wynn is, and likely will, remain a mystery and a source of disagreements.

What did Lois think about this friendship? We don't know because Lois never spoke or wrote about it publicly. Marriage is a private matter, and that is how Lois treated it. She likely understood Bill's need to relate to someone who experienced severe depression firsthand. Lois definitely knew about the relationship. Helen was a guest at Stepping Stones gatherings. On her calendar, Lois mentioned picking up Helen Wynn's son: "Bill and I drove to the office in a snow storm. Picked up 'Chips,' Helen Wynn's son, who had 3 boxes of old books for appraisal in New York."[29]

Lois and Bill by the fireplace in Stepping Stones living room. (Permission required for use.)

Regardless of the nature of Bill's relationship with Helen Wynn, in the Wilsons' times, if men had extramarital affairs, that was no cause for divorce. Bill and Lois lived within a cultural norm that tolerated men's marital infidelity. Marriages were to be preserved, commitments kept.

In any case, both Lois and Bill were committed to their marriage.

In October 1960, Bill, Lois, and Helen Wynn were all guest speakers at the twenty-fifth anniversary celebration of A.A. in Burlington, Vermont. After the mayor's welcome, Bill introduced Helen Wynn as "a girl whom I have seen with my own eyes do tremendous work inside and outside the office.... I give you Helen Wynn."[30]

Helen spoke about her journey getting sober and what it meant to her. She recalled having a recurring nightmare in early sobriety of speaking at an A.A. meeting in front of Bill—and here she now was, talking in front of Bill and Lois. She called it a "double indemnity for which I had no insurance" and added that it was wonderful to speak in their presence.[31]

Lois then described how she thought she could change Bill and discovered she couldn't. She acknowledged that, not having children, her only focus was on getting Bill to stop drinking: "Our whole lives simmered down to one terrific fight against alcohol, and I had to assume all family responsibilities, and look after him like a mother looks after a child."[32]

Bill maintained his friendship with Helen Wynn until he died. As the years of sobriety progressed for Bill and Lois, their marital relationship continued to grow.

CHAPTER 17

LOIS AND BILL'S LAST DECADE TOGETHER

For most Americans, the transition from the 1950s to the 1960s was an exciting and tumultuous time. Poodle skirts and soda shops were replaced by minidresses and lava lamps. But it was more than just a period with new fads. The social mores changed too. The Vietnam War, the civil rights movement, and the sexual revolution transformed how Americans defined themselves, sometimes leading to growth and, frequently, conflict.

Lois and Bill were no exception. Continued growth and the consequent conflicts faced Al-Anon and A.A. Their personal life in the sixties was marked by facing their aging, the loss of family and close friends, and Bill's declining health.

Facing Big Changes and Losses

In 1956, Bill moved his mother, now eighty-five, from California to Westchester so he could better care for her as she aged. Despite his difficulties with both parents growing up, Bill remained loyal to his mother and father until their deaths. Lois and Bill were now able to include his mother in their Sunday drives and trips back to Vermont. His mother spent her last five years in New York, near Bill and Lois, and passed away at age ninety-one.

The loss of his mother was preceded for Bill and Lois by other painful losses. Lois lost her sister Kitty in 1958. Then Fr. Ed Dowling, Bill's spiritual guide and the Wilsons' friend, died on April 21, 1960.

An A.A. member from Tennessee who knew both Fr. Ed and Bill wrote this a few days after Fr. Ed's death: "For Bill's sake I am glad that Father Ed's passing was so peaceful. The terrible—grotesque, almost—death of Fitz Mayo cast a spell on Bill and the rest of us for years. This departure out of our sight was fitting and in keeping with Father Ed's life and wishes."[1]

The 1960 International Convention in Long Beach was notable for the cold weather in southern California and the number of aging "friends of A.A." that were recognized for their contributions. Among the speakers, in addition to Bill and Lois, were Sr. Ignatia, Col. Edward Towns (son of Charlie Towns, founder of Towns Hospital), Ebby T., the Rev. Sam Shoemaker, Dr. Harry Tiebout, Warden Clinton Duffy of San Quentin Prison, and Marty Mann.

In January 1961, Bill wrote a letter of thanks to noted psychiatrist Carl Jung. In Bill's view, Dr. Jung had given hope to alcoholics during his treatment of Rowland H. when he told him he had a hopeless condition that required a "spiritual or religious experience" for treatment. Rowland H. had brought this message to Ebby T., who brought it to Bill, who brought it to Dr. Bob. Without this beginning, in Bill's mind, A.A. would not have become the movement it became. He acknowledged to Dr. Jung how his message was so powerful and persuasive: "Coming from you, one he so trusted and admired, the impact was immense."[2]

Dr. Jung replied to Bill's letter and Bill to him, but three months after Bill's second letter, Dr. Jung died, in June 1961.[3]

Frank Buchman, founder of the Oxford Group, died in the same year. Upon learning of his death, Bill expressed regret that he had never formally thanked Buchman for his contribution to the birth of A.A.

For those who live longer lives, the loss of friends becomes an ongoing experience. Lois and Bill knew an unusual number of people, entertained them at their home, and welcomed and offered comfort and encouragement to thousands. Their known losses later in the 1960s included the Rev. Sam Shoemaker in 1963 (whom Bill called "one of A.A.'s indispensables") and, in 1966, Bill's lifelong friend and sponsor Ebby T., Sr. Ignatia, and Dr. Harry Tiebout. After a lifetime of fighting alcoholism, Ebby T. is reported to have died, with two and a half years of sobriety, from emphysema, the same disease that was beginning to trouble his friend Bill and would eventually kill him.

Given the breadth of their friendships, Lois and Bill grieved often. In addition to their grief over those who died, they also grieved with those who were unsuccessful in finding sobriety and with their families. As early as 1955, Lois' sister Barbara wrote a poem about her drinking problem. The poem, with a note saying Barbara sent it to her brother Lyman in 1955, begins:

(Permission is required from the Stepping Stones Foundation for any further use, display, or duplication of the following material from its archive.)

They said I had a childhood kink
To make me always want to drink
So off to find a psycho gink
I went. Like that. Quick as a wink.

Doc asked and asked, "Why do you drink?
Do you know that you sometimes stink?"[4]

In 1964, Lois wrote to inform Barbara's lawyer of vacation plans so he could reach her about Barbara's declining health and need for institutional care. Barbara's attorney wrote back to Lois, reporting that Barbara had completed two of six treatments and was making progress. He referenced a prior hospitalization and raised serious concerns about Barbara's ability to live on her own. He concluded, "It is just not good for her to continue living alone."[5]

While Lois' correspondence with Barbara's attorney is discreet, there is reason to believe Barbara's health was impacted by her drinking. She managed to live sixteen more years, dying in 1980. It appears Lois' and Bill's love was not enough to get her sober.

Another scary moment occurred sometime between 1959 and 1964 when Marty Mann returned to drinking. She convinced herself she could drink bitters, which are 45 percent alcohol. Fortunately for Marty, a young woman with a year of sobriety who lived in her Bronxville, New York, neighborhood heard about Marty and wanted to meet her. Other women in her A.A. group encouraged her to visit Marty. "When she arrived unannounced at Marty and Priscilla's apartment, she was shocked to find Marty drunk, the place a mess, the dogs needing attention."[6]

Given Mann's leadership role in alcoholism education, a long-term relapse would have been deadly to her work. She chose to keep this to herself, and it is unclear who really knew. Bill was her sponsor and so likely knew. Historian Ernest Kurtz learned about it and once asked Marty about it in an interview. She indicated she didn't want to discuss it.

Fortunately, the relapse was brief, and there was no interruption to Marty's highly visible and successful education and advocacy efforts. Like other closely guarded confidences, it is unclear how much Lois and Bill knew or were able to support their friend during this stressful time.

Building a Movement

Lois and Bill continued living out their lives "of love and service" as Dr. Bob had encouraged in his last talk. For Lois, this meant continuing to partner with Anne Bingham and Al-Anon Family Groups' members to build the infrastructure for Al-Anon.

Having started in a small office in the old A.A. 24th Street Clubhouse in New York City, Lois successfully moved the Al-Anon office to 125 East 23rd. In 1956, the Al-Anon Board was created, and Lois was elected president and Anne Bingham vice president. This formality confirmed what everyone involved knew: Lois was the brains and engine for Al-Anon's birth and growth. From the outset, she saw leadership as something temporary and was guided by the groups and her Higher Power.

With Bill's help, Lois had drafted a pamphlet to give guidance to the growing number of Family Groups. With help from Margaret D., who became the first editor of *The Forum*, Al-Anon's equivalent to the *AA Grapevine*, the pamphlet became a book referred to as the Handbook in 1959. Al-Anon's World Services Office archives contain a copy of the *A.A. Service Manual* written by Bill with handwritten edits by Lois as she shaped this Al-Anon guide from A.A.'s experience. This basic text, called now *The Al-Anon Family Groups: Classic Edition* guided Al-Anon groups for decades and in the 1990s was supplemented by an expanded guide, *How Al-Anon Works*.

Freed in theory of the weight of leadership by the 1955 International Convention, Bill still actively contributed to A.A. He wrote frequently for the *AA Grapevine* throughout the late 1950s and early 1960s. His articles covered a wide range of topics. There were educational articles about A.A.'s "growth to maturity"—such as "Let's Be Friendly with Our Friends"—and articles about the importance of cooperating with psychiatrists, physicians, the clergy, and the media (press, radio, and television).

Three articles specifically seemed to sum up Bill's constant desire to grow emotionally and spiritually. In 1958, he wrote "The Next Frontier: Emotional Sobriety," where he pointed out that getting and staying sober were not enough for him or any recovering alcoholic. Bill wrote very directly about the risks of holding onto what he called "adolescent urges" for approval, security, and romance. He noted how this dependence on people and circumstances threatened sobriety. Bill concluded by suggesting that for him, prayer and surrender of his will to a Higher Power moved him along the path from dependence to emotional sobriety.[7]

Five months later, Bill wrote "Take Step Eleven" for the *AA Grapevine*, where he stated he was inexperienced in prayer and meditation, describing himself as a beginner. He cautioned against members who did not seek to further develop their prayer and meditation practice as described in Step Eleven.[8] Despite his humble professions, Bill prayed the St. Francis Prayer and Serenity Prayer regularly and began many mornings with quiet time and prayer with Lois.

In July 1960, he wrote "The Language of the Heart," a title chosen by A.A. in 1988 for a compilation of Bill's many *AA Grapevine* writings. Bill began this article by musing about his amazement at the growth of A.A. over twenty-five years and describing why he thought the communication between one recovering alcoholic and one seeking sobriety was so powerful. He explained that this was no usual communication but based on what he called "sacrificial love"—

that is, the desire of one alcoholic to help another. He dubbed this deep connection "the language of the heart."[9]

Lois and Bill both were working on putting in place foundations and guidelines to ensure A.A. and Al-Anon were available for future generations who needed help.

Lois had closely followed A.A.'s experience with developing a General Service Conference. After several years of study and consultation, the "Experimental Plan for Al-Anon World Service Conference" was sent to members in August 1960. The plan proposed an initial three-year trial, similar to the four-year trial period A.A. had used from 1951 to 1955.

Bill joined Lois at the initial meeting and made a short presentation. He explained how the launching of the World Service Conference in Al-Anon allowed Al-Anon to fully adhere to the Second Tradition, which reads: "For our group purpose there is but one authority—a loving God as he may express himself in our group conscience. Our leaders are but trusted servants—they do not govern."[10]

As Chair of the Board, Lois had a big role in shaping this first Al-Anon World Service Conference. Lois explained the purpose of the Policy Committee as assisting groups and Headquarters, when requested, in interpreting the Traditions and their application to the daily affairs of Al-Anon.

Lois also led what was the first of many discussions about Conference Approved Literature. This was a sensitive topic with groups, particularly those who had developed their own literature. Lois clarified why it was important for literature developed by Al-Anon World Service to have its stamp of approval. This would reassure members that literature was in line with Al-Anon. She explained that some local literature had a local or particular religious slant. Again, she was able to observe that A.A. had solved the same problem by developing "Conference Approved

Literature." Al-Anon adopted that same policy, requiring that only Conference Approved Literature be used at Al-Anon meetings.[11]

A year after Lois convened the first Al-Anon World Service Conference, Bill was successful in having the 1962 A.A. General Service Conference approve his draft of the Twelve Concepts. These ideas incorporate the values that Lois and Bill Wilson, Bob and Annie Smith, and others brought to the formation of A.A. and Al-Anon. The Twelve Concepts clarify lines of authority within the structure, ensure that every member and every group have a voice and are heard by protecting minority views, and affirm the importance of adhering to the spirit of A.A tradition.

Bill's one unresolved aim for A.A. was to change the balance of power in the General Service Board, which originally had two classes of Board members: nonalcoholics who brought business and other expertise and recovering alcoholics. As the Fellowship matured, Bill and others became eager to shift the majority to recovering alcoholics. The harder he pushed, the more the nonalcoholic members of the board resisted. At one point, after a fiery letter from Bill, several of the nonalcoholic board members resigned. Eventually, Board Chair Bernard Smith offered to try to work this out. With very little discussion, the board agreed to change the majority to recovering alcoholics. In 1966, the General Service Conference voted to have alcoholics represent a two-thirds majority of the Board.

Growing Attention to Alcohol and Drug Addiction

From its very early days, A.A. attracted members who self-described as having problems with both alcohol and drugs. Bill, Dr. Bob, and other early members, some of whom were dually addicted, had great compassion for men with drug problems and held firm that recovery from drug addiction was outside the primary purpose of A.A.

In 1950, Jimmy K. began attending A.A. meetings in New York City. Over time, he began meeting with other A.A. members who had both alcohol and drug problems. In 1953, Narcotics Anonymous (N.A.) was incorporated with Jimmy K. being elected president.

Since Lois and the early Al-Anon leaders shared Bill's view that recovery for people with drug addictions and their families required a separate program, Nar-Anon began meetings for families of persons with drug problems in 1968 and incorporated in 1971.

Throughout the 1960s, public attention and support for treatment for alcohol and drug addiction were growing. Senator Harold Hughes of Iowa, as a "self-declared recovered alcoholic," chaired public hearings of the Senate Subcommittee on Alcoholism and Narcotics, which included testimony by Bill Wilson (testifying as Bill W., with his back facing the camera), Marty Mann, and an Academy Award-winning actress in recovery, Mercedes McCambridge, on July 24, 1969.

Bill recounted for the Committee his own problems with alcohol, his recovery story, and the story of A.A.'s growth. These hearings and testimony contributed to the passage of the Comprehensive Alcoholism Prevention and Treatment Act of 1970.

One addiction recovery practitioner and historian summarized the importance of this legislation this way: "If there were a single piece of legislation that birthed today's system of addiction treatment, it was unquestionably the 1970 Comprehensive Alcoholism Prevention and Treatment Act."[12] This law provided the research, policy advocacy, and funding which sped up the recognition of alcoholism as a disease and public-health problem. It also launched a new treatment industry focused on alcoholism and drug abuse.

The Wilsons' Financial Security and A.A. and Al-Anon Cooperation

Bill was a good steward of his income from book royalties and attentive to ensuring income for Lois, Helen Wynn, and living heirs after he died. A review of the summaries of the General Service Conference meetings shows a number of discussions where some aspect of the royalty payments were discussed and clarified.

In 1964, the General Service Conference approved a written contract between Bill and A.A. World Service for Bill and Lois to continue to receive 15 percent royalties on books written by Bill during their lifetimes. After their deaths, living heirs were eligible to receive royalty payments which reverted to A.A. World Services upon the death of all heirs.[13]

Royalties received by the Wilsons had grown from $15,447 in 1954 to $28,790 in 1964. By 1984, four years before Lois died, the annual royalty income was $746,816.[14] After living in poverty with Bill, Lois became a wealthy woman.

Encouraging Humility

God is often found in serene spaces. Bill and Lois made space for serenity. They made music. They took walks. They had daily prayer. But despite any mystic and heroic qualities Bill might have had, he was still a flawed human with an ego. Lois helped keep his head on his shoulders and his feet on the ground.

In the late 1950s or so, Lois and Bill took a cross-country trip from New York to California. One place they stopped was a small town in the Mojave Desert. Barstow had been a small silver-mining town. The landscape featured long, sandy stretches punctuated by sword-shaped leaves on yucca plants and Joshua trees with their twisted bark capped by spiny leaves. Barstow's brown and dusty ter-rain, coupled with its broad and open sky, was very differ-ent from the green lawns and full, leafy trees of Westches-ter County, New York.

But the one thing the two places had in common was alcoholics.

"We learned there was an A.A. meeting that night at a local church," Lois recounted. Bill and Lois anonymously pulled up chairs, sat down, and listened to the speakers. When the meeting was over, Bill was greeted and chatted up just like any regular A.A. visitor. But instead of feeling welcomed, Lois saw that her husband was agitated.

"When we arrived, no one had any idea who Bill was. Since we were from back East, however, they wanted to know if we had met any of the old-timers who started the program. I could tell Bill was just bursting to tell them he not only met the founders but he was one of them. But I kept pinching his arm and we left the meeting without anyone being the wiser. Later, in the car Bill laughed and said it was good for his humility. I said, 'What humility?' and we laughed some more."[15]

CHAPTER 18

THE FINAL DAYS OF
THE WILSON MARRIAGE

On January 24, 1968, Lois achieved a milestone that not even her happily married parents had achieved. She and Bill each prepared for their fiftieth wedding anniversary in different ways.

Bill gave Lois an anniversary love letter which concluded: "Of all my blessings you are the greatest and most constant. God has been so good to us and most especially in his gift of you to me. I love you Lois, Bill."[1]

Lois summed up their fifty years in the opening sentences of her anniversary love letter this way: "Today completes our 50 years together – 50 years of deep & sustaining love & 50 years of meaningful activity, during which we've shared suffering from which we were miraculously released together. You led so many people to find a new life and your devoted wife was among the first to follow your lead." She concluded her note by apologizing that the surprise party prevented her from getting "the enclosed little ditties" nicely written in a card Bill could carry about.[2]

The little ditties included an updated version of the poem she had written to Bill in 1918 when they were first married. She noted the poem was written in the bathtub in their apartment in New Bedford, Massachusetts, when Bill was in Army training. She wrote of the robins singing "'Tis Spring" and how they were young and singing like the robins sing. In 1961, she had revised the poem with a note "written at our beautiful home, Stepping Stones, surrounded by the beautiful flowers you gave me," and she acknowledged they were both old and had gone where the road has led and "the song has not grown old."

She further revised the poem in 1968 "for our 50th anniversary":

(Permission is required from the Stepping Stones Foundation for any further use, display, or duplication of the following material from its archive.)

The robins sing "'Tis Spring," dear heart,
But you and I are old.
 Still as we've tread
 Where the road has led
We've sung the song they told.

The robins sing "'Tis Spring," Dear One,
Our guiding Father above,
 For fifty years.
 Thru smiles and tears,
Has warmed us with His love.

The robins sing "'Tis Spring," Dear Bill
Thank God for the Power that we
 And our hearts most deep
 That song could keep
Whatever the road might be.[3]

As the anniversary approached, Bill prepared the many details of their three-to-four-week vacation in the Caribbean, where they were meeting friends from Canada in Grenada. They also visited Tobago and Antigua.

Nell Wing, their loyal friend and surrogate daughter, took Bill and Lois out to lunch for their fiftieth wedding anniversary. She knew the couple was anticipating a big to-do and could see they were a little crestfallen when the only thing that happened was lunch.

It was when they returned home that they realized a huge surprise party was, in fact, waiting for them at Stepping Stones. The driveway was full of cars with license plates from a host of states. Lois' siblings and their spouses were there, as were Bill's half-sister, Helen, and her husband, along with nieces and nephews and A.A. and Al-Anon friends, locally and from as far away as the West Coast.

Love abounded as the Wilsons were surrounded by family and friends on this big day. Life was amazingly good, and there was much to be grateful for. Nell Wing summed up the love that kept Lois and Bill together for fifty years: "Certainly they had their little spats but they never dragged on. Lois and Bill not only adored each other but they respected each other. To me, I think that is what keeps people together for a long, long time—love and respect."[4]

After the anniversary party, when it was just the two of them, they talked about the days gone by and the memories they hoped to make going forward. But the clock was ticking for Bill. It had been apparent at the party that his strength was diminished and his stamina short due to his smoking.

Bill had started smoking during his war years, and he never stopped. Although Lois made it known she didn't like his smoking habit, eventually she stopped saying anything about it. By the 1960s, cigarettes had taken their toll. He had tried to stop. He had tried to hide his habit. He had tried to hide his bad health—to no avail. Dr. Leonard Strong, his brother-in-law, had told Bill the coughing, hacking, and chronic bronchitis were forerunners of heart and lung disease. By 1965, it was confirmed. He had emphysema.

Bill's Final Leadership Efforts

One of Bill's last major contributions to A.A. was to assist the Board in resolving how to best connect with and serve the rapidly growing number of emerging A.A. meetings and structures in countries around the world. In January 1968, Bill wrote a position paper with his thoughts.

Once again, Bill demonstrated his clarity of vision: "Long ago it became apparent that New York could not forever provide complete General Services to all the A.A. countries that occupy such vast regions of the world. The reasons for this are not hard to understand; our present centralized structure would develop serious defects: (1) If continued, growing centralization would tend to make New York and its service leadership the 'world capital' of A.A. Psychologically, such an ever-growing concentration would be most unwise. (2) It would foreclose the creation of effective world leadership overseas."[5]

Bill concluded by suggesting that A.A. leaders from around the world be convened in 1969 to decide together how to best organize worldwide. Despite his failing health, Bill participated in these discussions and witnessed the decision to establish a World Services structure for A.A.[6]

Later that year, Lois took steps to reduce her leadership role in Al-Anon. In October, she wrote an open letter to all Al-Anon members in the monthly publication *The Forum* about "letting go." She wrote: "Dear Longtimers in Al-Anon, We older members of Al-Anon play a very important role in our groups. By our attitudes and general bearing, we can prove to the new members that Al-Anon works.... On the other hand, if we try to dominate and do not give the newer member a chance to develop, we are stunting our groups and keeping newcomers away. From a place on the sidelines, old timers can give the group purpose and continuity, but not management."[7]

Lois demonstrated "letting go" by resigning her position as Chair of the Policy Committee. She remained involved by chairing ad-hoc committees and attending Policy, Board, and Executive Committee meetings and returned as cochair of the Policy Committee for a period. It would appear that Lois' personality and leadership style allowed her to be involved and not dominate. Bill's enthusiasm and personality perhaps made that more challenging for him.

Bill's Declining Health

Bill's inability to quit smoking was making everything he did more difficult. While he tried repeatedly to stop, he was never successful for more than a short time.

"He was trying so hard to stop smoking," Lois explained later. "He would often get angry with himself whenever he would light up another cigarette. I knew there was nothing I could say that would help. I had already said it all."[8]

"Sometimes when we were out walking together, Bill would begin coughing and gasping for breath. So he began carrying a pocket inhalator with him, a small device that would pump medication into his mouth and down into his lungs. It would help him to stop coughing and wheezing. It could be very frightening at times."[9]

Nell Wing noted a particularly poignant moment that involved the three of them. Nell and Lois were strolling together; Bill was up ahead. It was in late 1969 or early 1970, and Bill's health was in serious decline. Emphysema had weakened him, but on this day he had some of his old energy. Nell noticed something different about that moment.

> The three of us started on a walk, deciding to try out a new hilly road. At one point, Lois and I stopped to examine an unfamiliar species of flower. As Lois was telling me about it, I turned to see Bill walking on ahead of us, trudging along the upgrade, hands clasped behind his back, leaning forward as he always did. As his figure became smaller in the distance, I experienced a sudden but not unexpected premonition that this was to be the last walk the three of us would take together—which it was. I saw in that vision that Bill was literally and symbolically much ahead of us, while Lois and I were still attached to the things of this world, so to speak— to the roadside flowers and plants and nature. A moment later, Bill moved out of our sight."[10]

Prayer Unites Lois and Bill

Throughout their marriage, Lois and Bill began their days with quiet time and prayer as they had learned years ago from the Oxford Group. In an undated note, Lois commented on their prayer: "Morning Prayers said together for years. Last written down in the spring of 1970 when Bill was not too well. Bill often changed the wording + sometimes they were very beautiful. But the basic thoughts were always the same."[11]

Bill's prayers, like many of his talks, were not short. Instead, they expressed his deepest beliefs. This prayer meant so much to both Lois and Bill that a copy of it is kept on their bed for visitors to see at their Stepping Stones home:

O Lord, we thank Thee that Thou art; that we are, from everlasting to everlasting!

Blessed be Thy Holy name and all Thy benefactions to us of light, of love and of service.

May we find and do Thy Will in good strength and good cheer, today.

May Thy ever present Grace be discovered by family and friends—those here and those beyond; by our societies throughout the world; by men and women everywhere; and among those who must lead in these troubled times.

Nonetheless, O Lord, we know Thee to be all wonder, all beauty, all glory, all power, all love.—Indeed Thou art everlasting love; accordingly Thou has fashioned for us a destiny, passing through Thy Many Mansions ever in more discovery of Thee, and in no separation between ourselves.

For all of these great wonders, benefactions and assurances we now raise\hearts and minds unto Thee—O Father of Lights. We are filled with gratitude that shall be timeless How beautiful is Thy world, dear God!

It is a manifestation of Thy Spirit.

How beautiful is the spirit of man, dear Bill

It is a manifestation of God's love.[12]

While not indicated, it seems likely the last two lines were Lois' addition to the prayer. On Friday, January 29, 1937, Lois prayed:

God knoweth whereof we are and remembereth that we are dust. God understands us, knows our problems and is our friend to help us. Also we can't hide things from God, but if we go to him humbly he will help us out of any difficulty. Amen.... to think of God perversely, horrible thoughts come into my mind. Proving that love of God must first come from the heart.[13]

Saying Goodbye to Bill's A.A. Friends

Despite his declining health, Bill was adamant that he would attend A.A.'s International Convention in Miami in early July 1970. Bill and Lois went a few days early so he could rest and prepare for the speeches he would give. The day before the convention started, Bill's health plummeted as breathing became difficult, requiring oxygen. He was attended by a fellow A.A. member, Dr. Ed B., who was director of the Miami Heart Institute.

Despite his hallucinations and difficulty breathing, Bill insisted Dr. Ed get him to the convention. Arriving in an ambulance, Bill briefly attended the traditional Sunday morning spirituality session right before the close of the convention. When the thirteen thousand A.A. members and spouses saw Bill being wheeled to the stage, they leapt to their feet and welcomed him, tears flowing freely.

Lois described it this way: "I still choke up when I think about it. Everyone stood and shouted and applauded for almost five minutes. Bill kept raising his hand for them to be seated but they just had to let him know how much they loved him. His eyes filled up and he kept wiping away the tears."[14]

Finally, the beloved founder spoke:

Dear folks. There is always something new in one's A.A. life and what do you think it is with me this morning? It is that I am absolutely speechless. That is, almost absolutely speechless. As I look out across this crowd, there floats back to me a mighty assurance—and this is a mighty assurance for A.A.'s future that indeed it will go on for so long as God wants us. The other thing I would like to set on the record is my tremendous gratitude at being able to be with you in this finest hour of our closing meeting. So, I can only say May God bless you and keep you and Alcoholics Anonymous forever.[15]

Bill was quickly rushed back to Miami Heart Institute, where he stayed under the care of Dr. Ed, with Lois by his bedside, for the rest of July. Dr. Ed stayed in close contact with Bill and Lois once Bill and Lois returned to Stepping Stones.

Soon it was November 1970, the night of the Bill W. Dinner, New York A.A.'s largest sit-down dinner. This dinner was held annually to recognize the day Bill had his spiritual experience and got sober in Towns Hospital in 1935. Twenty-two hundred people were waiting to hear Bill Wilson speak, but Bill's condition had gotten too serious for him to attend. He had severe pneumonia, along with hallucinations.

Bill had prepared a speech, so Lois read it to the assembly. These remarks became known as "Bill's Last Message." From then on, at every Bill W. Dinner, Lois would deliver this speech. There was one especially memorable line, a paraphrase from an Arab quotation that Bill had heard somewhere. This quote was: "I salute you and I thank you for your lives."

As Bill's decline worsened, his hallucinations increased. Some are shocked that he is reported to have asked his nurse for a drink of alcohol on several occasions.[15] Those more familiar with the brain deterioration related to lack of healthy blood circulation see such cravings as normal.

As Bill's end neared, Dr. Ed offered one more possible treatment. Lois waited impatiently for a private plane to take Bill, Lois, and Nell to Miami. Bill was finally settled into his room at Miami Heart Institute, and, after spending most of the day with him, Lois and Nell left for the night. Bill died at 11:30 p.m. on January 24, 1971, despite numerous efforts to revive him.

Lois' Difficult Goodbye

It was early the next morning when the doctor came to the motel door with the bad news. Not only was Lois devastated by the death, she was devastated that she had not been called to be at his bedside when it was known he was close to death. "The missing of him would come later. But the hurt of not being at his side at this supreme moment was immediate. Why was I not called? Bill and I had shared so many of life's adventures; now, when the door opened for him into the greatest of mystical experiences, I was not there."[17]

Bill died on their fifty-third wedding anniversary. Lois, like most widows, was held and consoled by Nell and her close friends. She moved back and forth from deep grief to trying to be her organized, take-charge self. Quickly, the world knew of the loss of Bill W. With his death, *The New York Times* introduced him as Bill Wilson with a front-page obituary on January 26.

Newspapers around the world followed with tributes to Bill. Local A.A. groups in communities of all sizes around the world organized memorial services which stretched out over the next several months. In Baton Rouge, Louisiana, typical of many, they had a guest book that attendees signed. It was sent, along with a donation to a memorial fund at A.A. World Services in Bill's honor, to Lois.

While there were certainly many more memorial services held around the world, the Archives of Alcoholics Anonymous lists around twenty memorials between January 27 and February 14, including in Kiltegan, Ireland; Columbus, Ohio and Deer Park, New York in the United

States; Glascow, Scotland; Usulutan, El Salvador; and Port Elizabeth, South Africa.

February 14 became the day for organized memorials around the world. The A.A. list includes sixty-five communities from the United States, Canada, and around the world. There were seven services in Australia, two in South Africa, and more in communities as diverse as Seattle, Washington; Abilene, Texas; Hamilton, Ohio; Napa, California; Central Islip, New York; and St. Petersburg, Florida in the United States. Overseas commemorations happened in Aruba; Amsterdam, Holland; Grenada; Bombay, India; Colombo, Ceylon; Trinidad; Hamburg, Germany; and Karwar, India, among many others. Among the largest of gatherings were the ones in New York at St. John the Divine, in Washington, DC, at the National Cathedral, in Montreal at Notre-Dame Basilica, and in London at St. Martin-in-the-Fields.[18]

One of the A.A. trustees, who had also been a good friend of Bill's, delivered a eulogy at the New York service. Dr. Jack Norris said, "Bill's constant concern during almost all of the years that I knew him was that Alcoholics Anonymous should always be available for the suffering alcoholic—that the mistakes that led to the fading of previous movements to help alcoholics should be avoided. To me one measure of his greatness is the clarity of his vision of the future in his determination to let go of us long before we were willing to let go of him."[19]

Amidst the many accolades, perhaps it was this remark by an A.A. member at the Baton Rouge memorial service who said it best on behalf of all A.A. members. This fellow, also named Bill Wilson, said, "I'm not here mournful to remember Bill Wilson tonight because Bill Wilson is not dead. Neither is Dr. Bob... Because we are here tonight and we're all alive. They will never die."[20]

However, it wasn't until spring that Bill's body was finally laid to rest. The frigid New England January made the ground too cold and hard to dig a grave in his hometown of East Dorset, Vermont. Once the land thawed, a funeral was held on May 8, 1971. Lois joined her and Bill's families and their A.A. and Al-Anon family to bury Bill in his grandfather's plot. Bill's tombstone is silent on his role in cofounding Alcoholics Anonymous, as is Dr. Bob's in Akron.

Bill was buried humbly. His life was a testament to his desire to live out his favorite prayer by St. Francis by being an instrument of peace, love, and hope in the world.

CHAPTER 19

LIFE AFTER BILL: LOIS' LATER YEARS

What did Lois Wilson's life mean now that Bill was dead?

What was it like for her to live through all the celebration of Bill's life? How might she have felt as so many people talked of him as their personal savior? Repeatedly, she heard from recovering A.A. members: "Bill saved my life." "Without Bill and A.A., I'd be dead."

She and Bill had made peace with the accolades. They both knew they were but symbols of the power of the Twelve Steps and their way of healing.

Yet this was different. Lois was now alone without the love of her life. While grateful for the recognition of Bill and his life of service, she was reeling from the pain of not being with Bill the night he died.

We know a little from Lois about how she made it through those days and weeks of irreconcilable grief. She isolated herself with anguish and walled herself off from others. Even her close friend Nell Wing had a hard time getting her to eat or answer the phone.

A friend and biographer vividly described Lois' loss after Bill's death: "Lois sat by herself in the Spook Room for days on end, her Bible in her lap, listening to the March winds whistling through the eaves of the old house, and wondering, perhaps hoping, that somewhere in those strong, breath-like gusts she might hear Bill's voice whispering to her or feel his presence beside her.... So she sat and listened and softly murmured how much she missed him and still loved him."[1]

Despite her grief, Bill's presence was everywhere at Stepping Stones, and she refused to change a thing: the old violin he used to play when they had musical evenings together, the black-and-white picture in the photo album of Second Lieutenant William G. Wilson standing beside her just before he shipped out to war, views through the windows of the trails they walked together.

Despite this deep grief, Lois demonstrated her indefatigable resilience within weeks of Bill's death. Her calendar demonstrates her resilience and reveals where she turned for support. She found support where it had always come from—resuming her commitments to A.A. and Al-Anon and spending time with Nell Wing and other close friends.

On March 21, she met with Bob Thomsen, who was writing the official biography of Bill. Lois gave high priority to meeting with Bob Thomsen throughout 1971. Thomsen and his wife spent weekends at Stepping Stones. On March 26 and April 2, Lois noted her meetings with two other individuals interested in writing Bill's biography. Lois was obviously keen on getting Bill's story out and careful about whom she shared information with.

In May, Lois traveled to East Dorset for Bill's burial in his hometown. Part of the enigma of Lois Wilson was her openness and transparency on many events and issues alongside her privacy and reticence on those that were personal for her. Lois did not describe in her diary any of the details of Bill's funeral or what she felt.

Her interest in food came and went. Some days, she had an appetite; many days, she did not. So it was ironic that a food event helped her turn a major corner on her grief.

One day, in conversation with Nell Wing, Lois learned that the Al-Anon Fellowship members were trying to decide where to hold the Annual Stepping Stones Family Groups Picnic, which she had been hosting since recovering from her heart attack. Lois was shocked. The picnic was always held at Stepping Stones!

This was the wakeup alarm Lois needed. She did some Twelve Step self-examination and concluded that despite her deep emptiness and longing for Bill, it would be selfish not to go forward with the picnic. Her self-absorption had prevented her from being of service. Of course the annual picnic would happen, as it did every year.

As Nell reminded her, "Hundreds of Al-Anon and A.A. members and their families are anxiously waiting to hear from you. To see you. To be with you one more time."[2]

Lois reached deep to greet them for the first time by herself. "Tears ran down her cheeks when she spoke to the crowd about Bill's passing, but she went on to assure those in all three Fellowships that her husband's spirit was there among them and always would be.... The love and support Lois received that beautiful spring afternoon, together with the several thousand cards and letters piled up on her desk, helped Lois to return to society."[3]

In July, Lois traveled to South Carolina on a summer trip, much like what she and Bill had done for years. This time, she was accompanied by friends.

Twelve Step work fed Lois' spirit of service. She was in demand as a speaker. She suited up and showed up, but public speaking wasn't something she felt entirely comfortable doing. When another Al-Anon member expressed fear about public speaking, Lois told her: If you're not a little nervous, you don't have much to say. Being nervous was no match for being of service.

Although Al-Anon had Alcoholics Anonymous as a guide for how to serve and how to grow, Al-Anon still had its own trail to blaze. Creating its own literature, organizing a trustee board, hammering out issues via group conscience, recruiting adult sponsors for Alateen, planning and leading national conferences—there was plenty of work to do. And Lois did it.

Some habits and activities remained consistent. Lois was renewed by and took energy from her faith, her commitment to the Twelve Steps and involvement with A.A. and Al-Anon, her family and extended Twelve Step family, and her deep inner hunger to observe and live life to the fullest.

By December of 1971, Lois had decided she wanted to be with family during her first Christmas without Bill. So she flew to Tucson, Arizona, on December 23 to spend the Christmas holidays with Bill's half-sister Helen and her husband Guy. Helen had lived with Lois and Bill years earlier and was someone who loved Bill and could enjoy reminiscing about him.

Lois as World Ambassador for A.A. and Al-Anon

After catching up with the many notes and letters she had received, Lois would seem to be entitled to take a breath— to spend more time watching the seasons change, making notes on the birds and flowers at Stepping Stones, and reading whatever she wanted.

However, as 1972 approached—and less than a year after Bill's death—Lois, at the age of eighty, decided to travel around the world. And she didn't do it just for fun. Her diary entry on January 15, 1972, explains: "Bill and I had planned for several years to visit the A.A. and Al-Anon groups around the world. After he passed on, I decided that was what he would like me to do...so today we set off. Nell had come up to Stepping Stones to help me get ready for the trip."[4]

As Lois prepared for this trip in late 1971, she turned to her Al-Anon and A.A. families both for help in planning her itinerary and in selecting a travel companion. Her first choice, her friend and Al-Anon cofounder Anne Bingham, had just moved to California and was not available. So she turned to Evelyn C., also an early volunteer at the Al-Anon Clearinghouse, who was now sixty-five and a staff worker at the Al-Anon headquarters in New York.

Lois and Evelyn set out for Africa to begin their two-month trip around the world. Between her diary entries and her memoir, we get a vivid picture of two women on a mission of sharing the Al-Anon and A.A. message and having fun in the process.

Lois wanted to visit A.A. and Al-Anon in places she and Bill hadn't gone during their 1950 trip and countries where A.A. and Al-Anon developed since their 1950 trip. She was also grateful to have this trip to give purpose to her life at a time when she needed purpose.

The first stop was sightseeing in Nairobi and Victoria Falls. Just as Lois was fascinated by flowers and rock formations on her US travels, she took delight in being so close to wild animals. In recounting the trip, she rarely omitted her story of the night she and Evelyn stayed at a tourist center called the Ark.

One night, they were startled awake by five huge elephants at the nearby watering trough. Two hours later, they were awakened by a rare white rhinoceros in the light at the watering hole. They didn't sleep much that night and almost came closer than they wanted to some amazing animals!

But it was not the amazing animals or raw vegetation that evoked the greatest awe and wonder in Lois. It was Victoria Falls itself, an intense and tempestuous beauty.

> Seeing Victoria Falls was a highlight experience for me, dimmed only by not having Bill along. He would have been so greatly moved. In eight consecutive ravines, the mile-wide Zambezi River plunges into a deep, narrow crevice in the earth's crust with such force that the spray can be seen in the sky for miles around and forms a tropical rain forest on the downriver bank. The natives call the Falls "The Smoke that Thunders."[5]

In Johannesburg, South Africa, Lois reconnected with two A.A. members she and Bill had met at the 1969 A.A. World Service meeting in New York. Just like back home, Evelyn and Lois met with family members at Al-Anon meetings, and Lois spoke at A.A. meetings. The racial separation of apartheid presented a challenge in finding a hall large enough for the A.A. meeting. Blacks and whites were not allowed to be in the same hall, but the local A.A. members refused to participate in a segregated meeting. So they rented a small local hall where so many eager A.A. and Al-Anon members—black and white—attended, they overflowed the room, perching on the windowsills and congregating on the street.

Lois encountered segregation again in Sydenham, a suburb of Durban, this time involving Aryans from India as well. Again, A.A. and Al-Anon meetings brought all races and ethnic groups together. "The members were so warm and grateful that when we clasped hands—black, brown and white—and sang 'God be with you till we meet again,' tears wet all our cheeks."[6]

From Africa, Lois and Evelyn headed to Australia, where one thousand members participated in a meeting in Sydney. Their trip then took them to Hong Kong and on to Japan. Lois recounted how some of the ideas of A.A. and Al-Anon were beginning to take root in Tokyo, but existing programs to rehabilitate alcoholics veered from the A.A. model yet nevertheless seemed to make strides in helping Japanese people with drinking problems.

Their amazing journey concluded in Honolulu, where Lois noted that the locals had given her and Evelyn so many leis they looked like walking flowerpots!

Lois summed up the trip this way: "And so this was the end of the biggest adventure of my life (so far) and one I will never forget. I can only say that seeing and feeling the loving devotion and oneness of AA and Al-Anon across the world did much to submerge my sense of personal loss in an overwhelming sea of gratitude. The inspiration I received from this warm contact will long sustain me."[7]

The next few years continued with a pattern of Lois' devotion to A.A. and Al-Anon and enjoying her life. Her curiosity led her and Nell to take an Atlantic cruise in August 1972, which included a distinctly advantageous view of the eclipse of the sun. Lois contrasted this trip, which was both fun and informative, with a theatre tour of London in March 1973, again with Nell, which she described as just pure fun. Later that same year, Lois and Evelyn joined up for a trip to England to an A.A. and Al-Anon convention at Selsey-on-Sea.

With her direct style and powers of observation, Lois noted how the Brits, since her last visit in 1950 with Bill, had "lost their former self-consciousness, and there was much joyous camaraderie. And thousands more had joined A.A. and Al-Anon and Alateen were thriving. It was thrilling, and I know Bill would have been thrilled too."[8] Lois and Evelyn stayed on for the Al-Anon General Service Conference in London and then headed home.

In between her world trip and her trip to England, Lois began to experience fatigue and discovered a lump on her breast. Ruth L., a neighbor and Al-Anon friend, later commented on Lois' reaction to having her breast removed: "It didn't seem to faze her at all.... It was amazing how she went through that operation so calmly and with such a positive attitude. You could tell she really had the Twelve Steps in her life. Maybe that's why she recovered so well."[9]

The following spring, 1974, Nell again joined Lois on a trip to an A.A. convention in Cork, Ireland, followed by sightseeing in both north and south Ireland.

In 1976, she began work on her memoir, which she both wrote and illustrated. *Lois Remembers*, which details her life with Bill and the launching of A.A. and Al-Anon, was published by Al-Anon in 1979.

Lois continued to dedicate her life to A.A., Al-Anon, friends, learning, and having fun. Her A.A. and Al-Anon activities included attending and speaking at major events like Founders Day, a weekend conference each June in Akron where thousands of A.A.s and Al-Anons gather to remember the moment Dr. Bob and Bill met and A.A. was formed, when Dr. Bob had his last drink.

Lois' service to A.A. and Al-Anon included her home community and nearby states as she attended group anniversaries and continued her own recovery. One of many examples occurred in early 1985, when she was ninety-four. An Al-Anon group member from the Valley Stream group in Nassau County, New York, asked Lois if she would speak at their twenty-ninth group anniversary. Lois agreed and, on March 19, went and shared her story of recovery.

Lois' Leadership and Letting Go

Unlike Bill, who had been very conscious of wanting to move out of his founder role and be less involved in A.A. after the 1955 hand-off of A.A. to the members, Lois, from the outset, attempted to be "one among the many members." Though technically the cofounder of Al-Anon, her point of view and writings contributed to Al-Anon's development in a way that was less dominant than Bill's influence on A.A.

Lois saw herself as a symbol of the shared commitment of all members to practice the principles of the Twelve Steps and help carry the message. This commitment resulted in her regular attendance at Al-Anon General Service Conference meetings, serving for many years on the Policy Committee, and taking on various assignments as asked over the years.

Although Lois always gave the credit and the glory to her husband, she led in her own way after his death. She seemed to know intuitively the importance of working closely as an equal with others.

She found the balance of being hands-on when needed, the elder stateswoman when that was called for, and a continuous champion for A.A., Al-Anon, and Alateen. She was a dependable and inspiring presence and voice in Al-Anon and Alateen as those fellowships grew and developed.

Lois in Her Nineties

Lois' big heart and love for children was evident. When she was ninety-one, she was interviewed for an article for *Alcoholism* by Monica Getz. Getz opened the article by explaining how Lois mentioned she was getting shorter as she aged—having gone from five feet, three inches tall to just five feet. There was less of her all the time! Then Getz commented, "I find it difficult to accurately describe her in common human terms without sounding mushy and exaggerated.... Lois gives us a tour of the house. Pam (my daughter) is spellbound. There is no generation gap here. Lois' enthusiasm and directness are contagious."

In her interview, Getz asked a question that many have wondered about Lois, Why did she stay with Bill? She asked Lois directly: "But how does Al-Anon fit in with the future-shocked generation of serial monogamists who feel it is quaint 'to stand by your man' come hell or high water?" Lois, raised in a different and almost quaint era, had a ready answer.

> Each person has to look at his/her unique circum-
> stance. Al-Anon teaches us that we have choices.
> There is not one right way for everyone. It is very
> difficult to make these choices, but with the guid-
> ance of our higher power, chances are improved.
> In my own specific case, remember: Bill was never
> violent, not even mean. We had no children. I loved
> him. There was no treatment. And he had insight.
> Somehow, I knew it was an illness; I had not the
> slightest idea of leaving him. Think about it. *What
> good would leverage have done, when there was
> no treatment towards which to use leverage?*[10]

In 1983, when Lois was ninety-two, an Al-Anon member attending the World Service Conference was invited to Stepping Stones for a visit, as was Lois' custom. That member wrote about her experience:

> We were greeted by Lois. She stood in the doorway
> of her home, wearing a red sash declaring "Miss
> Alateen." In her hand was the newly published book

Alateen—A Day at a Time. Once inside, I sat on the couch next to Lois. While we were chatting, she spilled her cup of coffee. As people swarmed around her with towels, I told Lois that when I returned to my Area, I would tell everyone that she was not perfect, because she spilled things just like all of us do. Her eyes twinkled and she told me to do just that, because she did not like it when people put her on a pedestal. She paused and then spoke with an added passion in her voice, "Anyone can start a movement and that does not make them special. The special people are the people who keep the movement going."[11]

Lois remained active in Al-Anon as a trusted elder. She was part of the intense debate in the 1980s over how to best welcome to Al-Anon the adult children who grew up in homes with alcoholism. Like Alateen before it, the adult children issue caught on like a wildfire. A field of professionals grew with a range of ideas and treatments to heal those damaged by the trauma of growing up in a home with an alcoholic parent or sibling. For nearly a decade, Al-Anon conferences debated how to integrate the needs of adult children into Al-Anon.

At age ninety-three, Lois quietly and firmly took a stand to secure the position of the Twelve Concepts of Service, written by Bill for A.A. and adapted to Al-Anon. At the 1984 World Service Conference, "in response to a request by Lois W. that the Concepts be protected to the same degree as the Steps and Traditions, the Board of Trustees recommended that the words 'and Concepts of Service' be added to the Conference Charter."[12]

This meant that it would take a vote of two-thirds of A.A. and Al-Anon members to approve any change to the Twelve Steps, the Twelve Traditions, and the Twelve

Concepts. Bill and Lois Wilson both paid attention to the written word and to ensuring that what they considered important would not easily be changed. Lois honored Bill's belief in the Twelve Concepts and her own lifelong commitment to living by the Twelve Steps, the Twelve Traditions, and the Twelve Concepts.

Lois' Health Declines

Lois told everyone her hope was to live to be 100. She was also a realist and knew that someday her time on earth would end.

Like Bill, as he approached death, she began to muse and talk with close friends about how to leave her home and income from Bill's book royalties to Al-Anon. She, like Bill, was quickly reminded that the Twelve Traditions prohibited Al-Anon and A.A. from owning property and accumulating large reserves.

In the late 1970s, Lois had met with her trusted advisors about how to handle this quandary. The unanimous conclusion was to set up a nonprofit foundation and leave her home and other assets to the foundation. Lois set up the Stepping Stones Foundation along with Al-Anon friend Henrietta S., Nell Wing, and brother Lyman Burnham. Thus, "on December 24, 1979, the Stepping Stones Foundation was born.... Lois obviously chose to name the Foundation after her home so that it would always reflect the work she, Bill, and others had carried on there."[13]

Just as Lois intended, the Stepping Stones Foundation continues to welcome visitors to the Katonah, New York, home today, including the memorabilia "gallery" Lois set up, Bill's writing studio where he wrote many works (*Twelve Steps and Twelve Traditions* and more), and their personal papers, books, and other belongings. In addition, with Lois as President, the foundation continued the Wilsons' legacy of work in fostering public understanding of alcoholism, including such activities as coproducing public service announcements about alcoholism and hosting a symposium of educators, researchers, and other leaders in the alcoholism field.

As Lois aged, others had ideas of what she needed. Lois remained independent and said no to changes she didn't want. In her diary entry on January 19, 1988, at the age of ninety-seven, she asserted her independence one more time: "Man came to demonstrate a reading machine, but I do not need such a thing yet."[14]

As she aged, Lois got sick more often and had more accidents. In 1983 or so, she drew a picture of her body and made notes of her various illnesses and the years they occurred. She started at the top of her head and proceeded down her body. Among the illnesses and injuries she reported are: 6/83 Sprained neck muscle; 2/81 Bruised ribs; 1/22/54 Heart; 4/80 Broke right wrist; 60s Broke left wrist twice; 2/81 Broke fingers on left and right hands; 6/83 Broke left upper leg; 2/81 Broke left leg below the knee; 6/83 Tore ligaments on instep on right side.[15]

In June 1982, Henrietta S., the first General Secretary, and Margaret D., first editor of *The Forum*, met with Lois to discuss the early years of Al-Anon. This interview was published on audio and later excerpted on DVD.[16]

Despite this increase in health challenges, Lois continued to live and work from Stepping Stones, using it as a base for her travels. She had a favorite travel story that reminded her of the time in her twenties when she and Bill had become what she described as "motorcycle hobos," traveling the East Coast on a motorcycle with a sidecar.

During a trip to Palm Springs, California, in 1983, Lois was invited to speak to the Chapter Five A.A. group, consisting of recovering motorcycle riders, including many members of Hells Angels. "One huge, grinning biker gave

Lois his Chapter Five jacket and patch, along with a note that read: 'Since I gave you my patch, you are my "old lady."' Lois was ninety-two."[17]

A few months following this trip, Lois developed painful and debilitating digestive issues. Consequently, she attended fewer meetings and frequently canceled lunches.

Nineteen eighty-three also brought a painful ending to an over thirty-year relationship with Harriet Severino, her housekeeper. Harriet naturally knew both Bill and Lois intimately from her years working for them. Lois detailed in her diary a series of what she called "strange" events with Harriet and then reports of gossip and conflicts with other people Lois trusted. Harriet resigned as of June 1, 1983, a big change and loss for Lois. Lois was so upset by the accusations that she considered leaving Harriet out of her will. In the end, she included her.[18]

On the brighter side, Lois received the National Council of Alcoholism Humanitarian Award in 1983 on behalf of Al-Anon.

Courtesy Stepping Stones

Lois celebrates her birthday at Stepping Stones. (Permission required for use.)

The next year brought a continued slowdown in Lois' life. Her diary shows fewer trips to New York for Al-Anon meetings and business. She did speak at the opening luncheon of the April Al-Anon Conference, and in October, the Stepping Stones Foundation convened, under her leadership, a large group of psychologists, physicians, educators, and social workers from leading organizations involved in alcoholism research and treatment at Stepping Stones.

In 1985, Al-Anon held its first International Convention in Montreal at the same time and place with A.A. It was the last time, at age ninety-four, that Lois was with A.A., Al-Anon, and Alateen. She spoke from her wheelchair at the joint opening meeting and was greeted by thunderous applause.

In April of 1986, Lois had a particularly bright moment as she read a new article about her Bill. *Reader's Digest* published "Unforgettable Bill W." by Bob P., a Kansas native who came to New York for work and had a serious drinking problem. He described his first meeting with Bill when volunteering to help A.A. with public relations:

> Bill was slouched in a chair, his feet on a battered oak desk that was scarred with dozens of burn marks from cigarette stubs. When he stood, he was about six feet, two inches—slender and loose-limbed. He had a long face and sparkling blue eyes. He acted as if meeting me was the nicest thing that had happened to him in years. "I'm Bill," he said stretching out his hand. "I'm a drunk." I started mumbling how I owed

him my life, and Bill, embarrassed, looked at the floor and said: "Just pass it on."[19]

In 1987, at age ninety-six, Lois wrote a Happy Birthday article for Alateen Talk to celebrate Alateen's thirtieth birthday. She used an electric typewriter with large fonts so she could see what she was typing. Aware of the need to preserve history, she also used this special typewriter to type many of the photo and memorabilia descriptions on display on the second floor of Stepping Stones.

Lois continued to decline through 1987. By January 1988, her diary reports her basically staying at home. The resilience and vitality of her spirit and her feistiness remained evident in her final year of life.

She noted on January 5, 1988: "Ron [her long-time groundskeeper] brings me flowers continually so I always have some lovely ones. I usually stay in bed later; don't go downstairs till lunch time."[20]

Nell Wing described Lois' last few years this way: "She had her good days and her bad days. But while her body was getting weaker, her mind was still strong and alert. When one of us would tease her, she would always tease us right back."[21]

Nell Wing at her retirement party from A.A. World Services Office, New York. (Permission required for use.)

Lois' Death

Lois had her last stay at Northern Westchester Hospital in Mount Kisco in early October 1988. She had a breathing tube and was medicated for constant pain. Friends who visited could see her frustration at not being able to talk because of the breathing tube. At one point, she asked for paper and pencil. She wrote: "Tell them I want to see my Bill."[22]

They took the breathing tube out. She had a last word with Nell and her other close friends who were there and died on October 5, 1988.

Lois' death made *The New York Times*. Unlike Bill's obituary, which was on the front page, *The New York Times* reported Lois' death in the obituary section. Her obituary began, "Lois Burnham Wilson, a founder of the Al-Anon Family Groups, whose members are relatives and friends of alcoholics, died yesterday at Northern Westchester Hospital in Mount Kisco, N.Y. Mrs. Wilson, widely known as Lois W., was 97 years old and was a longtime resident of Bedford Hills, N.Y."[23]

As Lois W., she was revered as "the first lady of Al-Anon" and as a living reminder of the beginnings, five decades before, of "the Alcoholics Anonymous self-help movement."

The obituary, much shorter than Bill's, explained what Al-Anon was, whom it served, and its availability in the United States, Canada, and around the world. The *Times* editors found Al-Anon members' attitude toward alcoholism curious. The obituary commented: "Mrs. Wilson was said to never have voiced blanket condemnation of the drinking of alcoholic beverages, affirming that she opposed 'only the disease of alcoholism and the damage it does to a family.'"[24]

Newspapers across the country revealed Lois' last name and wrote about her amazing legacy. Al-Anon members around the world held memorial services. Al-Anon World Services organized a memorial service at Marble Collegiate Church in New York that was attended by thousands. As when Bill died, there was also a private memorial for Lois at Stepping Stones.

The memorial began with the Serenity Prayer, followed by remarks by close friends and associates of Lois. Norman Vincent Peale, a friend of the Wilsons, was too weak to preach; his associate observed in his remarks that Lois had "outchurched the church."[25]

American singer, songwriter, and activist Judy Collins sang "Amazing Grace" in her world-renowned a cappella style. As a person in recovery, Collins had benefited from the recovery movement begun by Bill and Lois. Collins had witnessed civil rights activist Fannie Lou Hammer sing "Amazing Grace" in 1964 at a voting and women's rights gathering. For her, it came to represent both the fight for equality and the personal fight she and other people with addictions experience and how relieved and joyful they are when they find recovery.[26]

On December 1, 1988, the Greater New York City Al-Anon Association (a service organization for Al-Anon groups in New York City and nearby counties) hosted a lunch in memory of Lois at a New York hotel. The program, called "A Celebration of Life," brought together hundreds of Lois' friends, along with members and staff of Al-Anon. Hank G. described his friendship and Al-Anon work with Lois. Hank lived in Chappaqua, a town not far from Stepping Stones, and went to many of the same Al-Anon meetings with Lois. As she aged and couldn't drive, he gave her a ride to meetings. Hank also volunteered generously with Al-Anon and became the chair of the Al-Anon World Services Board.

Over the following weeks, Nell Wing and her close friends grieved their loss. Wing reflected, "I anticipated the emotional loss but not the physical part, the exhaustion and depression that lasted several months. Not a day passes that I do not silently express my gratitude and love for her friendship and to Bill for his friendship too."[27]

Both before and after Lois and Bill Wilson died, millions of A.A. and Al-Anon members shared their deep and lasting gratitude to Lois and Bill Wilson and the founding mothers and fathers of A.A. and Al-Anon. Lois repeatedly reminded her admirers that she and Bill were symbols, stating that any gratitude should be for what the Twelve Step program had done to restore hope and lives. In one of these reminders, Lois said it this way: "I hope I understand correctly A.A. and Al-Anon members' special devotion to me. As the only survivor of the A.A. founders and their wives and as Bill's widow, I am a symbol to A.A.s of their beloved Fellowship. I shall always be grateful for the warmth and acceptance they show me."[28]

Lois Wilson's capacity to love touched hundreds of thousands of people. She ended her book *Lois Remembers* by summing up in a sentence the philosophy that guided her: "I used to believe *thinking* was the highest function of human beings. The A.A. experience changed me. I now realize *loving* is our supreme function. The heart precedes the mind.... Our hearts do not need logic. They can love and forgive and accept that which our minds cannot comprehend. Hearts understand in a way minds cannot."[29]

CHAPTER 20

THE WILSONS' IMPACT ON THE
ONGOING RECOVERY MOVEMENT

Lois and Bill Wilson were pivotal to the recovery movement as it has evolved for nearly a century. Without their love for each other and commitment to Twelve Step Recovery and their marriage, it is hard to imagine the recovery movement continuing to flourish as it does today. The Wilsons repeatedly gave credit to God or Higher Power and to many others for what they and others were co-creating. Their commitment to humble service—to being one among many—is part of what made the continued growth of the recovery movement possible. This chapter offers readers a brief introduction to the different dimensions of the recovery movement and connects these movements to the life and contributions of Bill and Lois Wilson and their marriage.

This chapter represents the views of the authors and is not offered as a comprehensive history of recovery, which is beyond the scope of this book.[1]

The Recovery Movements and Their Evolution

For the purpose of these reflections, we are distinguishing three "recovery movements":

1. the broader mental health recovery movement,
2. the modern alcoholism recovery movement, and
3. the new recovery advocacy movement.

The Mental Health Recovery Movement

A search for the term "recovery movement" will most likely bring results for the broader mental health recovery movement. This movement has its roots in the 1800s, when medical professionals and others began to talk about mental health challenges and experiment with remedies. In 1908, Clifford Beers wrote his own story of fighting the treatments of the time and regaining his mental health in his book *A Mind That Found Itself*.

The World Health Organization brought credibility to mental health treatment through a number of important long-term-outcome studies. Over thirty years, beginning in 1970, these studies found that people from every continent with "major mental illnesses" showed unexpectedly high rates of complete or partial recovery as a result of various mental health treatments.

In the 1980s and 1990s, the movement came into its own as mental health consumers—families of and people with mental health challenges—began to advocate for policies based on the belief that people with mental illnesses can recover and live productive lives in society even while still experiencing symptoms.

The deinstitutionalization campaign—to stop warehousing people with mental illness and support them living in community—fueled and expanded this broader mental health recovery movement. These efforts began in 1908 with what was called the Mental Hygiene movement, which was concerned about conditions in mental health institutions. The combination of lawsuits, the discovery of psychotropic drugs, concerns about costs, and grassroots advocacy made deinstitutionalization possible in the mid-twentieth century.[2]

The Wilsons' contribution to this broader movement is significant. Both Bill and Lois wrote and spoke about addiction as an illness that was mental, physical, and spiritual in nature. Bill established in *Alcoholics Anonymous*, backed up by a "doctor's opinion from Dr. William Silkworth," that alcoholism was the result of a mental obsession and physical compulsion. He described the strange "mental twist"[3] that preceded the first drink, "a hopeless condition of mind and body."[4]

Lois and Bill both contributed to the notion of emotional sobriety, a precursor to the mental health focus on emotional intelligence. They both realized that mental health issues impacted the family and that the entire family needed to recover for recovery to be successful.

Bill Wilson experienced and wrote extensively about his personal bouts with depression and his experiments with treatments. Nell Wing and others who knew and worked with Bill made the connection between his intense or manic periods of work for A.A. followed by depressive collapses. Bill publicly sought psychiatric help as the leader of an international organization in a period when seeking mental health treatment was seen as a sign of weakness.

Finally, and perhaps most significantly, the Wilsons launched a worldwide grassroots advocacy movement that brought respect and love to each person, regardless of mental health condition or income, race, gender, or sexual identity. Advocates for deinstitutionalization could look to this successful grassroots movement for encouragement and perhaps guidance.

The Modern Alcoholism Recovery Movement

The modern alcoholism recovery movement began on June 10, 1935, with the meeting of Bill Wilson and Dr. Bob Smith and the formation of Alcoholics Anonymous. This dimension of the recovery movement is about how the application of the Twelve Steps evolved in A.A. and was applied to families through the founding of Al-Anon in 1951.

This growth continued in many forms. The relationships developed through the informal networks of A.A., Al-Anon, Narcotics Anonymous, and other Twelve Step recovery programs resulted in the creation of formal organizations that nurtured the growth of awareness about both addiction and recovery. Most notably, Marty Mann, one of the first women in recovery in New York, was asked to lead the National Committee for Education on Alcoholism (NCEA) at Yale University in 1944. With much encouragement from Bill and Lois, NCEA became the National Council on Alcoholism in 1949 and later the National Council on Alcoholism and Drug Dependence. Marty Mann effectively led public education and advocacy in the United States for over thirty years until her death in 1980.

Marty Mann's relationships included prominent politicians such as President Lyndon Johnson and Senator Harold Hughes of Iowa, a self-reported person recovering from alcohol addiction. Senator Hughes convened a public hearing on July 24, 1969, where Bill W., Marty Mann, and Mercedes McCambridge testified.[5] This hearing led to

President Nixon signing the 1970 Comprehensive Alcoholism Prevention and Treatment Act.

While Bill didn't live to be part of it, this public witnessing by people in recovery took a huge step forward in 1976 as the battle against the stigmatism of alcoholism intensified. Marty Mann and the NCA organized a press conference in Washington, DC, on May 29, 1976, called Operation Understanding, that brought together fifty prominent leaders in entertainment, politics, government, sports, medicine, and other fields—all who were publicly acknowledging themselves as people in recovery. Television legends of the time Dick Van Dyke and Gary Moore, along with Mercedes McCambridge, joined baseball star Rollie Fingers and astronaut Buzz Aldrin and others to dispel the myth that all people with a drinking problem were skid row bums.

This event was followed on June 26, 1976, with Freedom Fest 1976 in Minnesota: A Celebration of Freedom from Alcohol and Drug Addiction. Organized by a Minnesota businessman and civic leader, this event brought together tens of thousands of people at a football stadium to celebrate and be proud about recovery. These events foreshadowed efforts today by Recovery Community Organizations around the nation and Faces and Voices of Recovery to improve awareness of people in recovery and the fact that recovery is a reality for millions.

Sadly, this momentum was hindered by the crusade in the 1980s to attack people with drug addiction and a return to using jail instead of recovery as the answer to addiction.[6]

Earlier, beginning around 1950, the paths to recovery for persons with alcohol-use disorders broadened beyond Twelve Step recovery. This included the rise of a number of mutual-aid societies that broadened the peer support found in A.A. through groups such as Women for Sobriety, Secular Organization for Sobriety, and Moderation Management, to name a few.

In response to expanding funding through the Hughes Act of 1970, treatment organizations and facilities also expanded and became an industry. This increased attention to addiction recovery contributed to growing public support for addiction recovery.

Over time, however, several factors led to a return to public policies that reinforced shame and incarceration in response to people with substance-use problems. The third phase of the recovery movement directly addressed this backsliding in public education and policies, pointing to the reality that recovery is possible for thousands of people and the appropriate solution for people with alcohol and other drug-use problems.

Meanwhile, Twelve Step recovery continued to expand as more organizations formed. Following the founding of Al-Anon in 1953, Narcotics Anonymous was formed in Los Angeles and adopted the Twelve Steps. In 1957, two men with gambling problems started Gamblers Anonymous. In 1960, Rozanne S. brought together some neighbors, also in Los Angeles, to form Overeaters Anonymous.

Bill Wilson and the General Service Conference allowed these early adapters to use the Twelve Steps and Twelve Traditions to help people address a wide range of other substance (cocaine, opioids, prescription drugs, smoking, etc.) and process (overeating, shopping, work, sex, gambling, debting, etc.) addictions over the past seventy years.

This is a movement with many parts and without any formal connections. All programs that embrace the Twelve Steps and Twelve Traditions abide by a tradition of singleness of purpose—meaning one attends A.A. for alcohol addictions, Narcotics Anonymous for drug addictions,

Food Addicts or Overeaters Anonymous for food addictions, etc. Each honors the traditions begun by A.A., which include singleness of purpose, no affiliation with other groups, and no opinions on outside issues—i.e., issues outside the primary purpose of that Twelve Step Fellowship. (See Traditions Four, Five, and Ten in the Appendix).

Bill Wilson, in consultation with Dr. Bob, spent years being concerned about what would happen to A.A. when he and Dr. Bob were gone. This resulted in what he called A.A. Coming of Age, the adoption of a structure which gave full power and authority for governance of A.A. to members acting through their groups.[7]

Lois played several major roles in supporting and ensuring the growth and survival of the Twelve Step movement. First, she stayed involved in Al-Anon and ensured it was built on the successful lessons of A.A. She learned from Bill and A.A. experience and made appropriate changes as the first adapter of the Traditions and Concepts so they better fit with the families Al-Anon was serving.

Lois attended A.A. events from after Bill's death until shortly before her death to bring Bill's presence and values to gatherings of A.A. members. Lois symbolized—in her person and what she said—their shared vision of recovery for individuals and families.

Lois and Al-Anon broadened awareness of the impact of addictions. This growth continued in the 1970s with the integration into Al-Anon of attention to the specific needs of people who grew up in alcoholic families. This heightened focus on the multi-generational impact of alcoholism and other addictions led to the formation of Adult Children of Alcoholics and Dysfunctional Families (ACA) in 1978 in New York and the founding of Co-dependents Anonymous in 1986, two years before Lois' death.

Bill encouraged the application of the Twelve Steps to other challenges. In a 1956 letter to a man named Ollie in California who was struggling with depression, Bill shared his enthusiasm for the work of psychotherapist Karen Horney. He suggested that someday A.A. might extend its moral inventory to psychic damages, including shame, guilt, and anger. He wrote: "I suppose someday a Neurotics Anonymous will be formed and actually do all this." Neurotics Anonymous was founded in 1964 in Washington, DC, seven years before Bill died.[8]

Bill recognized that while A.A. needed to honor its tradition of anonymity, there was a public education and advocacy job to be done if alcoholism was ever to be seen as different than a moral failure. He traveled and spoke at conferences of doctors, psychiatrists, and other people involved with mental health and recovery. He became involved in the Yale Summer School for Alcohol Studies when it was founded in 1943. He and Lois both attended and spoke during the final week of the Summer School annually. The Wilsons' friendship and role in helping Marty Mann get sober resulted in their involvement in and encouragement of her work to found the NCEA, which was started in conjunction with the Yale Summer School.

NCEA's educational focus broadened as the prevalence of drug addiction grew, becoming the National Council on Alcoholism and Drug Dependence (NCADD).

The Wilsons influenced the international growth of A.A. and the Twelve Step movement by their travels to Europe (Bill and Lois) and to South Africa, Australia, and New Zealand (Lois after Bill's death) to visit A.A. and Al-Anon groups. Their thoughtfulness about the organizational structure needed to support an international movement was also key. Bill wrote a position paper for the Alcoholic Foundation Board in 1968 outlining options for how

A.A. might support the international movement. He made it clear that a centrally controlled organization based in New York would fail. Instead, he proposed a structure that encouraged and supported the formation of World Services offices in countries around the world and regular meetings of the entire A.A. World Services network.

The Wilsons supported the growth of the Twelve Step movement by speaking at congressional hearings and key moments aimed at raising awareness of the pain of addiction and the possibility of recovery.

Finally, and most importantly perhaps, the Wilsons advocated for alcoholism to be declared a disease or illness. After years of debate, in 1956, the American Medical Association determined that alcoholism was an illness. Lois and Al-Anon introduced the notion of a "family disease" to begin to call attention to the negative consequences on families of living with a person with addiction.

As A.A. grew, its principles were adopted and further refined by faith-based organizations, recovery treatment programs, and people from a wide range of cultures. Native Americans in North Dakota, for example, have combined Twelve Step programs with circles of accountability and peer support groups known as Knights.

Harvard and Stanford Universities collaborated on a library review by Cochrane (a United Kingdom-based non-profit organization considered the gold standard for medical research on the effectiveness of A.A. in comparison with other treatment programs). This 2020 report brought the weight of scientific evidence to declare that the effectiveness of a Twelve Step Facilitated Treatment approach is comparable to or better than other addiction treatment modalities.[9] This study highlights how the A.A. Twelve Step approach is effective as part of alcoholism treatment.

The education and advocacy of the Wilsons and their successors have resulted in growing government support and involvement in the practice and study of addiction recovery. *Facing Addiction in America: The Surgeon General's Report on Alcohol, Drugs and Health in 2016* is a great resource to understand addictions, recovery, and the evolving public health support for the recovery movement.

The New Recovery Advocacy Movement

The New Recovery Advocacy Movement was launched in 2001 at a meeting in St. Paul, Minnesota. This meeting was the result of years of work to expand advocacy, acceptance, and treatment options for persons impacted by addiction and their families and communities. From its earliest days, all recovery movements sought to overcome societal stigmas and perceptions that addiction is a personal failing. This milestone meeting offered a forum for two hundred recovery advocates from thirty-six states to advance three goals: "(1) acknowledge and celebrate the multiple pathways to long-term recovery, (2) foster advocacy skills in the tradition of other American advocacy movements, and (3) produce principles, language, strategy, and leadership to carry the movement forward."[10]

Embedded in those goals are decades of work on multiple fronts. Building on the education work of Marty Mann, the recovery field had experienced cycles of progress and setbacks over a fifty-year period. The 1960s and 1970s brought progress in government support for treating alcohol and drug addiction as health crises. This period was followed by the shift back to blaming the victim and criminalizing addictions in the Nixon and Reagan eras of the 1980s and early 1990s.

Attendees at this 2001 meeting included members of local affiliates of NCADD, the successor organization to Marty Mann's NCEA; leaders of the Johnson Institute who, in the 1990s, had shifted focus from addiction-related education to policy advocacy; leaders of an emerging network of local grassroots Recovery Community Organizations (RCOs); and other practitioners, funders, and advocates. These leaders came together with the hope of building on a growing momentum and support for a new and broadened approach to addiction recovery and the multiple ways recovery was now being achieved.

These discussions solidified several shifts in understanding about addiction and addiction treatment and built an organizational framework to further advance the policy and practice shifts. One shift was to put the widely held and previously advocated "disease concept" in a larger context by coupling it with the message that long-term recovery is possible and has happened for thousands. One leader of this movement states unequivocally that focusing only on the recently emerging paradigm of addiction as a brain disease increases the stigma and harm to individuals and families facing alcohol and drug problems unless always accompanied by "two companion communications: (1) with abstinence and proper care, addiction-induced brain impairments rapidly reverse themselves, and (2) millions of individuals have achieved complete long-term recovery from addiction and have gone on to experience healthy, meaningful, and productive lives."[11]

A physician from California recovering from alcohol addiction was well known for his reminder, when he talked about getting sober, that if the mind focuses on a problem, the problem gets bigger. If it focuses on the solution— recovery through the Twelve Steps—there is progress on finding the solution.[12]

The St. Paul conference built on the tradition Bill and Lois established: Listen to everyday people and look for practical solutions. The "Movement Goals" coming out of the 2001 meeting were to:

1. portray alcoholism and addictions as problems for which there are viable and varied recovery solutions,
2. provide living role models that illustrate the diversity of those recovery solutions,
3. counter public attempts to dehumanize those with AOD (Alcohol and other Drugs) problems,
4. enhance the variety, availability, and quality of local/regional treatment and recovery support organizations, and
5. remove environmental barriers to recovery by promoting laws and social policies that reduce AOD problems and support recovery for those afflicted with AOD problems.[13]

These goals illustrate the direction the New Recovery Advocacy Movement has taken over the past two decades. Coming into the St. Paul meeting, there was growing perspective that arguing over the right way to recover is folly. People with addictions vary widely in terms of the nature and extent of addiction. While the Twelve Step Fellowships demonstrated results for millions, other approaches that were faith-based or treatment-based or used prescribed medicines and counseling also showed results. This broadened perspective was called the "multiple pathways" to recovery approach.

A twenty-two-person advisory committee was formed to guide the work on the goals. This group became a new nonprofit called Faces and Voices of Recovery[14] (a.k.a. Faces and Voices). The mission of Faces and Voices is: "To de-stigmatize addiction and normalize recovery through advocacy, education and leadership."[15] The work of Faces and Voices includes education around how to eliminate stigma-reinforcing language and advance language and understanding that demonstrates recovery is possible, advocating around policies and organizing events to demonstrate and give voice to the many people living in long-term recovery.

Faces and Voices makes real the 2001 Movement Goal of providing living role models who demonstrate the effectiveness of diverse pathways to recovery. Through local and national "recovery events," Faces and Voices encourages recovering people who may have been guarded about anonymity to stand up and be seen as persons in recovery. Neighbors seeing neighbors in recovery advances stigma reduction and raises awareness that there are proven ways to deal with addictions for individuals and families.

An independent 2013 documentary film *The Anonymous People* tells the story of the 23.5 million Americans who are living in long-term recovery from alcohol or drug addiction. The film specifically advances the goals of the 2001 Summit and Faces and Voices by shifting the focus from addiction as the problem to recovery as the solution.

Another effort that has emerged from this conference is the sustained growth of local and regional recovery community organizations. Faces and Voices has supported the formation of the Alliance of Recovery Centered Organizations (ARCO). This growing alliance includes recovery community organizations, centers and advocacy organizations, family and faith-based recovery organizations, recovery high schools and collegiate recovery programs, and a range of other organized ways to advance recovery.

Summary

All these efforts build on the basic work of Bill and Lois Wilson and the early Twelve Step members and allies. They look to manifest the power of mutual aid to achieve recovery and to educate the public to move beyond the denial and blaming of the individual to creating community services and systems that offer both multiple ways to provide help for individuals and families and clear evidence that recovery is possible and does work.

The Wilsons didn't view themselves as the founders of the recovery movement. They were both far too humble. They saw themselves as symbols and placeholders for hope. From their hope and years of commitment (thirty-eight for Bill, fifty-three for Lois) to advancing addiction recovery in the world, there indeed is a recovery movement and a lot more hope at a time when the ravages of addiction on families and communities continue to grow.

More will be revealed as more people recover and the power of addiction recovery is applied more broadly to the needs of individuals and families. We hope to encourage those actively in recovery to participate in carrying forward this broader message that recovery is possible and real for millions. It is true both that the Twelve Step Fellowships are a proven way to achieve recovery and that there are indeed many different starting points on the recovery journey and therefore many different recovery paths.

In the authors' opinion, the Wilsons' work is ongoing and incomplete until the recovery movement's aspiration that recovery is available to all has been realized. Those who come after the Wilsons in A.A. and other Twelve Step programs state their commitment to helping others when they say in their Responsibility Pledge: "I am responsible. When anyone, anywhere, reaches out for help, I want the hand of A.A. always to be there. And for that: I am responsible."[16] Extending these hands in a collaborative way will continue to build such a recovery movement.

AN AFTERWORD

WHERE FROM HERE?

While much has happened to build a broad and impactful recovery movement, much remains to be done.

If Bill and Lois Wilson were still alive, they might be bringing leaders of the larger Twelve Step Fellowships together at Stepping Stones to explore the broader questions of addiction, families, and recovery. But there is no academic center or organizing home specifically committed to research and education about the intersections of the many forms of addiction and their treatment for individuals, families, and communities.

One of the biggest barriers to addressing the interrelatedness of addictions is the reluctance of a capitalist economy and its government and institutions to move out of denial about the broader face of addiction and its impact on millions of families around the world. We admit obesity is a national health crisis yet do little to change the systems that feed and perpetuate eating addictions. Work addiction and sex addiction still remain in the humorous denial phase. Deep inside, we know they exist, but we remain largely in denial about them.

As a result of this collective cultural denial about the broader impact of addictions, millions of individuals suffer from addictions and even more children and adults—their families and friends—suffer negative mental-health and life-shortening implications.

Denial, complexity, and the segregation of addictions limit further progress. We wonder, if there were more leaders like Lois and Bill Wilson alive today, what advances might be underway to break through societal denial of the complexity and interrelation of addictions and the response to our addictive culture.

There are signs of hope in the Alliance for Recovery Centered Organizations and related efforts to bring recovering people, community leaders, and healthcare practitioners together to broaden and deepen the attention and resources devoted to facing and overcoming addictions.

This hopeful development points us to the dual challenge of respecting the Twelve Step Programs' Traditions of singleness of purpose and staying focused on a single mission and addiction while bringing people together across the many addictions to advance support, resources, and recovery for families and individuals.

The Wilsons built a powerful foundation with the many pioneers of the Twelve Step movement. What's next to speed up recovery for individuals, families, and communities around the world? The strength of the structure and system they built contains in it the safeguards that keep A.A., Al-Anon, and other Twelve Step programs healthy and available to those who need them. The question of how to preserve this legacy and continue to advance opportunities for recovery for individuals and families is one of the major challenges ahead.

Bill and Lois Wilson in their later years. (Permission required for use.)

Lois and Bill Wilson enjoyed many moments in nature, grateful for sobriety. We are grateful for the breadth and impact of the movement they launched.

Acknowledgments

This book is the product of a lifetime of living and learning. The authors wish to thank some of those we know have contributed and those we don't know personally who have nevertheless helped shape our lives and the lives of Lois and Bill Wilson and all who have followed them in recovery from addictions and their tentacles.

First, we acknowledge our families, who gave us life, a curiosity for learning, and values to guide our living. Our parents, grandparents, children, grandchildren, and partners and spouses all contributed to this book and its possibility.

We have learned and benefited from the pioneering research and writing of Ernest Kurtz, Mel B., Arthur S., and current A.A. history lovers Jackie B., Drew H., Mily T., Lee M., and Jay S., among many others.

Thanks to the foresight of Lois Wilson and the creation of Stepping Stones Archive, we have had unprecedented access to digital copies of original letters, diaries, and other writings of Lois and Bill Wilson and other early leaders. We thank the leadership of Stepping Stones—Sally Corbett-Turco, executive director; Sharon Wolff, CA, archive and collection manager; and the Stepping Stones Board—for their support of our research and learning. Among the Stepping Stones Foundation sources was their play, *Bill and Lois Wilson: In Their Own Words*, which was compiled from Stepping Stones Archive by Laurie Heffner Lewis, whom we thank.

From the first work on this book, Claire Ricewasser has shared generously everything she knew and encouraged persistence in completing this book. Her passion for recovery and knowledge of the history of the family recovery movement stayed with us and guided us even after she retired. You are now officially retired!

Similarly, William (Bill) White has encouraged this book and been a much-appreciated guide as it developed, as has Mike Fitzpatrick, through his counsel and through the many talented presenters on Recovery Speakers' weekly History Talk.

A book about Bill Wilson and his marriage to Lois requires exploration of the vast resources also available at Alcoholics Anonymous General Services office. Michelle Mirza, A.A.'s archivist, and her staff have been generous, supportive, and great allies in our research and learning.

We extend our thanks to the members of our Writing Group: Elizabeth Bruce, Phil Kurata, and Michael Oliver. We are also grateful to those who read this manuscript, in full or part, and offered helpful comments: Gail LaCroix, David Boehlke, Claire Ricewasser, Sally Corbett-Turco, Sharon Wolff, Evangelyn Ramsey, Kevin Hanlon, Michael Fitzpatrick, Bill Stauffer, William Lammers, Karen Casey, Greg Williams, and Tom Hill.

We have benefitted from a talented team of Sara Camilli as our agent, Shirin McArthur as our editor, Sharon Miller as designer and layout guide, and Nan Badgett as indexer. Readers will quickly see the attention to detail required for this complex book. This team made that possible!

We are also grateful for all the people who have generously share their experience on this subject and/or as writers, including John Kelly, William Cope Moyers, Nicole J. Burton, Linda Pippin, Dawn Eden Goldstein, William Schaberg, Jeffrey Roth, Christine Timko, Brandon Bowen,

Jonathan Shank, Myra Peabody Gossens, Eileen Guiliani, Jack Stansbury, William Borchert, Kathleen Cook Hunter, James LeBlanc, Mark Sanders, Francis Hartigan, and Malve Burns. We are also grateful for all the people who have told us of their experiences with Lois and/or Bill.

We are both especially grateful to our friends and family members who served as cheerleaders: Jacquelin Grice, James Amps, Laura Sturza, Shelley Gillon, Debbie M. Jackson, Mary O'Herron, Harvest Williams, Vita Washington, Mary Raphel, and Tom's wife, Geraldine. We appreciate the gift of love and encouragement from so many.

LOIS AND BILL WILSON AND THEIR MARRIAGE: IMPORTANT DATES

1879 – August 8 – A.A. cofounder Dr. Robert Holbrook Smith ("Dr. Bob") born in St. Johnsbury, Vermont.

1881 – March 3 – Anne Ripley born, who became Annie Smith, wife of Dr. Bob Smith.

1888 – Lois' parents, Clark Burnham and Matilda Hoyt, married.

1891 – March 4 – Lois Burnham born in Brooklyn, New York, oldest of six children (Lois, Barbara, Rogers, Kitty, Lyman, and Matilda, who died at age one).

1894 – Bill's parents, Gilman ("Gilly") Wilson and Emily Griffith, married.

1895 – November 26 – Bill Wilson born in East Dorset, Vermont, oldest of two children (Bill and Dorothy).

1906 – Bill's parents Gilly and Emily divorced; Emily moves to Boston. Bill and Dorothy raised by his mother's parents, Gardner Fayette Griffith and Ella Griffith, in East Dorset, Vermont.

Early 1900s – Lois attends private schools in Brooklyn, including kindergarten at Pratt Institute, eight years at Friends School, and five at Packer Collegiate Institute. Bill attends one-room schools in East Dorset and Rutland,

Vermont until 1909, when his grandfather sends him to Burr & Burton Seminary, a private school in Vermont.

1912 – November 19 – Bill's girlfriend at Burr & Burton dies from routine surgery. Bill suffers from depression and moves temporarily to Boston to be with his mother, attends Arlington High School; returns to Burr & Burton in 1913.

1913 – Bill meets Lois while she is summering in Vermont with her family.

1914–1915 – Lois and Bill begin to fall in love and become secretly engaged.

1915 – Dr. Bob Smith and Annie Ripley married. Bill enters Norwich University military school.

1917 – US enters World War I. Bill completes Officer Training School and becomes a Second Lieutenant in 66th Coast Artillery Corps of US Army. Bill begins drinking at social events with officers, socialites, and others before going to war.

1918 – January 24, Lois Burnham and Bill Wilson married at the Church of the New Jerusalem, a Swedenborgian Church in Brooklyn Heights, with reception at the Burnham home, 182 Clinton Street.

1918 – Dr. Bob and Annie Smith's biological son Robert Jr. (Smitty) born and their adopted daughter Suzanne Smith Windows born.

1918 – August – Bill departs for England and France (World War I). Lois unsuccessfully seeks job via YMCA in US to go overseas to be closer to Bill, writes daily to Bill, including while working stateside for the War Department with returning military at Walter Reed Hospital. Bill continues to drink while at war.

1919 – Bill returns home, struggles to adjust to civilian life and finding work.

1921 – Lois employed at Brooklyn Naval Hospital and Bellevue Hospital until 1922. Bill's drinking continues.

1921 – Lois' sister's husband helps Bill get job at USF&G. Bill begins studying at Brooklyn Law School; drinking continues.

1921–1924 – Lois experiences three miscarriages, learns she cannot have children. Frank Buchman starts the Oxford Group to encourage following the example of early Christians.

1923 – Lois encourages weekend hiking trips to the country to enjoy nature and remove Bill from opportunities to drink.

1923 – Dr. Bob and Annie Smith adopt Suzanne Smith.

1925–1926 – Bill and Lois sell everything to take a motorcycle trip (known as the motorcycle hobo experiment).

1925–1929 – Bill earns the trust of Frank Shaw, husband of Lois' friend Elise Valentine Shaw, and a position at a Wall Street company as a stock investigator. His financial success and drinking increase. Bill buys Lois a baby grand piano and expands apartment.

1929 – Wall Street/stock market crashes. Lois and Bill go to Montreal, where Bill finds temporary work

1930 – Wilsons return to New York and move in with Lois' parents at her childhood home. Lois' mother is ill, and Lois helps with her care.

1930 – December 24 – Lois' mother dies. Bill gets drunk and misses funeral.

1931–1933 – Bill's drinking worsens. He seeks treatment twice at Towns Hospital and returns to drinking; Lois works at Macy's Department Store. Annie Smith and her friend Henrietta Seiberling begin attending Oxford Group meetings in Akron.

1934 – Visit from Bill's childhood friend Ebby Thacher introduces Bill to Oxford Group.

1934 – December 11–- Bill takes his last drink, returns to Towns Hospital, and has spiritual experience which gets him sober.

1935 – Lois and Bill seek to help other alcoholics, open their home to men with drinking problems, attend Oxford Group. Lois works at another department store and supports Bill and guests.

1935 – May – Bill goes to Akron for business venture which ultimately fails, seeks out someone to help, and is introduced by Henrietta Seiberling to Dr. Bob Smith, who has a drinking problem. Bill and Dr. Bob meet at her residence at the Gate Lodge on the Seiberling estate on Mother's Day.

1935 – June 10 – Dr. Bob takes his last drink and A.A. is born. Bill remains in Akron until August.

1935 – June – Lois goes to Akron to be with Bill and meets Bob and Annie Smith.

1935–1939 – Wilsons and Smiths attend Oxford Group meetings and work with other people with drinking problems and their families. Lois curses and throws her shoe at Bill because of jealousy over his newfound Oxford

Group friends. Family meetings take place in New York/ New Jersey, Akron, and Cleveland. New York group breaks from Oxford Group.

1938 – Alcoholic Foundation formed.

1939 – Lois and Bill lose her childhood home at 182 Clinton Street to foreclosure. Lois and Bill are homeless and stay in fifty or more places with friends and at 24th Street Club House over two-year period.

1939 – Big Book of *Alcoholics Anonymous* is published, which includes the Twelve Steps first drafted by Bill with support from Dr. Bob, Hank Parkhurst, and others. Lois rejected by Bill in her desire to write the chapter To Wives.

1941 – March 1 – *Saturday Evening Post* article by Jack Alexander about A.A. published, leads to increased sales of the book and initial growth spurt for A.A. Lois takes lead in organizing responses to hundreds of letters.

1940–1950 – Growing pains for Wilsons and Smiths and A.A. Lois and Annie are all-in with Bill and Bob's A.A. work. Bill calls this the "flying blind" period. Lois and Bill travel and see growth and problems facing groups. Bill begins work on Twelve Traditions. Annie Smith in Akron and Lois in New York continue meeting with wives of A.A. members.

1941 – Spring – Lois and Bill receive help to buy their first home after 23 years of marriage and move to Town of Bedford, New York. House is initially called Bil-Lo's Break and later renamed Stepping Stones.

1943 – Akron group breaks from Oxford Group. Lois and Bill take their first cross-country trip to visit A.A. groups.

1945–1955 – Bill has recurrence of depression and is unable to work for some periods. Dr. Bob diagnosed with cancer (1948).

1949 – June 1 – Annie Smith dies.

1950 – First A.A. International Convention held in Cleveland, Ohio: Twelve Traditions approved, agreement to experiment with what becomes the General Service conference and governing body for A.A. Dr. Bob gives farewell talk. Bill returns from US and Canada travels and encourages Lois to unify the family groups by forming a Clearing House.

1950 – November 16 – Dr. Bob Smith dies.

1951 – April 20–22 – First experimental A.A. General Service Conference held. Lois and Anne Bingham (Lois' neighbor) bring together wives of A.A. General Service Conference Delegates involved in family groups and local family group members to discuss forming a Clearing House for the Family Groups. Lois and Anne Bingham poll by mail 87 known family groups nationally and by May the majority agree to starting the Clearing House, adopting the A.A. Twelve Steps and the Al-Anon name.

1955 – A.A. International Convention held in St. Louis, Missouri. A.A. is handed off from the founders' leadership to the fellowship through its General Service Conference.

1955–1970 – Lois and Bill continue to support growth of A.A. and Al-Anon while expanding travel and other interests.

1957 – Alateen for teenagers becomes part of the Al-Anon Family Group Headquarters. First Alateen group starts in

California (1956) and grows quickly to 45 communities by 1958.

1970 – July – Bill makes final appearance at A.A. International Conference in Miami, Florida, having been transported from the hospital where he was being treated for emphysema by his doctor and an A.A. friend.

1971 – January 24 – Bill Wilson dies at Miami Heart Institute at the age of 76 after long illness. *The New York Times* reports his death on front page and many memorial services held around the world in February.

1972 – Lois visits newly formed A.A. groups around the world with a several-month-long visit to A.A. and Al-Anon groups in Africa, China, Japan, Australia, and New Zealand, among other countries.

1973 – Lois finishes writing *Diary of Two Motorcycle Hobos*, published by Al-Anon and Alcoholics Anonymous.

1979 – Lois completes her memoir, *Lois Remembers*, published by Al-Anon Family Services.

1979 – The Stepping Stones Foundation incorporated as a nonprofit tax-exempt organization with Lois Wilson as president to "foster public understanding of alcoholism and inspire recovery by preserving and sharing the historic home, archives and legacy of Bill and Lois Wilson."

1970–1988 – Lois continues to live at Stepping Stones, participates in the development of Al-Anon's service structure through selected committees in her capacity as an Honorary Lifetime Trustee of Al-Anon Family Group Headquarters. She participates in Al-Anon meetings, attends A.A. meetings as Bill's surrogate, and enjoys travel and friends as she ages. She remains mentally alert and engaged until her death.

1984 – Lois convenes leading professionals at Stepping Stones to discuss public outreach and education about alcoholism as a disease.

1988 – October 5 – Lois dies at a hospital near Bedford Hills, New York at age of 97. Her death is reported in obituary section of *The New York Times* and memorial services are held at Stepping Stones, Marble Collegiate Church in New York, and around the world.

Some Important Dates in the Evolution of the Addiction Recovery Movement

Note: This is intended to introduce the topic and not as an exhaustive or full history. *Slaying the Dragon* by William White and the William White Papers (https://www.chestnut.org/william-white-papers/) provide a comprehensive history of addiction treatment and recovery in America and were important sources for this timeline.

Late 1700s – Native American named Wyoming Woman leads recovery mutual aid circle in 1750s. Other Native experiments.

1784 – Dr. Benjamin Rush describes excessive drinking as "odious disease."

Late 1840s – Washingtonians organize first society of recovered alcoholics, which goes out of existence after brief period of growth.

1935 – Alcoholics Anonymous co-founded by Bill Wilson and Dr. Bob Smith.

1940s – Dr. E. M. Jellinek starts the Yale School of Alcohol Studies. Marty Mann involved with the Yale University program and is funded by Yale University to start the National Committee for Education on Alcoholism (NCEA) in 1944.

1945 – First A.A. groups for African Americans organized in St. Louis, Chicago (Evans Avenue Group), and Washington, DC (Cosmopolitan Group).

1946 – First translation of A.A. Big Book into Spanish by Cleveland A.A., second Spanish translation in 1950 for use in US, Puerto Rico, Mexico, and Caribbean.

1951 – Al-Anon co-founded by Lois Wilson and Anne Bingham.

1952 – American Medical Association (AMA) defined alcoholism and, in 1956, declared that the alcoholic should be viewed as a sick person.

1953–present – Founding of other Twelve Step organizations for individuals and families: Narcotics Anonymous (1953), Gamblers Anonymous (1957), Overeaters Anonymous (1960), NARANON (1971), Sex and Love Addicts Anonymous (1976), Workaholics Anonymous (1983), Codependents Anonymous (1986), among many others.

1969 – Bill Wilson (as Bill W., without face showing on camera), Marty Mann, and Mercedes McCambridge testify before Senate Subcommittee on Alcohol and Narcotics (Hughes Committee), which led to legislation signed in 1970 by President Nixon and funding of the National Institute of Alcohol Abuse and Alcoholism (NIAAA).

1970 – Gay activists in recovery begin to challenge A.A., petitioning A.A. for the right to establish "special interests" gay A.A. groups. This built on members of the LGBTQ community joining A.A. without "coming out," beginning with Marty Mann and gay people she introduced to A.A. in 1940s and 1950s.

1970s–1990s – Broadening of types of addiction recovery mutual aid groups to include religious recovery mutual-aid societies like Alcoholics for Christ (1976), Jewish Alcoholics, Chemically Dependent People and Significant Others (1979), Millati Islami (1989), Celebrate Recovery (1990), and the Buddhist Recovery Network (2008). The same period also saw the growth of secular recovery mutual-aid societies which included Women for Sobriety (1975), Secular Organization for Sobriety (1985), Rational Recovery (1986), SMART Recovery (1994), and Moderation Management (1994).

1980s–1990s – Growth of the crack cocaine epidemic in US, resulting in a "get tough on crime" campaign that increased the stigma attached to drug and other addictions and resulted in record numbers of Black and Brown people being incarcerated.

1996 – Purdue Pharma puts OxyContin on the market and, through promotional efforts, the sales of OxyContin escalate from $44 million (316,000 prescriptions dispensed) in 1996 to combined sales of nearly $3 billion (over 14 million prescriptions) in 2001 and 2002. A second opioid crisis begins in 2000s.

1997 – Dr. Alan Leshner, in his role as director of National Institute on Drug Abuse, publishes *Addiction Is a Brain Disease, and It Matters*. His idea of the "hijacked brain" reaches broad audiences through a PBS special, *Moyers on Addiction: Close to Home* (1998), and later by a *Time* magazine cover story, "How We Get Addicted," in 2007.

2001 – Founding meeting of the New Recovery Advocacy Movement in St. Paul, Minnesota. Its aim includes developing resources focused on recovery, building recovery community, and celebrating recovery as a transformative process, while furthering research to understand the positive impact of recovery to more effectively spread recovery in diverse communities across America.

2001 – Faces & Voices of Recovery organized to support action on the goals adopted at the St. Paul Summit.

2012 – Faces & Voices organizes the Association of Recovery Community Organizations (now the Alliance for Recovery Centered Organizations).

2013 – *The Anonymous People* documentary released to demonstrate the reality of many people being in long-term recovery from addictions.

2016 – President Obama signs the Comprehensive Addiction and Recovery Act of 2016, which expands treatment for persons with alcohol and drug addictions.

2017 – Mobilize Recovery organized with a mission of "raising up the voices of people whose lives are affected by addiction."

2018 – Congress passes the Opioid Crisis Response Act of 2018 to address the number of people dying from opioid addiction and provide increased funding for opioid treatment and innovations in treatment and recovery.

2019 – Latino Recovery Advocacy (LARA) founded "to build culturally appropriate addiction recovery services and language accessibility for the Hispanic and Latino speaking population" and to advance "a world where no one suffers from language disparities in addiction recovery services."

2020 – Faces & Voices amends its mission "to de-stigmatize addiction and normalize recovery through advocacy, education, and leadership" and "commits to use of a race equity lens in all its work and a focus on diverse voices at all levels."

2022 – Faces & Voices agrees to manage International Recovery Day, begun in 2018 by recovery activist John Winslow, and continues efforts through the National Recovery Institute and public policy to focus on raising voices and aiding efforts to combat stigma and promote the power and proof of long-term recovery.

Recovery Resources

Twelve Step Fellowships

There are many Twelve Step organizations, some with similar purposes. The following are a few of the better-known programs. A web search will help you find other resources. Each group is autonomous, so meetings all follow the Twelve Steps and Twelve Traditions and do vary as to topic and type of meeting and culture. Potential new members are encouraged to attend different groups and look for meetings and a sponsor that are helpful to you. The links are to the national or worldwide service organization. In many cases, there are state, county, or city websites with local information.

For persons with substance or process addictions

Alcoholics Anonymous: https://www.aa.org/
212-870-3400

All Addicts Anonymous https://alladdictsanonymous.org/

Debtors Anonymous: https://debtorsanonymous.org/
781-453-2743

Emotions Anonymous: https://emotionsanonymous.org/
651-647-9712

Gamblers Anonymous: https://www.gamblersanonymous.org/ga/ 909-931-9056

International Conference of Young People in Alcoholics Anonymous: https://www.icypaa.org/

International Women's Conference: https://internationalwomensconference.org/

Narcotics Anonymous: https://www.narcotics. com/ 800-683-0146

Nicotine Anonymous: https://www.nicotine-anonymous. org/ 877-879-6422

Overeaters Anonymous: https://oa.org/ 505-891-2664

Secular Alcoholics Anonymous: https://www.aasecular. org/ secularAA@gmail.com

Secular Narcotics Anonymous: https://secularna.org/

Sex and Love Addicts Anonymous: https://slaafws.org/ 210-828-7900

Under Earners Anonymous: https://www. underearnersanonymous.org/

Workaholics Anonymous: https://workaholics-anonymous.org/ 515-415-8468

For family members and friends of persons with substance or process addictions

Adult Children of Alcoholics and Dysfunctional Families: https://adultchildren.org/ 310-534-1815

Al-Anon Family Groups: https://al-anon.org/ 757-563-1600

Alateen:
https://al-anon.org/newcomers/teen-corner-alateen/
757-563-1600

Families Anonymous: https://familiesanonymous.org/
US: 800-736-9805 INT: 847-294-5877

Gam-Anon: https://www.gam-anon.org/   718-352-1671

Nar-Anon: https://www.nar-anon.org/ 310-534-8188;
800-477-6291

S-Anon: https://sanon.org/ 615-833-3152

Historic Landmark Homes and Archives of A.A. and the A.A. Cofounders

A.A. General Service Office Archives: https://www.
aa.org/gso-archives

Dr. Bob's Home, Akron, Ohio: https://www.drbobshome.
org/

Stepping Stones – Historic Home of Bill & Lois Wilson®
(The Stepping Stones Foundation®), 62 Oak Rd.,
Katonah, NY 10536: https://www.steppingstones.org/
914-232-4822

Wilson House (Birthplace of Bill Wilson), East Dorset,
Vermont: https://wilsonhouse.org/

Other Recovery Organizations

There are multiple pathways to recovery. Here are some
examples. Scientific studies show the varying success
rates of different approaches. No endorsement is
intended for any of the programs listed.

Faith-based: Celebrate Recovery: https://celebraterecovery.com/about/

Secular: SMART Recovery: https://smartrecovery.org/ 440-951-5357

SMART Recovery Family and Friends: https://smartrecovery.org/family 440-951-5357

Women: Women for Sobriety: https://womenforsobriety.org/about/ 215-536-8026

Young People in Recovery: https://youngpeopleinrecovery.org/

Recovery Education, Advocacy, and Community Organizations

Alliance for Recovery Centered Organizations (Local Recovery Community Organizations): https://facesandvoicesofrecovery.org/programs/arco/

Center for African American Recovery Development: https://www.thecaard.org/

Faces & Voices of Recovery: https://facesandvoicesofrecovery.org/ 202-737-0690

International Doctors in Alcoholics Anonymous (IDAA): https://www.idaa.org/

Latino Recovery Advocacy: https://lararecovery.org/ 561-727-7588

Mobilize Recovery: https://www.mobilizerecovery.org/

National Alliance on Mental Illness (NAMI) Family-to-family: https://www.nami.org/f2f

National Alliance on Mental Illness (NAMI) Ending the Silence (for teens): https://www.nami.org/ets 800-950-6264

National Association for Children of Addiction (NACoA): https://www.nacoa.org, 888-554-2627

Online Museum of African American Addictions, Treatment and Recovery: https://www. museumofafricanamericanaddictionsrecovery.org/

Recovery Research Institute: https://www. recoveryanswers.org/

Recovery Speakers: https://www.recoveryspeakers.com/

Shatterproof: https://www.shatterproof.org/ 800-597-2557

White Bison and Wellbriety Movement: https:// whitebison.org/ 877-871-1495

APPENDIX

THE TWELVE STEPS, THE TWELVE TRADITIONS, AND THE TWELVE CONCEPTS

Note: What follows are the A.A. and Al-Anon Steps, Traditions, and Concepts. Al-Anon studied and adapted from the A.A. language. Differences in the Al-Anon language are underlined.

The Twelve Steps of Alcoholics Anonymous

(See https://www.aa.org/the-twelve-steps for more information. Reprinted with permission.)

1. We admitted we were powerless over alcohol—that our lives had become unmanageable.
2. Came to believe that a Power greater than ourselves could restore us to sanity.
3. Made a decision to turn our will and our lives over to the care of God *as we understood Him.*
4. Made a searching and fearless moral inventory of ourselves.

5. Admitted to God, to ourselves, and to another human being the exact nature of our wrongs.

6. Were entirely ready to have God remove all these defects of character.

7. Humbly asked Him to remove our shortcomings.

8. Made a list of all persons we had harmed, and became willing to make amends to them all.

9. Made direct amends to such people wherever possible, except when to do so would injure them or others.

10. Continued to take personal inventory and when we were wrong promptly admitted it.

11. Sought through prayer and meditation to improve our conscious contact with God, *as we understood Him*, praying only for knowledge of His will for us and the power to carry that out.

12. Having had a spiritual awakening as the result of these Steps, we tried to carry this message to alcoholics, and to practice these principles in all our affairs.

The Twelve Steps of Al-Anon

These Twelve Steps, adapted nearly word-for-word from the Twelve Steps of Alcoholics Anonymous, have been a tool for spiritual growth for millions of Al Anon/Alateen members. At meetings, Al Anon/Alateen members share with each other the personal lessons they have learned from practicing these Steps.

1. We admitted we were powerless over alcohol—that our lives had become unmanageable.
2. Came to believe that a Power greater than ourselves could restore us to sanity.
3. Made a decision to turn our will and our lives over to the care of God *as we understood Him.*
4. Made a searching and fearless moral inventory of ourselves.
5. Admitted to God, to ourselves, and to another human being the exact nature of our wrongs.
6. Were entirely ready to have God remove all these defects of character.
7. Humbly asked Him to remove our shortcomings.
8. Made a list of all persons we had harmed, and became willing to make amends to them all.
9. Made direct amends to such people wherever possible, except when to do so would injure them or others.
10. Continued to take personal inventory and when we were wrong promptly admitted it.
11. Sought through prayer and meditation to improve our conscious contact with God *as we understood Him*, praying only for knowledge of His will for us and the power to carry that out.

12. Having had a spiritual awakening as the result of these steps, we tried to carry this message to <u>others</u>, and to practice these principles in all our affairs.

© *Al-Anon's Twelve Steps, copyright 1996 by Al-Anon Family Group Headquarters, Inc. Reprinted with permission of Al-Anon Family Group Headquarters, Inc.*

The Twelve Traditions of Alcoholics Anonymous (Short Form)
(Visit https://www.aa.org/the-twelve-traditions for the long form and more information. Reprinted with permission.)

1. Our common welfare should come first; personal recovery depends upon A.A. unity.
2. For our group purpose there is but one ultimate authority—a loving God as He may express Himself in our group conscience. Our leaders are but trusted servants; they do not govern.
3. The only requirement for A.A. membership is a desire to stop drinking.
4. Each group should be autonomous except in matters affecting other groups or A.A. as a whole.
5. Each group has but one primary purpose—to carry its message to the alcoholic who still suffers.

6. An A.A. group ought never endorse, finance, or lend the A.A. name to any related facility or outside enterprise, lest problems of money, property, and prestige divert us from our primary purpose.
7. Every A.A. group ought to be fully self-supporting, declining outside contributions.
8. Alcoholics Anonymous should remain forever non-professional, but our service centers may employ special workers.
9. A.A., as such, ought never be organized; but we may create service boards or committees directly responsible to those they serve.
10. Alcoholics Anonymous has no opinion on outside issues; hence the A.A. name ought never be drawn into public controversy.
11. Our public relations policy is based on attraction rather than promotion; we need always maintain personal anonymity at the level of press, radio, and films.
12. Anonymity is the spiritual foundation of all our traditions, ever reminding us to place principles before personalities.

The Twelve Traditions of Al-Anon Family Groups

The Traditions summarize the Al-Anon principles that have proven to help Al-Anon groups function effectively.

1. Our common welfare should come first; <u>personal progress for the greatest number depends upon unity</u>.

2. For our group purpose there is but one authority—a loving God as He may express Himself in our group conscience. Our leaders are but trusted servants— they do not govern.

3. <u>The relatives of alcoholics, when gathered together for mutual aid, may call themselves an Al-Anon Family Group, provided that, as a group, they have no other affiliation. The only requirement for membership is that there be a problem of alcoholism in a relative or friend.</u>

4. Each group should be autonomous, except in matters affecting another group or Al-Anon or <u>AA</u> as a whole.

5. Each Al-Anon Family Group has but one purpose: <u>to help families of alcoholics. We do this by practicing the Twelve Steps of AA ourselves, by encouraging and understanding our alcoholic relatives, and by welcoming and giving comfort to families of alcoholics.</u>

6. Our Family Groups ought never endorse, finance or lend our name to any outside enterprise, lest problems of money, property and prestige divert us from our primary <u>spiritual aim. Although a separate entity, we should always co-operate with Alcoholics Anonymous</u>.

7. Every group ought to be fully self-supporting, declining outside contributions.

8. <u>Al-Anon Twelfth Step</u> work should remain forever non-professional, but our service centers may employ special workers.
9. Our groups, as such, ought never be organized; but we may create service boards or committees directly responsible to those they serve.
10. <u>The Al-Anon Family Groups</u> have no opinion on outside issues; hence our name ought never be drawn into public controversy.
11. Our public relations policy is based on attraction rather than promotion; we need always maintain personal anonymity at the level of press, radio, films, <u>and TV. We need guard with special care the anonymity of all AA members</u>.
12. Anonymity is the spiritual foundation of all our Traditions, ever reminding us to place principles above personalities.

The Twelve Concepts of Alcoholics Anonymous (Short Form)

I. Final responsibility and ultimate authority for A.A. world services should always reside in the collective conscience of our whole Fellowship.

II. The General Service Conference of A.A. has become, for nearly every practical purpose, the active voice and the effective conscience of our whole society in its world affairs.

III. To insure effective leadership, we should endow each element of A.A.—the Conference, the General Service Board and its service corporations, staffs, committees, and executives—with a traditional "Right of Decision."

IV. At all responsible levels, we ought to maintain a traditional "Right of Participation," allowing a voting representation in reasonable proportion to the responsibility that each must discharge.

V. Throughout our structure, a traditional "Right of Appeal" ought to prevail, so that minority opinion will be heard and personal grievances receive careful consideration.

VI. The Conference recognizes that the chief initiative and active responsibility in most world service matters should be exercised by the trustee members of the Conference acting as the General Service Board.

VII. The Charter and Bylaws of the General Service Board are legal instruments, empowering the trustees to manage and conduct world service affairs. The Conference

Charter is not a legal document; it relies upon tradition and the A.A. purse for final effectiveness.

VIII. The trustees are the principal planners and administrators of over-all policy and finance. They have custodial oversight of the separately incorporated and constantly active services, exercising this through their ability to elect all the directors of these entities.

IX. Good service leadership at all levels is indispensable for our future functioning and safety. Primary world service leadership, once exercised by the founders, must necessarily be assumed by the trustees.

X. Every service responsibility should be matched by an equal service authority, with the scope of such authority well defined.

XI. The trustees should always have the best possible committees, corporate service directors, executives, staffs, and consultants. Composition, qualifications, induction procedures, and rights and duties will always be matters of serious concern.

XII. The Conference shall observe the spirit of A.A. tradition, taking care that it never becomes the seat of perilous wealth or power; that sufficient operating funds and reserve be its prudent financial principle; that it place none of its members in a position of unqualified authority over others; that it reach all important decisions by discussion, vote, and whenever possible, substantial unanimity; that its actions never be personally punitive nor an incitement to public controversy; that it never perform acts of government; that, like the Society it serves, it will always remain democratic in thought and action.

The Twelve Concepts of Al-Anon

The Twelve Concepts of Service summarize the Al-Anon principles that have proven to help Al-Anon's service organizations function effectively together.

1. The ultimate responsibility and authority for Al-Anon world services belongs to the Al-Anon groups.
2. The Al-Anon Family Groups have delegated complete administrative and operational authority to their Conference and its service arms.
3. The right of decision makes effective leadership possible.
4. Participation is the key to harmony.
5. The rights of appeal and petition protect minorities and insure that they be heard.
6. The Conference acknowledges the primary administrative responsibility of the Trustees.
7. The Trustees have legal rights while the rights of the Conference are traditional.
8. The Board of Trustees delegates full authority for routine management of Al-Anon Headquarters to its executive committees.

9. Good personal leadership at all service levels is a necessity. In the field of world service the Board of Trustees assumes the primary leadership.
10. Service responsibility is balanced by carefully defined service authority and double-headed management is avoided.
11. The World Service Office is composed of selected committees, executives and staff members.
12. The spiritual foundation for Al-Anon's world services is contained in the General Warranties of the Conference, Article 12 of the Charter.

© *Al-Anon's Twelve Concepts of Service, copyright 1996 by Al-Anon Family Group Headquarters, Inc. Reprinted with permission of Al-Anon Family Group Headquarters, Inc.*

General Warranties of the Conference

In all proceedings the World Service Conference of Al-Anon shall observe the spirit of the Traditions:
1. that only sufficient operating funds, including an ample reserve, be its prudent financial principle;
2. that no Conference member shall be placed in unqualified authority over other members;
3. that all decisions be reached by discussion, vote and whenever possible by unanimity;

4. that no Conference action ever be personally punitive or an incitement to public controversy;

5. that though the Conference serves Al-Anon it shall never perform any act of government; and that like the fellowship of Al-Anon Family Groups which it serves, it shall always remain democratic in thought and action.

NOTES

Cover image by Art D. (Colorized detail), 1953: Courtesy Stepping Stones Foundation, Katonah, NY, WR-101-- 35_Y-3_001. Reproduced by permission from Stepping Stones Archive, Stepping Stones Foundation®. (Stepping Stones – Historic Home of Bill & Lois Wilson®, 62 Oak Rd., Katonah, NY 10536, archive@steppingstones.org, steppingstones.org, 914-232-4822. Hereafter referred to as SSF. (Permission required for use.)

Unless otherwise noted, all photos are the property of the Stepping Stones Foundation and not available for reproduction without permission. To inquire about the use of image(s), contact Stepping Stones, archive@stepping-stones.org.

Abbreviations Key

GSO - The Archives at the General Service Offices of Alcoholics Anonymous, 475 Riverside Drive, 11th Floor, New York, NY, 10115, 212.870.3400.

SSF – Stepping Stones Archive, Stepping Stones Foundation (Stepping Stones – Historic Home of Bill and Lois Wilson) 62 Oak Road, Katonah, NY, 10536, archive@steppingstones.org, steppingstones.org, 914.232.4822.

Foreword by William B. Stauffer

1. National Institute on Alcohol Abuse and Alcoholism, "Alcohol-Related Emergencies and Deaths in the United States," 2024, https://www.niaaa.nih.gov/alcohols-effects-health/

alcohol-topics/alcohol-facts-and-statistics/alcohol-related-emergencies-and-deaths-united-states#:~:text=The%20Alcohol%2DRelated%20Disease%20Impact.

2. Jim Zarroli, "'Deaths of Despair' Examines the Steady Erosion of US Working-Class Life," March 18, 2020, https://www.npr.org/2020/03/18/817687042/deaths-of-despair-examines-the-steady-erosion-of-u-s-working-class-life.

Preface

1. For more on the stigma and language related to people with addictions, see "Addictionary" (https://www.recoveryanswers.org/addiction-ary/) and "Overview" (https://www.recoveryanswers.org/recovery-101/) from Recovery Research Institute and "Language Matters: It Is Time We Change How We Talk About Addiction and Its Treatment," *Faces and Voices of Recovery*, https://facesandvoicesofrecovery.org/resource/language-matters-it-is-time-we-change-how-we-talk-about-addiction-and-its-treatment/.

2. Bill Wilson introduced the idea of anonymity in the Foreword to the first edition of A.A.'s basic text, *Alcoholics Anonymous* (referred to hereafter as the Big Book, as it is known in the A.A. community), written in 1939. He explained: "It is important that we remain anonymous because we are too few, at present to handle the overwhelming number of personal appeals which may result from this publication" (4th edition, xiii). Later, in the 1950s, in writing the Twelve Traditions of A.A., he suggested anonymity was an important spiritual principle that fostered humility. The Twelfth Tradition states: "Anonymity is the spiritual foundation of all our Traditions, ever reminding us to place principles before personalities." For more information on anonymity, see Alcoholics Anonymous, *Twelve Steps and Twelve Traditions* (Alcoholics Anonymous World Services, 1952).

Chapter 1

1. Lois B. Wilson, *Lois Remembers* (Al-Anon Family Group Headquarters, 1979), 3. Referenced as "memoir" in this book.

2. *Vignettes of the Past*, written by Lois Wilson, date not available, LBW_203_Bx-035_F-0015_Item-001_Pg_024. Stepping Stones Archive, Stepping Stones Foundation®. (Stepping Stones – Historic Home of Bill & Lois Wilson®, 62 Oak Rd., Katonah, NY 10536, archive@steppingstones. org, https://steppingstones.org, 914-232-4822. Hereafter referred to as SSF.

3. Vicky L. Dixon, "The Story of Swedenborg and the Swedenborgian Church" (Central Office, General Convention of the New Jerusalem, 1977) as found at Stepping Stones Archive, Lois Wilson Papers, LBW_201-9_Bx-011_F-0004_Item-003_Pg 9.

4. "Swedenborg and Life Recap: Spiritual Marriage 2/8/16," *Swedenborgian Foundation*, https://swedenborg.com/ spiritual-marriage.

5. Wilson, *Lois Remembers*, 12.

Chapter 2

1. Bill Wilson, *Bill W.: My First 40 Years* (Hazelden, 2000), 29.

2. Alcoholics Anonymous, *'Pass It On': The Story of Bill Wilson and How the A.A. Message Reached the World* (Alcoholics Anonymous World Services, 1984), 36.

3. Wilson, *Bill W.: My First 40 Years*, 29–30.

4. For more details, see *The Laundry List: 14 Traits of an Adult Child* (Adult Children of Alcoholics/Dysfunctional Families, 2006) x, 10–18. For more information on the Twelve Step organization Adult Children of Alcoholics and Dysfunctional Families, visit https://adultchildren.org.

5. Bill was reluctant to publish an autobiography, but concluded others would tell his story and decided to tell it himself. He personally dictated his autobiography, *Bill W.: My First 40 Years*, beginning in 1954. This book was given to Robert Thomsen, who wrote Bill's official biography, *Bill W.: The Absorbing and Deeply Moving Life Story of Bill Wilson, Co-Founder of Alcoholics Anonymous*, with Lois' assistance. It was published in 1975.

6. Wilson, *Bill W.: My First 40 Years*, 5.

7. Susan Cheever, *My Name Is Bill: Bill Wilson—His Life and the Creation of Alcoholics Anonymous* (Simon & Schuster, 2004), 18.
8. See Wilson, *Bill W.: My First 40 Years*, 12–13 and Robert Thomsen, *Bill W.: The Absorbing and Deeply Moving Life Story of Bill Wilson, Co-Founder of Alcoholics Anonymous* (Harper & Row, 1975), 8–11.
9. Thomsen, *Bill W.*, 8.
10. Cheever, *My Name Is Bill*, 16.
11. Wilson, *Bill W.: My First 40 Years*, 3–24.
12. Wilson, *Bill W.: My First 40 Years*, 18.
13. Alcoholics Anonymous, *'Pass It On,'* 30.
14. Wilson, *Bill W.: My First 40 Years*, 19.
15. Burr & Burton is still in operation. It was called Burr & Burton Seminary when Bill attended, though it was not a school for theological training or ministry preparation, as the term is used today. Today's students can now choose from 170 courses, and those who don't bring their lunch in a pail can dine in the school cafeteria on locally sourced food.
16. Thomsen, *Bill W.*, 56.
17. Cheever, *My Name Is Bill*, 61–62.

Chapter 3

1. Wilson, *Bill W.: My First 40 Years*, 35.
2. © Stepping Stones Foundation play *Bill and Lois Wilson: In Their Own Words*, compiled by Laurie Hefner Lewis.
3. Wilson, *Lois Remembers*, 16.
4. This diary is preserved by the Stepping Stones Foundation along with letters between Lois and Bill and other writings. The mission of the Stepping Stones Foundation, as stated on its website, is "to foster public understanding of alcoholism and inspire recovery by preserving and sharing the historical home, archives, and legacies of Bill and Lois Wilson, cofounders, respectively, of Alcoholics Anonymous and Al-Anon Family Groups." See https://www.steppingstones. org/about/.
5. Letter from Bill Wilson to Lois Wilson, October 1915, WGW_102-4_Bx-027_F-0019, SSF.
6. Letter from Bill Wilson to Lois Wilson, September 1915, WGW_102-4_Bx-027_F-0018, SSF.

7. Letter from Bill Wilson to Lois Wilson, no date, WGW_102-4_Bx-027_F-0019_Item-006_Pg_001, SSF. Underlines changed to italics.

8. Lois kept many of Bill's letters from the beginning of the relationship; Bill began later and kept fewer letters that were recovered. Therefore, we have many more of Bill's letters than Lois'.

9. Letter from Bill Wilson to Lois Wilson, 1915, WGW_102-4_Bx-027_F-0019_Item-018, SSF.

10. Letter from Bill Wilson to Lois Wilson, 1915, WGW_102-4_Bx-027_F-0019_Item-009_Pg_002, SSF.

11. Cheever, *My Name Is Bill*, 68.

12. Letter from Bill Wilson to Lois Wilson, December 1916, WGW_102-4_Bx-027_F-0027_Item-002_Pg_002, SSF. Underlines changed to italics.

13. Emily Post, *Etiquette in Society, in Business, in Politics and at Home* (Kessinger, 1922), "Chapter VII: Conversation, Need for Reciprocity."

14. Letter from Bill Wilson to Lois Wilson, 1917, WGW_102-4_Bx-027_F-0029_Item-002_Pg_002, SSF. Underlines changed to italics.

15. Cheever, *My Name Is Bill*, 81.

16. Letter from Bill Wilson to Lois Wilson, Summer 1917, WGW_102-4_Bx-027_F-0030_Item-003_Pg, SSF.

17. Cheever, *My Name Is Bill*, 75.

18. Wilson, *Lois Remembers*, 23.

19. Poem by Lois Wilson, Spring 1918, LBW_210_Bx-048_F-0015-0016_Item-040_Pg_007, SSF.

Chapter 4

1. Wilson, *Bill W.: My First 40 Years*, 53 and 56.

2. Letter from Lois Wilson to Bill Wilson, January 24, 1919, LBW_202-4_IN_WGW_Bx-027_F-0041_Item-002_Pg_001, SSF.

3. *Alcoholics Anonymous* (Alcoholics Anonymous World Services, 1976), 1. See "Bill's Story" for details.

4. Wilson, *Lois Remembers*, 34.

5. Wilson, *Bill W.: My First 40 Years*, 62.

6. Lois Wilson, *Diary of Two Motorcycle Hobos* (self-published, 1973). Available at Stepping Stones Foundation Archive.
7. *Alcoholics Anonymous*, 3.
8. Thomsen, *Bill W.*, 141.
9. Bill Wilson Pledge, New Year's Day, 1927, WGW_102-4_Bx-027_F-0045_Item-001_Pg_001, SSF. Underlines changed to italics.
10. Alcoholics Anonymous, *'Pass It On,'* 80.
11. The piano and original receipt are on display at the Wilsons' historic home in Katonah, New York, where they lived from 1941 until their deaths. The Stepping Stones Foundation now manages the home; tours are offered. For more information, visit https://www.steppingstones.org.
12. Personal conversation, as quoted in William G. Borchert, *The Lois Wilson Story*: *When Love Is Not Enough* (Hazelden, 2010), 96. Some of Borchert's quotes are from taped interviews and some are from his recollection of personal conversations.
13. Taped interview and personal conversation, as quoted in Borchert, *The Lois Wilson Story*, 98.
14. Personal conversation, as quoted in Borchert, *The Lois Wilson Story*, 100.
15. Borchert, *The Lois Wilson Story*, 101.
16. Wilson, *Lois Remembers*, 79.

Chapter 5

1. Borchert, *The Lois Wilson Story*, 101–102.
2. Borchert, *The Lois Wilson Story*, 101.
3. Borchert, *The Lois Wilson Story*, 114–115.
4. Wilson, *Lois Remembers*, 78–79.
5. Lois essay, undated, LBW_202-4_IN_WGW_Bx-027_F-0057_Item-001. Reply from Bill dated January 1928, same file, SSF.

Chapter 6

1. Wilson, *Lois Remembers*, 82.
2. Thomsen, *Bill W.*, 173–174.
3. Borchert, *The Lois Wilson Story*, 135.

4. Taped interview and personal conversation, as quoted in Borchert, *The Lois Wilson Story*, 131.
5. Michael Hiltzik, *The New Deal: A Modern History* (Free Press, 2011), 69.
6. Taped interview and personal conversation, as quoted in Borchert, *The Lois Wilson Story*, 142.
7. Arthur S., ed., *A Narrative Timeline of AA History: Public Version for Public Posting* (Arlington, TX: Self-published, 2014), 20, https://www.chestnut.org/resources/5038dfdf-7183-4e2a-802b-49612e2df64d/2014-percent-20Narrative-percent-20Timeline-percent-20of-percent-20AA-percent-20History.pdf.
8. "Bill's Story," *Alcoholics Anonymous*, 1–16.

Chapter 7

1. Alcoholics Anonymous, *'Pass It On,'* 83–84. The relationship between Bill Wilson and Ebby Thacher was complex. There were often Bill's version and Ebby's version of the same events. How often they drank together (Ebby said only once; Lois and Bill said they drank together often) and what happened in Manchester are two instances where perhaps the details are not as important as the result of the relationship.
2. Bob S., *Ebby in Exile: A Vital AA Link* (Self-published, 2016), 5.
3. *Alcoholics Anonymous*, 27.
4. There are multiple versions of this story, regarding the timing of Ebby's visit to Bill and who was present. We have chosen to tell the story from Bill's perspective as he reported it over time.
5. *Alcoholics Anonymous*, 9.
6. Alcoholics Anonymous, *'Pass It On,'* 113.
7. Personal conversation, as cited in Borchert, *The Lois Wilson Story*, 160.
8. *Alcoholics Anonymous*, 9.
9. Alcoholics Anonymous, *'Pass It On,'* 115.
10. *Alcoholics Anonymous*, 10.
11. Taped interview and personal conversation, as cited in Borchert, *The Lois Wilson Story*, 165. Bill's response from personal conversation, as cited in Borchert, *The Lois Wilson Story*, 165.

12. Note from Bill to Lois, December 11, 1934, WGW_102-4_ Bx-027_F-0068_Item-001, SSF.
13. Taped interview and personal conversation, as cited in Borchert, *The Lois Wilson Story*, 167.
14. Alcoholics Anonymous, *'Pass It On,'* 121.
15. Alcoholics Anonymous, *'Pass It On,'* 121.
16. Alcoholics Anonymous, *'Pass It On,'* 125.
17. Borchert, *The Lois Wilson Story*, 168.

Chapter 8

1. Thomsen, *Bill W.*, 233–234.
2. Alcoholics Anonymous, *'Pass It On,'* 133.
3. *Alcoholics Anonymous*, xxviii.
4. Thomsen, *Bill W.*, 232.
5. Wilson, *Lois Remembers*, 91.
6. Taped interview and personal conversation, as cited in Borchert, *The Lois Wilson Story*, 169.
7. © Stepping Stones Foundation play *Bill and Lois Wilson: In Their Own Words*, compiled by Laurie Hefner Lewis.
8. Borchert, *The Lois Wilson Story*, 170.
9. *Alcoholics Anonymous*, 62.
10. Taped interview, as cited in Borchert, *The Lois Wilson Story*, 173.

Chapter 9

1. The word "movement" is used here and later in the book to denote different periods of development following the founding of Alcoholics Anonymous in 1935. Initial growth mostly broadened the Twelve Step program to address other substance and process addictions. Over time, as explained in Chapter 20, there were other adaptations, some of which built from the Twelve Steps while others did not. For the purposes of this book, we refer to these developments as the alcoholism recovery movement.
2. This term is somewhat out of date, as he would now be called a colon and rectal surgeon or colorectal surgeon.
3. Alcoholics Anonymous, *Dr. Bob and the Good Oldtimers* (Alcoholics Anonymous World Service, 1980), 10.
4. Alcoholics Anonymous, *Dr. Bob and the Good Oldtimers*, 27.

5. Alcoholics Anonymous, *Dr. Bob and the Good Oldtimers*, 28.

6. Alcoholics Anonymous, *Dr. Bob and the Good Oldtimers*, 16.

7. Paula Mejia, "The Lucrative Business of Prescribing Booze During Prohibition," *Atlas Obscura*, November 15, 2017, https://www.atlasobscura.com/articles/doctors-booze-notes-prohibition.

8. Alcoholics Anonymous, *Dr. Bob and the Good Oldtimers*, 32.

9. Bob Smith and Sue Smith, *Children of the Healer: The Story of Dr. Bob's Kids* (Hazelden, 1993), 111.

10. Smith and Smith, *Children of the Healer*, 114.

11. Smith and Smith, *Children of the Healer*, 116.

12. Smith and Smith, *Children of the Healer*, 121.

13. Alcoholics Anonymous, *Dr. Bob and the Good Old Timers*, 56.

14. For more on the Oxford Group and its connection to Akron and the founding of A.A., see Ray R., "The Oxford Group Connection," *Silkworth*, August 25, 1959, https://silkworth.net/alcoholics-anonymous/the-oxford-group-connection.

15. Alcoholics Anonymous, *Dr. Bob and the Good Oldtimers*, 57.

16. Charlotte Hunter, Billye Jones, and Joan Ziegler, *Women Pioneers in 12 Step Recovery* (Hazelden, 1999), 25.

17. Hunter, Jones, and Ziegler, *Women Pioneers in 12 Step Recovery*, 27 and 31.

18. All these ideas are found in A.A.'s Twelve Steps. In fact, "recent research has established some twenty-eight Oxford Group ideas that substantially influenced the language and program of *Alcoholics Anonymous* Big Book and its Twelve Steps" (Hunter, Jones, and Ziegler, *Women Pioneers in 12 Step Recovery*, 31). The twenty-eight Oxford Group ideas are detailed on pages 31–34 of *Women Pioneers in 12 Step Recovery*.

19. Some A.A. historians observe that interventions only became a popular approach for supporting family members forty years later when First Lady Betty Ford's daughter Sue organized an intervention meeting in April 1978.
20. Alcoholics Anonymous, *Dr. Bob and the Good Old Timers*, 58.

Chapter 10

1. Personal conversation, as cited in Borchert, *The Lois Wilson Story*, 176.
2. Alcoholics Anonymous, *'Pass It On,'* 157–158.
3. Alcoholics Anonymous, *'Pass It On,'* 135.
4. Alcoholics Anonymous, *'Pass It On,'* 136.
5. Alcoholics Anonymous, *Dr. Bob and the Good Old Timers*, 59.
6. Alcoholics Anonymous, *Dr. Bob and the Good Oldtimers*, 59–60.
7. Borchert, *The Lois Wilson Story*, 180.
8. Alcoholics Anonymous, *Dr. Bob and the Good Oldtimers*, 66.
9. *Alcoholics Anonymous Comes of Age: A Brief History of A.A.* (Alcoholics Anonymous World Services, 1957), 69.
10. Alcoholics Anonymous, *'Pass It On,'* 142.
11. *Alcoholics Anonymous*, 180. Italics in text.
12. Ernest Kurtz, *A.A.: The Story* (Harper & Row, 1988), 32.
13. *Alcoholics Anonymous*, 180. Italics in text.
14. *Alcoholics Anonymous Comes of Age*, 68.
15. Matthew J. Raphael, *Bill W. and Mr. Wilson: The Legend and Life of A.A.'s Cofounder* (University of Massachusetts Press, 2000), 99.
16. Smith and Smith, *Children of the Healer*, 83.

Chapter 11

1. The Smith home is now preserved and serves as a museum and archive of the life and work of Dr. Bob and Annie Smith. Visitors are welcome. More information and a virtual tour of the home can be found at https://www.drbobshome.org/about/our-home-campus/.
2. Alcoholics Anonymous, *Dr. Bob and the Good Oldtimers*, 69.

3. Smith and Smith, *Children of the Healer*, 37.
4. *Alcoholics Anonymous*, 10.
5. Alcoholics Anonymous, *Dr. Bob and the Good Oldtimers*, 73.
6. Alcoholics Anonymous, *Dr. Bob and the Good Oldtimers*, 73.
7. Smith and Smith, *Children of the Healer*, 39.
8. Alcoholics Anonymous, *'Pass It On,'* 148.
9. There are multiple points of view about the actual date that Dr. Bob had his last drink and A.A. was born. Dr. Bob stated in "Dr. Bob's Nightmare" in *Alcoholics Anonymous* that June 10, 1935 was the date of his last drink. More recently, researchers discovered that the American Medical Association (AMA) conference that Dr. Bob attended in Atlantic City occurred the following week, between June 10 and 14. This would make it impossible for Dr. Bob's last drink to be on June 10. Nevertheless, A.A. proudly celebrates Founders Day as June 10, 1935, with an annual major weekend conference in Akron.
10. Smith and Smith, *Children of the Healer*, 41.
11. Alcoholics Anonymous, *Dr. Bob and the Good Oldtimers*, 77–82.
12. Alcoholics Anonymous, *Dr. Bob and the Good Oldtimers*, 81.
13. Alcoholics Anonymous, *Dr. Bob and the Good Oldtimers*, 82.
14. Alcoholics Anonymous, *Dr. Bob and the Good Oldtimers*, 84.
15. Alcoholics Anonymous, *Dr. Bob and the Good Oldtimers*, 86.
16. Alcoholics Anonymous, *Dr. Bob and the Good Oldtimers*, 84.
17. *Alcoholics Anonymous*, 3rd Edition, 301.
18. *Alcoholics Anonymous*, 3rd Edition, 301.
19. Letter from Bill Wilson to Lois, May 1935, WGW_102-4_Bx-027_F-0071_Item-001_Pg, SSF.
20. William G. Wilson Correspondence, May 1935, WGW_102-4_Bx-027_F-0072_Item-001_Pg_001, SSF.
21. Borchert, *The Lois Wilson Story*, 185.

22. Borchert, *The Lois Wilson Story*, 188.
23. Alcoholics Anonymous, *Dr. Bob and the Good Oldtimers*, 56.
24. See Dick B., *Anne Smith's Journal 1933–1939: A.A.'s Principles of Success* (Paradise Research Publications, 1994) for more details.
25. Alcoholics Anonymous, *Dr. Bob and the Good Old Timers*, 101.
26. Alcoholics Anonymous, *Dr. Bob and the Good Oldtimers*, 137–141 and William H. Schaberg, *Writing the Big Book: The Creation of A.A.* (Central Recovery Press, 2019), 131–132.
27. WGW Correspondence, August 1935, WGW_102-4_Bx-027_F-0088_Item-001_Pg_001, SSF.
28. Alcoholics Anonymous, *'Pass It On,'* 158.
29. Smith and Smith, *Children of the Healer*, 43.
30. Ernest Kurtz, *Not God: A History of Alcoholics Anonymous* (Hazelden, 1991), 41.
31. Nancy Moyer Olson, *Biographies of the Writers of the Stories in the Big Book*, ed. Glenn Chestnut (Hindsfoot Foundation, 2019), 166.

Chapter 12

1. As relayed by Ernest Kurtz in an interview for the documentary film *Bill W.*, directed by Dan Carracino and Kevin Hanlon (Page 124 Productions, 2012), https://www.imdb.com/title/tt2275549/.
2. Schaberg, *Writing the Big Book*, 24.
3. Schaberg, *Writing the Big Book*, 25.
4. Schaberg, *Writing the Big Book*, 18.
5. Schaberg, *Writing the Big Book*, 36.
6. Schaberg, *Writing the Big Book*, 44.
7. Schaberg, *Writing the Big Book*, 61.
8. Schaberg, *Writing the Big Book*, 86.
9. Letter from Bill Wilson to Dr. Bob Smith, June 22, 23, or 24, 1938, Alcoholics Anonymous, the General Service Office (hereafter GSO) Archives, Box 59, 1938, Folder B, Documents 1938-25 to 1938-30.
10. Schaberg, *Writing the Big Book*, 121–123.
11. Schaberg, *Writing the Big Book*, 117.

12. Lois Wilson Diary, June 27, 1938, LBW_201-10_Bx-011B_F-0005_Item-001_Pg_039, SSF.
13. Alcoholics Anonymous, *'Pass It On,'* 200.
14. Alcoholics Anonymous, *Dr. Bob and the Good Oldtimers*, 153.
15. *Alcoholics Anonymous,* 18.
16. Schaberg, *Writing the Big Book*, 320–321.
17. *Alcoholics Anonymous*, 59, italics added by author.
18. Personal conversation, as quoted in Borchert, *The Lois Wilson Story*, 243.
19. Schaberg, *Writing the Big Book*, 102.
20. Inscription by Bill Wilson in *Alcoholics Anonymous*, December 25, 1939, AA1ed, SSF.
21. Lois Wilson Diary, April 26, 1939, LBW_201-10_Bx-011B_F-0006_Item-001_Pg_060, SSF.

Chapter 13

1. Alcoholics Anonymous, *'Pass It On,'* 214.
2. Alcoholics Anonymous, *'Pass It On,'* 215–216.
3. Not much was known about Bobbie B., her work with Bill, and her contribution to the growth of A.A. until the 2022 publication of *Bobbie B.: The Untold Story of A.A.'s "Fantastic Communicator"* by Gary Neidhardt. This book draws on personal letters obtained from Bobbie B.'s family and archival research to offer new insights about her role, this period of A.A. history, and Bill's and Lois' lives.
4. Alcoholics Anonymous, GSO Archives, Box 46, R22, File NY B, 15, 16.
5. Alcoholics Anonymous, *'Pass It On,'* 317.
6. Glenn Chestnut, "Early Black Leaders," unpublished paper, July 2016, Gary, Indiana.
7. *Alcoholics Anonymous*, 4th edition, 244.
8. "Recollections of Vi Scott," Hotel Bedford, Bedford Springs, NY, November 10, 1954. From Washington Area Intergroup Association Archives and archives of Washington, DC Cosmopolitan Group, folder 6–7.
9. "Recollections of Vi Scott," folder 9.
10. Alcoholics Anonymous, *'Pass It On,'* 241.
11. Dawn Eden Goldstein, *Father Ed: The Story of Bill W.'s Spiritual Sponsor* (Orbis, 2022), 124–131.

12. Goldstein, *Father Ed*, 131.
13. Edward Dowling, SJ, "Alcoholics Anonymous," *The Queen's Work* (March 1944), 30–31, as cited in Goldstein, *Father Ed*, 131–132.
14. Goldstein, *Father Ed*, 133.
15. Ernest Kurtz, as quoted in Goldstein, *Father Ed*, 148.
16. Wilson, *Lois Remembers*, 125.
17. Letter from Father Ed Dowling to Bill Wilson, May 27, 1942, AA_309_Bx-003_F-0005_Item-007_Pg_001, SSF.
18. Bill Wilson to Fr. Ed Dowling, May 20, 1946, AA_309_Bx-003_F-0005_Item-021_Pg_001, SSF.
19. Michael Fitzpatrick, *We Recovered Too: The Family Groups' Beginnings in the Pioneers' Own Words* (Hazelden, 2011), 10.
20. Alcoholics Anonymous, *'Pass It On,'* 249.
21. *Alcoholics Anonymous Comes of Age*, 87.

Chapter 14

1. Wilson, *Lois Remembers*, 133.
2. Wilson, *Lois Remembers*, 134.
3. Wilson, *Lois Remembers*, 135–136.
4. Alcoholics Anonymous, *'Pass It On,'* 262–263.
5. Wilson, *Lois Remembers*, 137.
6. Mary C. Darrah, *Sister Ignatia: Angel of Alcoholics Anonymous* (Hazelden, 2001), 127–128, as found in Anne Ripley Smith's Oxford Group notebook, GSO Archives (Anne Ripley Smith Archives, Box 33A).
7. Darrah, *Sister Ignatia*, 128.
8. Alcoholics Anonymous Archives, New York, NY, 42 from Anne Ripley Smith's Oxford Group Notebook.
9. *Alcoholics Anonymous Comes of Age*, 195.
10. "Origin of the Serenity Prayer: A Historical Paper," Service Material from the A.A. GSO, 2009.
11. Lois Wilson Diary, March 4, 1941, LBW_201-10_Bx-011A_F-0009_Item-001_Pg_121, SSF.
12. Bill Wilson to Ruth Hock, WGW_102-2_Bx-014_F-0001-_Item-058_Pg_001, SSF.
13. *A Visual History of Alcoholics Anonymous* (Alcoholics Anonymous World Services, 2021), 41.

14. Jackie B. is to be acknowledged for her research on the beginnings of A.A. meetings in prisons and on the role of Ricardo M. in organizing prisoners at San Quentin for A.A. meetings, as presented in "The Untold Story of AA in San Quentin Prison," *Recovery Speakers*, May 7, 2021, https://www.recoveryspeakers.com/the-untold-story-of-aa-in-san-quentin-prison-presented-by-jackie-b-5-7-2021/.

15. Sally Brown and David R. Brown, *A Biography of Mrs. Marty Mann, the First Lady of Alcoholics Anonymous* (Hazelden, 2001), 155–156.

16. Marty Mann's work with NCEA, which became the National Council on Alcoholism and Drug Dependence, is often credited as the beginning of the modern recovery movement. (See Chapter 18 for more on the recovery movement.)

17. Wilson, *Lois Remembers*, 146.

18. Lois Wilson Diary, October 28–30, 1943, LBW_201-10_Bx-011A_F-0009_Item-001_Pg_148, SSF. Also *Vignettes of the Past*, written by Lois Wilson, Date not available, LBW_203_Bx-035_F-0015_Item-001_Pg_031, SSF.

19. Wilson, *Lois Remembers*, 143.

20. From November 22, 1943 letter from Bobbie B. to Pat C. of Minneapolis, as found in footnote CXXXIV in Neidhardt, *Bobbie B.*, 178.

21. Alcoholics Anonymous, *'Pass It On,'* 292.

22. Lois Wilson Diary, LBW_201-10_Bx-011A_F-0009_Item-001_Pg_184–185, SSF.

23. Lois Wilson Diary, LBW_201-10_Bx-011A_F-0009_Item-001_Pg_186–189, Pg_193–194, SSF.

24. Lois Wilson Diary, LBW_201-10_Bx-011A_F-0009_Item-001_Pg_195, SSF.

25. Lois Wilson Diary, LBW_201-10_Bx-011A_F-0009_Item-001_Pg_195, SSF.

26. Lois Wilson Diary, LBW_201-10_Bx-011A_F-0009_Item-001 Pg 204, SSF.

27. Neidhardt, *Bobbie B.*, 195.

28. Neidhardt, *Bobbie B.*, 196–200.

29. Neidhardt, *Bobbie B.*, 201.

30. "Where Willpower Comes In," *The Language of the Heart: Bill W.'s Grapevine Writings* (*AA Grapevine*, 2005), 274.

31. Alcoholics Anonymous, *'Pass It On,'* 293.
32. Francis Hartigan, *Bill W.: A Biography of Alcoholics Anonymous Cofounder Bill Wilson* (St. Martin's Griffin, 2001), 166–167.
33. Alcoholics Anonymous, *'Pass It On,'* 294.
34. "Twelve Suggested Points for AA Tradition," *Language of the Heart*, 21.
35. "Anne S.," *Language of the Heart*, 353–354.
36. *Alcoholics Anonymous*, 335.
37. Alcoholics Anonymous, *'Pass It On,'* 335.
38. Alcoholics Anonymous, *'Pass It On,'* 337.
39. Alcoholics Anonymous, *'Pass It On,'* 337.
40. *Alcoholics Anonymous*, 339–342.

Chapter 15

1. There were two Annes involved in the founding of Al-Anon who worked closely with Lois. The first is Anne Smith (often called Annie and referred to as Annie in this text) who was the wife of A.A.'s cofounder Dr. Bob Smith. As noted earlier in the text, Annie Smith played a vital role in both shaping the spirituality of A.A. and in welcoming family members who attended early A.A. meetings informally. Annie Smith died in June 1949 and was not a part of the formal founding of Al-Anon in 1951. Anne Bingham and Lois met at the informal meetings for families near Lois' Westchester County home. Lois asked Anne Bingham to assist her in the launch of Al-Anon. Lois and Anne Bingham worked side by side in developing communications and literature for early Al-Anon members.
2. *First Steps: Al-Anon 35 Years of Beginnings* (Al-Anon Family Group Headquarters, 1986), 43.
3. Wilson, *Lois Remembers*, 98.
4. Wilson, *Lois Remembers*, 98.
5. Wilson, *Lois Remembers*, 99–100.
6. Wilson, *Lois Remembers*, 173.
7. Smith and Smith, *Children of the Healer*, 74.
8. *First Steps*, 20.
9. Al-Anon Family Groups, *Many Voices, One Journey* (Al-Anon Family Groups, 2011), 21.

10. Al-Anon Family Groups, *Many Voices, One Journey* (Al-Anon Family Groups, 2011), 21.
11. Wilson, *Lois Remembers*, 173.
12. *First Steps*, 44.
13. *First Steps*, 48.
14. *First Steps*, 46.
15. See *Al-Anon World Service Office 2023 Annual Report* (Al-Anon World Services, 2023), 10 for detailed breakdown of meetings in the US, Canada, other countries, and of electronic and in-person Al-Anon and Alateen meetings.

Chapter 16

1. Letter from Bill Wilson to Lois, January 24, 1954, WGW_102-4_Bx-027_F-0102_Item-016_Pg, SSF.
2. Lois Wilson Diary, LBW_201-10_Bx-011A_F-0010_Item-001_Pg_146, SSF.
3. Borchert, *The Lois Wilson Story*, 292.
4. Taped interview, as quoted in Borchert, *The Lois Wilson Story*, 293.
5. *Many Voices, One Journey*, 74–75.
6. Read the pamphlet "Circles of Love and Service" (A.A. World Services, 2018) for more details: https://www.aa.org/sites/default/files/literature/P-45_0624.pdf.
7. The Archives GSO, Box 33, R15, File 24.1, p. 21.
8. For more information on A.A.'s rapid international growth, see *A Visual History*, 272–332.
9. The contribution of Captain Jack to A.A.'s international growth is becoming better known due to mention in *A Visual History of Alcoholics Anonymous* (pages 258–261) and the release of previously unavailable communications between Captain Jack and A.A. through A.A. GSO Internationalists History Collection Folder 2 1946–1948.
10. *A Visual History*, 261.
11. *A Brief History of the Big Book/Una Breve Historia del Libro Grande/L'histoire du Gros Livre En Bref* (A.A. World Services, 2017).
12. Borchert, *The Lois Wilson Story*, 286. Also, regarding Uncle Clarence's instrument, see Wilson, *Bill W.: My First 40 Years*, 25–26.
13. Alcoholics Anonymous, *'Pass It On,'* 381.

14. *Alcoholics Anonymous Comes of Age*, 226.
15. *Alcoholics Anonymous Comes of Age*, 224.
16. *Alcoholics Anonymous Comes of Age*, 226.
17. *Alcoholics Anonymous Comes of Age*, 228.
18. See Appendix for A.A.'s Twelve Concepts.
19. *Many Voices, One Journey*, 119.
20. Alcoholics Anonymous, *'Pass It On,'* 275.
21. Cheever, *My Name Is Bill*, 239.
22. Cheever, *My Name Is Bill*, 241.
23. Nell Wing, *Grateful to Have Been There: My 42 Years with Bill and Lois, and the Evolution of Alcoholics Anonymous* (Parkside, 1992), 80.
24. Cheever, *My Name Is Bill*, 178–179.
25. Personal conversation, as quoted in Borchert, *The Lois Wilson Story*, 316–317.
26. Personal conversation, as quoted in Borchert, *The Lois Wilson Story*, 317.
27. Biographers Susan Cheever, Nan Robertson, and Francis Hartigan all cite evidence of Bill flirting or having relationships with women. Other biographers—William Borchert and Ernest Kurtz—believe Bill is falsely accused of inappropriate relationships by people disappointed or angry with him.
28. Amendment to Bill's Agreement with A.A. WSO, April 29, 1963, in Arthur S., *A Narrative Timeline of AA History*, 76.
29. Lois Desk Calendar, January 7, 1969, LBW_201-10_Bx-011c_F-0017_Item-001_Pg_002, SSF.
30. Bill and Lois Wilson and Helen Wynn were all guest speakers at the twenty-fifth anniversary celebration of Alcoholics Anonymous at University of Vermont in Burlington on October 22, 1960. The transcript of their remarks is available at Brown University archives, Tom Powers Collection of Bill Wilson public talks (ms.2010.002) Box A and Helen Wynn Box 3, Box 5, Item T048.2.
31. Tom Powers Collection, Brown University archives, Box 3, Box 5, Item T048.2.

32. Tom Powers Collection, Brown University archives, Box 3, Box 5, Item T048.2.

Chapter 17

1. Letter from Paul H., GSO Archives, Box 30, File 18.2, p. 4.
2. Letter from Bill Wilson to Dr. Carl Jung, January 23, 1961, AA_325_Bx-004_F-0015_Item-007_Pg_001, SSF.
3. All three of Bill Wilson's communications with Dr. Jung are available in the Stepping Stones Archive.
4. Poem written by Lois' sister Barbara Burnham Jones in 1955 and sent to her brother Lyman Burnham, Lois Wilson Correspondence, LBW_201-1_Bx-001_F-0012_Item-011_Pg_001, SSF.
5. Letter from Barbara Burnham Jones' attorney to Lois Wilson, August 7, 1964, Lois Wilson Correspondence, LBW_201-1_Bx-001_F-0012_Item-014_Pg 1, SSF.
6. Brown and Brown, *Biography of Mrs. Marty Mann*, 262.
7. Bill Wilson, "The Next Frontier: Emotional Sobriety," January 1958, as reprinted in *Language of the Heart*, 236.
8. Bill Wilson, "Take Step Eleven," *Language of the Heart*, 239.
9. Bill Wilson, "The Language of the Heart," *AA Grapevine*, July 1960, 243, 249.
10. See Appendix for A.A. and Al-Anon Twelve Traditions.
11. *Many Voices, One Journey*, 98–99.
12. William L. White, *Slaying the Dragon: The History of Addiction Treatment and Recovery in America* (Chestnut Health Systems, 1998), 377.
13. Arthur S., ed., *A Narrative Timeline of AA History*, 77.
14. See Arthur S., *A Narrative Timeline of AA History*. Royalties on A.A. publications are reported by year in Appendix 2.
15. Borchert, *The Lois Wilson Story*, 305–306.

Chapter 18

1. Anniversary letter, Bill to Lois, January 24, 1968, WGW Correspondence, WGW_102-4_Bx-027_F-0102_Item-035_Pg_002, SSF.
2. Anniversary letter, Lois to Bill, January 24, 1968, WGW Correspondence, WGW_102-4_Bx-027_F-0103_Item-013_Pg_002, SSF.

3. Anniversary poem from Lois to Bill, 50th wedding anniversary, January 24, 1968, Lois Wilson Correspondence, 1968, WGW_102-4_Bx-027_F-0043_Item-001_Pg_001, SSF.
4. Interview of Nell Wing, as quoted in Borchert, *When Love Is Not Enough*, 320.
5. "The Future of AA's World Services Overseas; Position Paper – Suggested by Bill," January 1968, WGW_103_Bx-034_F-0001_Item-001_Pg, SSF.
6. The organizational structure of A.A. is unique. A summary chart and reference to a fuller description in the Service Manual can be found at https://www.aa.org/structure-conference-us-and-canada.
7. *Many Voices, One Journey*, 147.
8. Personal conversation, as quoted in Borchert, *The Lois Wilson Story*, 321.
9. Personal conversation, as quoted in Borchert, *The Lois Wilson Story*, 322.
10. Wing, *Grateful to Have Been There*, 69–70.
11. Lois Wilson note, undated, LBW_210_Bx-048_F-0007_Item-002_Pg_004, SSF.
12. Bill and Lois Wilson prayer, undated, LBW_210_Bx-048_F-0007_Item-002_Pg_005, SSF.
13. Lois Wilson Diary, January 29, 1937, LBW_201-10_Bx-011A_F-0009_Item-001_Pg_004, SSF.
14. Borchert, *The Lois Wilson Story*, 323.
15. "Bill's Last Talk" at 1970 A.A. International Convention in Miami, July 5, 1970, as found on A.A. GSO DVD *Markings on the Journey*, 1987, revised 2002.
16. Cheever, *My Name Is Bill*, 248–249.
17. Borchert, *The Lois Wilson Story*, 326.
18. Cheever, *My Name Is Bill*, 250.
19. "Talk by Dr. Norris," Memorial Service for Bill Wilson, New York, NY, February 14, 1971, transcript posted at https://club12.org/reference/.
20. "Bill W. Memorial Service from Baton Rouge on February 14th, 1971," *Recovery Speakers*, February 14, 2021, https://www.recoveryspeakers.com/bill-w-memorial-service-from-baton-rouge-on-february-14th-1971/.

Chapter 19

1. Borchert, *The Lois Wilson Story*, 329.
2. Interview of Nell Wing, as quoted in Borchert, *The Lois Wilson Story*, 330.
3. Borchert, *The Lois Wilson Story*, 331.
4. Lois Wilson trip log, January 15, 1972, LBW_201-4_Bx-009_F-0006_Item-003_Pg_001, SSF.
5. Wilson, *Lois Remembers*, 163.
6. Wilson, *Lois Remembers*, 163.
7. Lois Wilson Travel Diary, 1972, LBW_201-4_Bx-009_F-0006_Item-003_Pg, SSF.
8. Wilson, *Lois Remembers*, 166.
9. Anonymous Al-Anon friends and taped interview, as quoted in Borchert, *The Lois Wilson Story*, 336.
10. Getz, *Lois W.*, A.A. GSO Archives, Bx 33, File 24.1 R 15 Pg 32 (b).
11. *Many Voices, One Journey*, 233.
12. *Many Voices, One Journey*, 236.
13. Taped interview, as quoted in Borchert, *The Lois Wilson Story*, 339.
14. Lois Wilson Diary, January 19, 1988, LBW_201-10_Bx-011d_F-0009_Item-001_Pg_010, SSF.
15. From a body diagram with illnesses noted, drawn by Lois Wilson around 1983, LBW_210_Bx-041_F-0014_Item-001_Pg_001, SSF.
16. "Lois W. and the Pioneers Audio Interview," Al-Anon Family Groups, https://al-anon.org/media/1982_Lois_Pioneers.
17. Borchert, *The Lois Wilson Story*, 336.
18. Lois Wilson Diary, 1983, LBW_201-10_Bx-011d_F-0002_Item-001_Pg, SSF.
19. The article, "Unforgettable Bill W.," first appeared in *Reader's Digest* in August 1986 and was reprinted in its entirety in the June 1999 *AA Grapevine*.
20. Lois Wilson Diary, January 5, 1988, LBW 207, Box 011d, F0009, Item 001, Pg_002, SSF.
21. Borchert, *The Lois Wilson Story*, 343.
22. Taped interview of anonymous Al-Anon friend, as quoted in Borchert, *The Lois Wilson Story*, 344.

23. Lois Burnham Wilson obituary, *The New York Times*, October 6, 1988, https://www.nytimes.com/1988/10/06/obituaries/lois-burnham-wilson-a-founder-of-al-anon-groups-is-dead-at-97.html.
24. Lois Burnham Wilson obituary, *The New York Times*, October 6, 1988.
25. Norman Vincent Peale was eighty years old in 1980 and in declining health.
26. Judy Collins shared her story as a person in long-term recovery from alcohol and food addiction in her 2017 book *Cravings*, where she acknowledges the role Bill and Lois Wilson and Twelve Step programs played in her recovery and that of thousands. She expressed her gratitude for her recovery by singing "Amazing Grace" at A.A. conferences and the Akron Founders Day gathering.
27. Interview of Nell Wing, as quoted in Borchert, *The Lois Wilson Story*, 344.
28. Wilson, *Lois Remembers*, 168.
29. Wilson, *Lois Remembers*, 196.

Chapter 20

1. William White, an emeritus research consultant and retired addiction recovery professional, clinical director, researcher, and writer of over 400 articles and twenty books, offers a detailed review of the history of addiction, recovery, and the recovery movement in his book *Slaying the Dragon: The History of Addiction Treatment in America* and on his website at https://www.chestnut.org/william-white-papers/.
2. See "Our History of Mental Health," *International Mental Health Collaborating Network*, https://imhcn.org/deinstitutionalisation/ and Michael Hlebechuk, "History of Insanity and the Evolution of the Peer Recovery Movement" (2011) available online at https://www.oregon.gov/deiconference/Documents/Hlebechuk_Michael%20History%20of%20Insanity%20and%20the%20Evolution%20of%20the%20Peer%20Recovery%20Movement.pdf.
3. *Alcoholics Anonymous*, 33.
4. *Alcoholics Anonymous*, 20.

5. See Chapter 17 for more on Senator Hughes, the Hughes Bill, and the role of Academy Award-winning actress Mercedes McCambridge. See https://aainthedesert.org/wp-content/uploads/2019/01/BILL-WILSON-SENATE-TESTIMONY.pdf for Bill Wilson's testimony before the Senate hearing.

6. For more on the history and evolution of the recovery movements, see White, *Slaying the Dragon* and the documentary movie *The Anonymous People* (4th Dimension, 2013).

7. See Chapter 17 for more on the General Service Conference and the structure of A.A.

8. Robert Fitzgerald, *The Soul of Sponsorship: The Friendship of Fr. Ed Dowling, S.J., and Bill Wilson in Letters* (Hazelden, 1995), 40–42.

9. John F. Kelly, Keith Humphreys, and Marica Ferri, "Alcoholics Anonymous and Other 12-Step Programs for Alcohol Use Disorder," *Cochrane Database of Systematic Reviews 2020*, Issue 3. Art. No.: CD012880.

10. White, *Slaying the Dragon*, 484.

11. White, *Slaying the Dragon*, 512.

12. *Alcoholics Anonymous*, 4th edition, 419.

13. White, *Slaying the Dragon*, 484.

14. Faces and Voices of Recovery is a leading force in public education and policy advocacy around recovery. See https://facesandvoicesofrecovery.org/ for more on their work.

15. "About, Our Mission," *Faces and Voices of Recovery*, https://facesandvoicesofrecovery.org/about/.

16. Alcoholics Anonymous, "I Am Responsible Pledge," https://www.aa.org/participating-in-aa.

Bibliography

A., Tony. "The Laundry List: 14 Traits of an Adult Child of an Alcoholic." Adult Children of Alcoholics & Dysfunctional Families World Service Organization, 1978. https://adultchildren.org/literature/laundry-list/.

A Visual History of Alcoholics Anonymous. Alcoholics Anonymous World Services, 2021.

"About." *Faces and Voices of Recovery.* Accessed November 16, 2024. https://facesandvoicesofrecovery.org/about/.

"About." *Stepping Stones Foundation.* Accessed November 12, 2024. https://www.steppingstones.org/about/.

"Addictionary." *Recovery Research Institute.* Accessed November 15, 2024. https://www.recoveryanswers.org/addiction-ary/.

"Adult Children of Alcoholics & Dysfunctional Families." *Adult Children of Alcoholics & Dysfunctional Families.* World Service Organization. Accessed November 11, 2024. https://adultchildren.org.

Al-Anon. *Al-Anon's Twelve Steps & Twelve Traditions.* Al-Anon Family Group Headquarters, 1981.

Al-Anon. *First Steps: Al-Anon 35 Years of Beginnings.* Al-Anon Family Group Headquarters, 1986.

Al-Anon. *Many Voices, One Journey.* Al-Anon Family Groups Headquarters, 2011.

Alcoholics Anonymous. World Publishing Company, 1939.

Alcoholics Anonymous. 3rd ed. Alcoholics Anonymous World Services, 1976.

Alcoholics Anonymous. 4th ed. Alcoholics Anonymous World Services, 2001.

Alcoholics Anonymous. *A Brief History of the Big Book / Una Breve Historia del Libro Grande / L'histoire du Gros Livre En Bref.* Alcoholics Anonymous World Services, 2017.

Alcoholics Anonymous. *Alcoholics Anonymous Comes of Age: A Brief History of A.A.* Alcoholics Anonymous World Services, 1957.

Alcoholics Anonymous. *Dr. Bob and the Good Oldtimers: A Biography, with Recollections of Early A.A. in the Midwest.* Alcoholics Anonymous World Services, 1980.

Alcoholics Anonymous. *'Pass It On': The Story of Bill Wilson and How the A.A. Message Reached the World.* Alcoholics Anonymous World Services, 1984.

Archives at the General Service Offices of Alcoholics Anonymous, New York, New York.

B., Dick. *Anne Smith's Journal 1933–1939: A.A.'s Principles of Success.* Paradise Research Publications, 1994.

B., Jackie. "The Untold Story of AA in San Quentin Prison." *Recovery Speakers*, May 7, 2021. Video, 1:32:45. https://www.recoveryspeakers.com/the-untold-story-of-aa-in-san-quentin-prison-presented-by-jackie-b-5-7-2021/.

"BBA by the Numbers." *Burr and Burton Academy.* Accessed November 15, 2024. https://www.burrburton.org/about/bba-by-the-numbers.

"Bill W. Memorial Service from Baton Rouge on February 14th, 1971." *Recovery Speakers*, February 14, 2021. Video, 1:30:44. https://www.recoveryspeakers.com/bill-w-memorial-service-from-baton-rouge-on-february-14th-1971/.

"Bill Wilson's 1969 U.S. Senate Testimony." *Alcoholics Anonymous Central Intergroup Office of the Desert.* Accessed November 06, 2024. https://aainthedesert.org/wp-content/uploads/2019/01/BILL-WILSON-SENATE-TESTIMONY.pdf.

"Bill's Last Message." *Alcoholics Anonymous.* Accessed November 20, 2024. https://www.aa.org/bills-last-message.

Borchert, William. *The Lois Wilson Story: When Love Is Not Enough.* Hazelden, 2005.

Brown, Sally, and David R. Brown. *A Biography of Mrs. Marty Mann, the First Lady of Alcoholics Anonymous*. Hazelden, 2001.

Carracino, Dan, and Kevin Hanlon, directors. *Bill W*. Page 124 Productions, 2012. Video, 1:44. https://www.amazon.com/Bill-W-William-G-Wilson/dp/B08RWF1JSB.

Cheever, Susan. *My Name Is Bill: Bill Wilson—His Life and the Creation of Alcoholics Anonymous*. Simon & Schuster, 2004.

Chesnut, Glenn. "Early Black A.A. Leaders." Unpublished presentation. July 26, 2014, Gary, Indiana.

Chesnut, Glenn. *Heroes of Early Black AA: Their Stories and Their Messages*. BookPatch, 2017.

"Circles of Love and Service." *Alcoholics Anonymous*, 2018. https://www.aa.org/sites/default/files/literature/P-45_0624.pdf.

Collins, Judy. *Cravings: How I Conquered Food*. Anchor, 2017.

Darrah, Mary C. *Sister Ignatia: Angel of Alcoholics Anonymous*. Hazelden, 2001.

Fitzgerald, Robert. *The Soul of Sponsorship: The Friendship of Fr. Ed Dowling, S.J., and Bill Wilson in Letters*. Hazelden, 1995.

Fitzpatrick, Michael. *We Recovered Too: The Family Groups' Beginnings in the Pioneers' Own Words*. Hazelden, 2011.

Goldstein, Dawn Eden. *Father Ed: The Story of Bill W.'s Spiritual Sponsor*. Orbis, 2022.

Hartigan, Francis. *Bill W.: A Biography of Alcoholics Anonymous Cofounder Bill Wilson*. St. Martin's Griffin, 2001.

Hlebechuk, Michael. "History of Insanity and the Evolution of the Peer Recovery Movement." Oregon, 2011. https://www.oregon.gov/deiconference/Documents/Hlebechuk_Michael%20History%20of%20Insanity%20and%20the%20Evolution%20of%20the%20Peer%20Recovery%20Movement.pdf.

Hunter, Charlotte, Billye Jones, and Joan Ziegler. *Women Pioneers in 12 Step Recovery*. Hazelden, 1999.

365

K., Mitchell. "Dr. Bob's Last Drink." *Harbor Area Central Office of Alcoholics Anonymous*. Accessed November 17, 2024. https://hacoaa.org/wp-content/uploads/Dr.-Bobs-Last-Drink.pdf.

Kelly, John, Keith Humphreys, and Maricia Ferri. "Alcoholics Anonymous and other 12-step programs for alcohol use disorder." *Cochran Database of Systematic Reviews*, Issue 3, (2020). https://www.cochranelibrary.com/cdsr/doi/10.1002/14651858.CD012880.pub2/full.

Kurtz, Ernest. *A.A.: The Story*. Harper & Row, 1988.

Kurtz, Ernest. *Not God: A History of Alcoholics Anonymous*. Hazelden, 1991.

"Language Matters: It Is Time We Change How We Talk About Addiction and its Treatment." *Faces & Voices of Recovery*. Accessed November 10, 2024. https://facesandvoicesofrecovery.org/resource/language-matters-it-is-time-we-change-how-we-talk-about-addiction-and-its-treatment/.

"Lois W. and the Pioneers Audio Interview," *Al-Anon Family Groups*. Accessed November 18, 2024. https://al-anon.org/for-members/wso/archives/lois-w-pioneers-audio-interview/.

Lois Wilson's Diaries and Letters. Stepping Stones Foundation Archives, Stepping Stones Foundation® (Stepping Stones - Historic Home of Bill & Lois Wilson®), Katonah, New York. steppingstones.org.

Mejia, Paula. "The Lucrative Business of Prescribing Booze During Prohibition." *Atlas Obscura*, November 15, 2017. https://www.atlasobscura.com/articles/doctors-booze-notes-prohibition.

"Memorial Service for Bill Wilson: Talk by Dr. Norris." *Club 12*, February 14, 1971. https://club12.org/reference/.

Neidhardt, Gary. *Bobbie B. The Untold Story of A.A.'s "Fantastic Communicator": A Window into the Alcoholic Foundation Office in the 1940s*. Independently Published, 2022.

Olson, Nancy. *Biographies of the Authors of the Stories in the Big Book*. Hindsfoot, 2019.

"Origin of the Serenity Prayer: A Historical Paper." Service Material from the General Service Office. Alcoholics Anonymous, Revised July 30, 2009. https://www.aa.org/sites/default/files/literature/assets/smf-129_en.pdf.

"Our History of Mental Health." *International Mental Health Collaborating Network.* Accessed November 5, 2024. https://imhcn.org/deinstitutionalisation/.

"Overview." *Recovery Research Institute.* Accessed November 15, 2024. https://www.recoveryanswers.org/recovery-101/.

P., Bob. "Unforgettable Bill W." *AA Grapevine*, June 1999. https://www.aagrapevine.org/magazine/1999/jun/unforgettable-bill-w?srsltid=AfmBOopv_ddMYaqUwaIWFWV95hD4KWWfgx3MTY52gxm68jlrg_nmzcw3.

Pace, Eric. "Lois Burnham Wilson, a Founder of Al-Anon Groups, Is Dead at 97." *The New York Times*, October 6, 1988. https://www.nytimes.com/1988/10/06/obituaries/lois-burnham-wilson-a-founder-of-al-anon-groups-is-dead-at-97.html.

Post, Emily. *Etiquette in Society, In Business, in Politics, and at Home.* Kessinger, 1922.

R., Ray, "The Oxford Group Connection." *Silkworth*, August 25, 1959. https://silkworth.net/alcoholics-anonymous/the-oxford-group-connection.

Raphael, Matthew. *Bill W. and Mr. Wilson: The Legend and Life of A.A.'s Cofounder.* University of Massachusetts Press, 2000.

Robertson, Nan. *Getting Better: Inside Alcoholics Anonymous.* iUniverse.com, 1988.

S., Arthur. *A Narrative Timeline of AA History: Public Version for Public Posting.* Self-published, 2014.

S., Bob. "Ebby in Exile: A Vital AA Link." *Alcoholics Anonymous North Halton / Erin*, 2016. https://aanorthhaltonerin.org/wp-content/uploads/2020/04/Ebby_In_Exile.pdf.

Schaberg, William. *Writing the Big Book: The Creation of A.A. Central Recovery Press*, 2019.

Smith, Bob and Sue Smith. *Children of the Healer: The Story of Dr. Bob's Kids*. Hazelden, 1993.

"The Start and Growth of A.A." *Alcoholics Anonymous*. Accessed November 17, 2024. https://www.aa.org/the-start-and-growth-of-aa.

"Structure of U.S./Canada General Service Conference." *Alcoholics Anonymous*. Accessed November 10, 2024. https://www.aa.org/sites/default/files/literature/smf-179_Structure_of_the_Conference_EN_0122.pdf.

"Swedenborg and Life Recap: Spiritual Marriage 2/8/16." *Swedenborgian Foundation*. Accessed November 8, 2024. https://swedenborg.com/spiritual-marriage.

Thomsen, Robert. *Bill W.: The Absorbing and Deeply Moving Life Story of Bill Wilson, Co-Founder of Alcoholics Anonymous*. Harper & Row, 1975.

Tom Powers collection. Brown University Archives, Providence, Rhode Island.

Twelve Steps and Twelve Traditions. Alcoholics Anonymous World Services, 1952.

"2023 World Service Office Annual Report." *Al-Anon Family Groups*. Accessed November 17, 2024. https://al-anon.org/pdf/World-Service-Office-Annual-Report-2023.pdf .

Washington Area Intergroup Association Archives, Washington DC.

White, William L. *Slaying the Dragon: The History of Addiction Treatment and Recovery in America*. Chestnut Health Systems, 1998.

Williams, Greg, director. *The Anonymous People*. 4th Dimension Productions, 2013. 1 hr., 28 min. https://www.amazon.com/People-Kristen-Johnston/dp/B00IX1KCGA.

Wilson, Bill. *The A.A. Service Manual Combined with Twelve Concepts for World Service*. Alcoholics Anonymous World Services, 2021.

Wilson, Bill. *Bill W.: My First 40 Years*. Hazelden, 2000.

Wilson, Bill. *The Language of the Heart: Bill W's Grapevine Writings*. A.A. Grapevine, 1988.

Wilson, Lois. *Diary of Two Motorcycle Hobos.* Gratitude Press, 1998.

Wilson, Lois. *Lois Remembers.* Al-Anon Family Group Headquarters, 1979.

Wing, Nell. *Grateful to Have Been There: My 42 Years with Bill and Lois, and the Evolution of Alcoholics Anonymous.* Parkside, 1992.

Continued from the Copyright Page:

The excerpts from *Alcoholics Anonymous, 'Pass It On,' Alcoholics Anonymous Comes of Age, Dr. Bob and the Good Oldtimers*, and archival materials from the General Service Office Archives are reprinted with permission of Alcoholics Anonymous World Services, Inc. ("A.A.W.S."). Permission to reprint these excerpts does not mean that A.A.W.S. has reviewed or approved the contents of this publication, or that A.A.W.S. necessarily agrees with the views expressed herein. A.A. is a program of recovery from alcoholism only—use of these excerpts in connection with programs and activities which are patterned after A.A., but which address other problems, or in any other non-A.A. context, does not imply otherwise.

The excerpts from *Lois Remembers, Many Voices, One Journey*, and *First Steps* are reprinted by permission of Al-Anon Family Group Headquarters, Inc. Permission to reprint these excerpts does not mean that Al-Anon Family Group Headquarters, Inc. has reviewed or approved the contents of this publication, or that Al-Anon Family Group Headquarters, Inc. necessarily agrees with the views expressed herein. Al-Anon is a program of recovery for families and friends of alcoholics—use of these excerpts in any non-Al-Anon context does not imply endorsement or affiliation by Al-Anon.

Index

Note: Page numbers in *italics* indicate page references for pictures. Those followed by "n" refer to endnotes.

A

A.A. *See* Alcoholics Anonymous

A.A. Auxiliary, 220

AA Grapevine
    Al-Anon growth and, 222
    Annie Smith tribute in, 206
    Bill's writings, 249–251
    development of, 196
    Twelve Traditions articles, 205, 230
    voting members from, 213

A.A. Service Manual, 249

adult children of alcoholics, 15, 117, 279

Adult Children of Alcoholics and Dysfunctional Families (ACA), 117, 295

African Americans, 173–177

"The Aims and Purposes of the Non-Alcoholic Group," 220

Akron, Ohio. *See also* Sister Ignatia; Smith, Anne; and Smith, Robert
    Bill and Dr. Bob meeting, 128–131
    Bill and Dr. Bob's work in, 139–142
    Bill's proxy fight, 106–107, 109–110, 123–125, 147–148
    Lois in, 144–145, 147
    Oxford Group, 117–121, 126, 145–146

Akron Alcoholic Squad meeting (1937), 154–157

Akron City Hospital, 140

Al-Anon Family Group Headquarters, 224

Al-Anon Family Groups
    at A.A. convention (1955), 235–237

S

ABOUT THE AUTHORS

Tom Adams, MSW, is a retired nonprofit executive and consultant and an active student of the history and development of Alcoholics Anonymous and other Twelve Step programs. As a person in recovery, he is passionate about broadening awareness that recovery from addiction is possible for the individual with the addiction and their family. He is the author of *The Nonprofit Leadership Transition and Development Guide* and the *Critical Conversations* Blog (www.thadams.com). He posts often on spirituality, recovery, and racial justice.

Joy Jones is the author of six books for adults and children and the winner of the 2022 PEN/Phyllis Naylor Grant for her novel-in-progress, *Walking the Boomerang.* She is a popular speaker on topics of culture and literacy. Jones is former director of community relations for the Psychiatric Institute of Washington and cofounder of a creative expression program at St. Elizabeths Hospital. Currently, she works for DC Public Library. She became interested in A.A. when someone told her A.A. is closer to God's concept of the church than the church is. Visit her at www.joyjonesonline.com.

www.ingramcontent.com/pod-product-compliance
Lightning Source LLC
Chambersburg PA
CBHW071701120626

46550CB00001B/66